Transnational Crime, Crime Control and Secur[...]

Series editors: **Anastassia Tsoukala** University o[...] [...], [...], and **James Sheptycki**, York University, Canada

Editorial board:

Peter Andreas, Brown University, Providence, Rhode Island; **Vida Bajc**, Methodist University, Fayetteville, North Carolina; **Benjamin Bowling**, King's College London; **Stanley Cohen**, London School of Economics and Political Science; **Andrew Dawson**, University of Melbourne; **Benoît Dupont**, University of Montreal; **Nicholas Fyfe**, University of Dundee; **Andrew Goldsmith**, University of Wollongong, Australia; **Kevin Haggerty**, University of Alberta; **Jef Huysmans**, Open University, UK; **Robert Latham**, York University, Toronto; **Stéphane Leman-Langlois**, Laval University, Quebec; **Michael Levi**, Cardiff University; **Monique Marks**, University of KwaZulu-Natal, South Africa; **Valsamis Mitsilegas**, Queen Mary, University of London; **Ethan Nadelmann**, Drug Policy Alliance, USA; **John Torpey**, City University of New York Graduate Center; **Federico Varese**, University of Oxford.

Titles include:

Vida Bajc
SECURITY, SURVEILLANCE AND THE OLYMPIC GAMES (*forthcoming*)

Sophie Body-Gendrot
GLOBALIZATION, FEAR AND INSECURITY
The Challenges for Cities North and South

Alexander Kupatadze
ORGANIZED CRIME, POLITICAL TRANSITIONS AND STATE FORMATION IN POST-SOVIET EURASIA

Georgios Papanicolaou
TRANSNATIONAL POLICING AND SEX TRAFFICKING IN SOUTHEAST EUROPE
Policing the Imperialist Chain

Leanne Weber and Sharon Pickering (*editors*)
GLOBALIZATION AND BORDERS
Death at the Global Frontier

Transnational Crime, Crime Control and Security
Series Standing Order ISBN 978–0–23028945–1 hardback
                          978–0–23028946–8 paperback
(*outside North America only*)

You can receive future titles in this series as they are published by placing a standing order. Please contact your bookseller or, in case of difficulty, write to us at the address below with your name and address, the title of the series and one of the ISBNs quoted above.

Customer Services Department, Macmillan Distribution Ltd, Houndmills, Basingstoke, Hampshire RG21 6XS, England

Globalization, Fear and Insecurity

The Challenges for Cities North and South

Sophie Body-Gendrot

First published 2012 by
PALGRAVE MACMILLAN

Palgrave Macmillan in the UK is an imprint of Macmillan Publishers Limited,
registered in England, company number 785998, of Houndmills, Basingstoke,
Hampshire RG21 6XS.

Palgrave Macmillan in the US is a division of St Martin's Press LLC,
175 Fifth Avenue, New York, NY 10010.

Palgrave Macmillan is the global academic imprint of the above companies
and has companies and representatives throughout the world.

Palgrave® and Macmillan® are registered trademarks in the United States,
the United Kingdom, Europe and other countries.

ISBN: 978–0–230–28421–0 hardback
ISBN: 978–1–137–00792–6 paperback

This book is printed on paper suitable for recycling and made from fully
managed and sustained forest sources. Logging, pulping and manufacturing
processes are expected to conform to the environmental regulations of the
country of origin.

A catalogue record for this book is available from the British Library.

Library of Congress Cataloging-in-Publication Data

Body-Gendrot, Sophie.
    Globalization, fear and isecurity : the challenges for cities north and
south / by Sophie Body-Gendrot.
        p. cm.
    ISBN 978–1–137–00792–6 (pbk.)
        1. Urban policy. 2. Urban violence. 3. Fear. 4. Cities and towns. I. Title.

HT151.B564 2012
307.76—dc23   201201232

10 9 8 7 6 5 4 3 2 1
21 20 19 18 17 16 15 14 13 12

Printed and bound in Great Britain by
CPI Antony Rowe, Chippenham and Eastbourne

People only ever have the degree of liberty that their audacity wins from fear.

Marie-Henri Beyle; pen name, Stendhal

Contents

Illustrations

Figures

Tables

Acknowledgements

I am deeply grateful to Richard Sennett, Ricky Burdett and Philipp Rode, who devised and organized the Urban Age conferences in New York, Shanghai, London, Mexico City, Johannesburg, Berlin, Mumbai, Sao Paulo, Istanbul and Hong Kong between 2005 and 2011; and to Wolfgang Nowak, director of the Alfred Herrhausen Society at the Deutsche Bank, who financially supported such programs at the London School of Economics (LSE). They generously invited me to be part of the Urban Age 'nomadic' group from the very start. I was then able to conduct a dialogue with local experts on security in all the mega-cities around the world that from 2005 onwards we visited, explored and attempted to understand. The field experiences and the lessons – in terms of fears and insecurity – I drew from these 'endless cities' and from living in them are the subject of this book.

I wish to express my gratitude to the Institute of Public Knowledge (IPK) at New York University (NYU) which, thanks to Craig Calhoun, Richard Sennett, Sam Carter and Jessica Coffey, provided a supportive environment for my research for a few weeks in 2010 and 2011. Although I was never granted any leave of absence or grant or research assistance from my academic institutions, it was stimulating to share the NYU intellectual environment. I was also privileged to sit in at the NYU Law School and the Straus Institute for the Advanced Study of Law and Justice monthly meetings, thanks to the generous invitations of David Garland and James Jacobs. Doctoral student Fanny Lauby provided me with research assistance during the time I carried out my research at the IPK.

I also wish to thank my friend, Saskia Sassen: our conversations (and laughter) and her books and articles have been a great source of inspiration and support. I have been extremely fortunate in receiving valuable feedback and shrewd comments from Malcolm Anderson and splendid editing of chapters 3 and 5 by B. Loveday: asking friends to spend hours reading one's work can put a strain on friendship, and only the most generous will comply. Aziz Huq, Mira Kandar, Carolina Grillo, Alan Mabin and Betsy Stanko offered very useful suggestions on some of my chapters. Friends and colleagues also offered advice, in particular Vera Telles and Daniel Richman. I had a very fruitful conversations in New York with Michael Jacobson at the Vera Institute of Justice and with

Jeremy Travis at John Jay College of Criminal Justice. I owe a great deal to my colleagues and friends at Centre de recherches sociologiques sur le droit et les institutions pénales (CESDIP)/Centre National de Recherche Scientifique (CNRS), to my students at the Centre d'études littéraires et scientifiques avancées (Centre d'études littéraires et scientifiques avancées (CELSA) at Université-Paris-Sorbonne) and to my doctoral students, who are too numerous to be individually mentioned here. They helped me explore and test further my findings. I wish to thank them all.

Finally, the idea for this book began at a conference of the RC21 committee International Sociology Association (ISA) in Tokyo, where S. Zukin urged me to write this book. Then A. Tsoukala, my French editor for the series *Transnational Crime, Crime Control and Security* at Palgrave Macmillan, invited me to be an author in her series. At Palgrave Macmillan continuous support was offered, first by Philippa Grand and Andrew James, then Julia Willan, Ellie Shillito and the production team at Newgen Knowledge Works, India.

Some of the material herein was drawn from earlier published work, including:

Body-Gendrot, S. 'Urban "riots" in France: Anything New?', in L. Cachet, S. de Kimpe, P. Ponsaert and A. Ringeling (eds) *Governance of Security in the Netherlands and Belgium* (Den Haag, Netherlands: Boom Juridische Uitgevers, 2008), 263–80.

Body-Gendrot, S. 'Confronting Fear', in R. Burdett and D. Sudjik (eds) *The Endless City* (London: Phaidon, 2008), 352–63.

Body-Gendrot, S. *La peur détruira-t-elle la ville?* (Paris: Bourin, 2008).

Body-Gendrot, S. 'Police Marginality, Racial Logics, and Discrimination in the *Banlieues* of France', *Ethnic and Racial Studies* 33 (4) (2010a), 656–74.

Body-Gendrot, S. 'European policies of social control Post 9–11', *Social Research*, 77, 1, (2010b), 181–204.

Body-Gendrot, S. 'Uneven landscapes', in R. Burdett and D. Sudjik (eds) *Living in the Endless City* (London: Phaidon, 2011), 360–67.

Body-Gendrot, S. 'Power and Powerlessness in Global Cities' http://www.opendemocracy.org, February 7, (2011a), last accessed: March 8, 2012.

Body-Gendrot, S. 'Disorders in World Cities' http://www.opendemocracy.org, August 15 (2011b), last accessed: March 8, 2012.

Body-Gendrot, S. and Savitch, H.V. 'Urban Violence in the United States and France: Comparing Los Angeles (1992) and Paris (2005)', in

K. Mossberger, S. Clarke and P. Jones (eds) *Oxford Handbook of Urban Politics* (Oxford: Oxford University Press, 2012, forthcoming).

I wish to thank the following for permission to use copyright material by arrangement with:

Gary LaFree and Laura Dugan (2009) for Table 3.1 on the distribution of incidents by regions of the world

Frank Zimring (2012) for Table 3.2 on crime rates in 2007 in London and New York from *The City That Became Safe: New York's Lessons for Urban Crime and Its control*, Oxford, 2012.

Ajay Mehra (2011) for Table 3.3 on terrorist attacks in Mumbai since 1993

Alan Mabin (2001) for Table 4 on the levels of reported crime in Johannesburg versus the RSA average-2001

Jeremy Travis, President of John Jay College for Figures 3.1 and 3.2 borrowed from the Jones-Brown and J. Gill (2010) Report 'Stop, Question and Frisk Policing Practices in New York City: a primer'.

Foreword

The city has long been a strategic site for the exploration of many major subjects confronting society and the social sciences. But it has not always served us to understand some of the major transformations of an epoch. In the first half of the twentieth century, the study of cities was at the heart of sociology. This is evident in the work of Simmel, Weber, Benjamin, Lefebvre and the Chicago School, especially Park and Wirth, both deeply influenced by German sociology. These sociologists confronted massive processes – industrialization, urbanization, alienation and a new cultural formation they called 'urbanity'. Studying the city was not simply studying the urban. It was about studying the major social processes of an era.

By the 1950s, the study of the city had gradually lost this privileged role as a lens for the discipline and as producer of key analytic categories. There are many reasons for this: most important among which are questions of the particular developments of method and data, and the major questions driving social science. The social sciences, we might say, lost their capacity to 'see' the city and all it made visible. Most of what remained of traditions of 'seeing' was focused on 'social problems'.

Sophie Body-Gendrot brings us back to the use of the city as a lens for understanding larger processes for which the city is one acute and concentrated instance. She does so across four continents, with all their organizational, political and cultural differences. But she does so with twenty years of experience researching the pertinent subjects. And she does so armed with a powerful conceptual architecture centred on globalization, insecurity and cities. This larger assemblage of elements enables the city to work as a window onto challenges that go beyond cities, but for which the city is an acute and particularly contradictory instance. Body-Gendrot's research includes inter-ethnic relations, citizens' participation, power relations and public policies.

This mix of acute and contradictory challenges brings with it the need for detailed empirical study and careful tracking of policies, responses by governments and citizens, evolutions of the central condition at issue here, insecurity and its consequences. Fieldwork and access to those in charge of security in cities was critical. Her fieldwork in New York City included work with the NYPD and the justice system, with tenants from public housing projects, schools and various institutions. For fifteen years she was a member of the Eisenhower Foundation whose project was to replicate what works well in disadvantaged American neighbourhoods. In London, she was welcomed by the New Scotland Yard anti-terrorist unit, by the police chief from the Metropolitan Police Service at Southwark Police Station, and had multiple exchanges with aides to Mayor Livingston, in matters of security. In Paris, she was a member of the Police Complaints Authority for five years; this allowed her to conduct hearings and hear conflicting accounts of both the police and citizens mostly from poor neighbourhoods. She did multiple research trips to São Paulo, including a whole summer at the Center for the study of violence, and did interviews in *favelas*. And she made several trips to Johannesburg, doing fieldwork and meeting with experts.

This extraordinary twenty-year voyage across some of the most complex and powerful cities in the world does indeed deliver its promise. This is evident in the author's keen sense that it would be a mistake to apply the same categories to the cities in the North as to the cities in the South, to European as to American cities. It is of course easier to do so. But the author engages with the material, political and subjective conditions in each city. The comparative analytics are centred in how each city handles the security question – it is this shared question that is applied to these very diverse cities. As the author puts it, her challenge was 'to mix particularisms and generalizations in order to find the appropriate questions and, if lucky, answers. ... The city is both a practiced and a felt space, an experience and an ideal, an idea and sometimes a utopia'.

There is a challenge in the effort to recover place in the context of globalization and insecurity. It is an unexpected turn of events that the start of the new century brings back some of the old questions of the early Chicago School of Urban Sociology and some of the questions later raised by Jane Jacobs. One could ask if their methods might be of particular use in recovering the category place at a time when dominant forces such as globalization and telecommunications seem to signal that place and the details of the local no longer matter. Large cities around the world are the terrain where multiple globalization processes assume concrete, localized forms. These localized forms are, in good part, what globalization is about.

If we consider further that large cities also concentrate a growing share of disadvantaged populations – immigrants in Europe and the United States, African-Americans and Latinos in the United States, masses of shanty dwellers in the mega-cities of the developing world – then we can see that cities have become a strategic terrain for a whole series of conflicts and contradictions.

We can then also think of cities as one of the sites for the contradictions of the globalization of capital. On one hand, they concentrate a disproportionate share of corporate power and are among the key sites for the over-valorization of the corporate economy; on the other hand, they concentrate a disproportionate share of the disadvantaged and are one of the key sites for their de-valorization. This joint presence happens in a context in which (1) the transnationalization of economies has grown sharply and cities have become increasingly strategic for global capital, and (2) marginalized people have found their voice and are making claims on the city as well. This joint presence is further brought into focus by the sharpening of the distance between the two.

These joint presences have made cities a contested terrain. The global city concentrates diversity. Its spaces are inscribed not only with the dominant corporate culture, but also with a multiplicity of other cultures and identities, notably through immigration. The slippage is evident: the dominant culture can encompass only part of the city. And while corporate power inscribes non-corporate cultures and identities with 'otherness', thereby devaluing them, they are present everywhere.

Recovering place means recovering the multiplicity of presences in this landscape. The large city of today has emerged as a strategic site for a whole range of new types of operations – political, economic, 'cultural', subjective.

To all of this, Sophie Body-Gendrot adds the question of security in its multiple concrete manifestations. The cities she has studied provide a range of security concerns and the effects of the response by the forces of order and by citizens themselves. They range from the most lethal cases, notably terrorism, move on to criminal cartels and gangs challenging city authorities and, at the other extreme, socially destructive urban violence. The author gives us a valuable examination of the language within which the question of insecurity is embedded. This varies, depending on the actors involved in each city in her study, but also varies sharply across these cities.

Under conditions of insecurity, states are likely to enter the picture armed with powerful instruments. Body-Gendrot notes states have a choice between policies of redistribution and/or punishment. The politicization of fear is a conservative choice. The author writes

> What gives terrorism its specific place in current fears is the idea of an alleged presence of infiltrated enemies, ready to commit

unpredictable and blind actions.…Currently, political authorities dealing with public anxieties take initiatives translating into constraints on civil liberties. In the scenario anticipating terrorist actions, suspicion does not spare anyone'

Other options beyond the politics of fear are always possible. For Body-Gendrot, a critical and difficult question for our times then becomes: How can global cities alleviate social tensions when the sense of solidarity is eroded? What is possible? 'Confronting this diffuse rise of fears – or at least tensions – focussing on the collective experiences of living together within diversity, are states indeed the most competent players or just one among many?'

Today we are seeing a partial unbundling of national space and of the traditional hierarchies of scale centred on the national, with the city nested somewhere between the local and the region. This unbundling, even if partial, makes it problematic to conceptualize the city as nested in such hierarchies. Major cities have historically been nodes where a variety of processes intersect in particularly pronounced concentrations. In the context of globalization, many of these processes are operating at a global scale that cuts across historical borders, with the added complexities this brings with it.

This is not, however, the city as a bounded unit, but the city as a complex structure that can articulate a variety of cross-boundary processes and reconstitute them as a partly urban condition. Further, this type of city cannot be located simply in a scalar hierarchy that puts it beneath the national, regional and global. It is one of the spaces of the global, and it engages the global directly, often bypassing the national. Some cities may have had this capacity long before the current era; but today these conditions have been multiplied and amplified to the point that they can be read as contributing to a qualitatively different urban era. Cities have also long been sites where major trends interact with each other in distinct, often complex manners, in a way they do not in just about any other setting. Today all of this holds also for studying the global in its urban localizations.

In a brilliant move, Body-Gendrot focuses on the broad and diverse range of capabilities cities offer. She focuses on actors that allow cities to move beyond their difficulties by using a city's accumulated knowledge as reservoirs of action. She highlights specifically urban capabilities such as urban cultures and public spaces as resources.

The city is one of the places where the formation of new claims by citizens materializes and assumes concrete forms. Citizens can actively criticize and reject specific conditions or decisions and they can ask for change in ways that transcend the formality of participation in national politics – voting. Further, the loss of power of national states in the current context, even when the executive branch of government is, in my view, gaining power, produces the possibility for new forms of power and politics at the subnational level, especially cities. Further, insofar as the national as container of social process and power is cracked it opens up possibilities for a geography of politics that links subnational spaces across borders. Cities are foremost in this new geography. One question this engenders is how and whether we are seeing the formation of a new type of transnational politics that localizes in these cities. Global capital and the new immigrant workforce are two major instances of transnationalized actors with features that constitute each as a somewhat unitary actor overriding borders while at the same time in contestation with each other inside cities.

The centrality of place in a context of global processes engenders a transnational economic and political opening in the formation of new claims and, hence, in the constitution of entitlements, notably rights to place and, at the limit, in the constitution of 'citizenship'. The city has indeed emerged as a site for new claims: not only by global capital which uses the city as an 'organizational commodity', but also by disadvantaged sectors of the urban population, which frequently is as internationalized a presence in large cities as is capital. Cities are the terrain where people from many different countries are most likely to meet and a multiplicity of cultures can come together. The international character of major cities lies not only in their telecommunications infrastructure and international firms, but also in the many different cultural environments in which these people at work (in the firms) exist. One can no longer think of centres for international business and finance simply in terms of the corporate towers and corporate culture at its centre.

Today, as we enter a new century, the city is once again emerging as a strategic site for understanding some of the major new trends reconfiguring the social order. The city and the metropolitan region emerge as one of the strategic sites where major macro-social trends materialize and, hence, can be constituted as an object of study. Among these trends are globalization, the rise of the new information technologies, the intensifying of transnational and translocal dynamics, and the strengthening presence and voice of specific types of socio-cultural diversity.

To this extensive set of subjects, Sophie Body-Gendrot has added the most critical emergent issues we now face: insecurity and fear, in their many diverse manifestations. Each of these trends has its own specific conditionalities, contents and consequences. The urban moment is but one moment in often complex multi-sited trajectories. But it is an important one: the urban moment of a major process makes the latter susceptible to empirical study in ways that other phases of such a process might not.

Saskia Sassen
London, 2012

Introduction

This book links the issues of urban safety, laws, law enforcement and justice to the more general studies related to cities. Most research on cities deal with policymaking, local institutions, governance and service delivery, while issues of threats, risks, insecurity and fear relative to the well-being of populations are usually left to criminological studies. Yet the well-being of cities depends on public safety.

The research focuses on global cities. As economic and production activities have dispersed in various locations where labour costs are cheap, a centralization in the functions of command, control, profit-maximizing and planning has appeared as a necessity for multinational headquarters and financial institutions in search of economics of scale, cooperation and skills. The concentration of the management and financing of operation networks is located in the business centres of some very large metropolises which form new centralities, working more in cooperation than in competition. The current influence of finance on economic activities allows multinational headquarters and financial institutions to gather complementary resources, form central alliances and dictate requests to their partners within an increasing development of transnational interactions. As 'nodes and hubs' of the world finance and economy, they subcontract sophisticated services, helping them make the best decisions in regard to their competitors. The best minds and skills in the knowledge economy thus work and live in these cities along with workers in the shadow, frequently first-generation male and female immigrants, who provide services at the bottom of the assembly line of the global economy (Sassen, 2001).

I first show that although residents of cities have lived in fear throughout history, current forms of globalization have fostered new types of threats. The attack on the Twin Towers of the World Trade

1

Center in New York City by terrorists is the most spectacular of such new threats, but other macro-changes affect people's daily lives and need to be studied. How do such global insecurities insert themselves into everyday life? What do people do about them? (Pain and Smith, 2008, 2) Do they just gate themselves in? Do they become insurgent citizens and express demands forcefully, if the context offers opportunities for them to do so?

In this book, I look at both ends of the connection, from top down and down up. I then explore the idea that if cities have so much to lose from new threats linked to globalization, then it is a must for them to be on the front line and find solutions. I examine the specific strategies that cities can develop when their capacity for independent action is limited by the exercise of sovereign powers (executive, legislative, judicial) of state and global institutions such as the European Commission and by the necessity for attracting and maintaining private financial and economic investors. There is no nostalgia here for city states as they were in sixteenth-century Italy: some of their residents lived in constant fear of assassination by rival families (Putnam, 1993), but today some very large cities demonstrate that they can overcome global constraints and the state domination for survival's sake.

The meaning of words conveying a wide range of emotions such as fear, insecurity, risk, danger, urban violence, and the precautionary principle needs to be specified. The very elusive character of terms loaded with images conveniently allows political maneuvering. 'Bombarding the world with messages about new and renewed risks allows governments to capitalize on fears by governing through beliefs, behaviours and assent of the "neurotic citizen"'[1] (Ibid., 1). They legitimize restrictions on citizens' rights and freedoms and the buttressing of order.

We believe that we think with words

Terms like fear, insecurity, risk and violence do not simply evoke a difference in degree; the very nature of the terms is different.

Fear and insecurity

According to philosopher Lars Svendsen, *fear* 'has become the emotion that controls the public, acts as a magnifying glass through which we consider the world' (2008, 12). Fear is a positive signal against danger, a warning sent to the mind. When fear becomes dysfunctional, problems appear. Such dysfunctions as applied to cities are studied here. Anglo-Americans refer to fear of crime, 'an emotional response of dread or anxiety to crime or symbols that a person associates with crime' (Ferraro, 1995:4). For Sessar and Kury (2008), fear of crime is a political issue resulting from surveys in a politically usable construction. According to Baker (2010), Europe governs less through fear as in America, and more through security with an emphasis put on offenders' due process of law rather than on an expansion of victims' rights.

Insecurity, also a slippery and contested term, conveys numerous meanings and has referent objects ranging from the individual to the state to the global economy, and so on (Zedner, 2009, 10). It functions with its opposite, security. Its lack of definitional clarity allows a wide range of interpretations and responses. Why is it that people think that problems of insecurity are worsening? Are insecurity and the feeling of insecurity the same phenomenon? One should differentiate general and fluctuating opinions on the problem of insecurity, fears regarding one's daily life, those of one's kin and the experience of victimization (Mucchielli, 2011). Those are different phenomena and are measured via surveys. Jackson (2006:261) compares them to 'a sponge, absorbing all sorts of anxieties about related issues of deteriorating moral fabric, from family to community to society'. The feeling of insecurity reached a peak in France before the presidential elections of 2002: sixty per cent of those polled said that security should be the first governmental priority. Ten years later in France, security ranks fifth or sixth among national concerns. At the same time, those expressing strong concerns about insecurity add that in their daily life, they do not feel unsafe. Only 8 per cent of those surveyed in the Parisian region in 2010 feel unsafe at home, as was the percentage in 2000. Deconstructing the sample reveals that those who feel unsafe have never been victimized (Zauberman, 2012). Their feeling of vulnerability may be due to their age, gender or socio-economic status and attitudes. Convergences emanate from the type of places they have chosen, or been forced, to live. An aged woman living in suburb not far from public housing estates will typically express such feelings.

Regarding cities, feelings of insecurity are increased by signs of disorder. Yet, such perceptions are selective. We remark on them all the more as they appear in social contexts which are not familiar to us. We do not notice graffiti along the banks of the Seine in Paris or the Thames in London, where we feel safe, but they strike us on the walls of a railway station in an unfamiliar locality. Actors of disorders, however, frequently live in the same spaces as those who fear them. But the feared may also be the fearful and vice versa (as in the case of former bullied children turning into violent teenagers). Insecurity may not be caused by acts one has witnessed, but merely by rumours circulating among people who know each other more or less or by intensive crusades launched by the media after a very unusual incident. The collective contamination of negative perceptions – a feeling of powerless when signs of order have vanished, an 'ontological' disenchantment – all testify to the solitude of individuals in cities confronted with macro-changes that they cannot grasp and that the state, supposedly invested with the duty to protect them, seems unable to alleviate. For Bauman (1998, 11; Zedner, 2009, 98), the demand for security results from a 'transfer of anxiety'. This observation marks a contrast with village life where everyone knows each other in a familiar environment. For Wirth (1938), in cities anonymity is both a protection and a cause of insecurity. It betrays a loss of markers, which makes the interpretation of changes difficult for vulnerable and lonely individuals, but shields them when these dense urban spaces send too many stimuli.

Risk

Feelings of insecurity are frequently unrelated to risk. Risk is defined as a potential danger, more or less anticipated, and varies greatly across time and space. Beck (1992, 96) points out that risk awareness is frequently based on second-hand information, but also on second-hand non-experiences. The conception according to which everything can happen is widespread. 'Anything can be a risk; it all depends on how one analyzes the danger and consider[s] the event ... [D]anger is not an objective condition. As Kant might have put it, the category of risk is a category of the understanding; it cannot be given in sensibility or in intuition. Not all risks are equal and not all risks are interpreted as dangers' (Campbell, 1998, ix). Some risks cause fear, some just concerns, while others appear attractive in some circumstances. Living (increasingly, in a very large city) is to accept living with risks. Yet risks which are statistically insignificant are given a great deal of attention; they are constructed by the discourses of experts, media, economic interests and politicians. It is in their interest to do so. Communication on responses given to urban risks (for instance, installing CCTVs in the public space) allows governing elites to divert attention when they have so little control over major threats (global warming, earthquakes, economic instability, and so on), and to refocus larger anxieties into concern for insecurity, to conceal their limits and avoid answering impossible demands from citizens always requiring ever more secure environments.

Risk is socially situated and varies from culture to culture. People, however, tend to employ puzzling rationalities in selecting the risks that they want to be concerned with. They orient their mode of thinking on specific situations or behaviours and are mentally prepared to confront danger within what Douglas and Wildavski (1984) call 'a portfolio of risks'. Risk is consequently a socially and individually constructed element, defined through comparisons, in an architecture itself characterized by a necessary oblivion of all other potential risks. There is no scientific basis to such a construction. People are scared of aspects which objectively cause few casualties, such as the transportation of toxic goods.[2] There is frequently confusion between risk and insecurity, yet these notions are dissimilar (Katane, 2005). They relate to different social logics, modes of construction and interpretations of situations which are not linked. Risks are examined and evaluated one by one while, by contrast, insecurity is a more general feeling that one tries to escape by building or requiring protection. Risk can be managed by the individual or by the community, via trusted individuals or experts' informed advice, while experts or science rarely alleviate feelings of insecurity (Ibid.). One should specify that urban insecurity for the middle classes is mostly a concern (Furstenberg, 1971; Robert, 1999, 76–77). Governing elites take insecurity seriously because middle classes have a power of sanction and express their discontent. By contrast, urban insecurity is physically and emotionally experienced day to day by those who know what it means to find oneself alone, powerless, in a hostile and brutal environment. For instance, artists with scarce resources, living in low-life streets controlled by drug dealers may need, evening after evening, to negotiate access to their apartments. The situation is the same in both North and South mega-cities.

Urban violence

Within the field of insecurity, politicians, media and researchers also refer to another concept, that of urban violence. Violence belongs to the repertoire of common language. Criminal court judges rarely use it. Although it becomes more common in criminological writing, its demarcation is often ignored, according to Dutch historian Spierenburg (2008, 14). There is little agreement on the definitions of violence, a slippery term covering huge and frequently changing ranges of heterogeneous physical and emotional behaviours, situations and victim–offender relationships (Levi and Maguire, 2002, 796). Either the notion is underdefined or overdefined. It remains a morally charged notion running along a continuum, 'from an angry and hostile glare … through verbal abuse, a verbal threat, threatening gestures, a single blow, an attack causing minor injuries, an attack causing major injuries to an attack causing death' (Waddington, Badger and Bull 2004, 145). Yet, as correctly remarked upon by de Haan (2008, ch. 2), such a definition focuses on visible, intentional, interpersonal harm, while excluding institutions or administrations. It ignores the social implications of violent processes such as racism and sexism. Finally, it excludes symbolic violence, that 'gentle, invisible form of violence which is never recognized as such and is not so much undergone as chosen, the violence of credit, confidence, obligation, personal loyalty, hospitality, gifts, gratitude, piety' (Bourdieu, 1987). In our discussion, the use of violence is limited to urban violence.

Sherman (1995, 36–7) wonders why there is so much focus on crime-prone individuals and not on dangerous spaces. Examining crime reports in Minneapolis, he found that crime was highly concentrated in a few locations to which he referred as 'hot spots'. 'Why aren't we thinking more about wheredunit, rather than just whodunit?' he asked. Shaw and McKay (1942) had reached the same conclusions in their seminal study of high-crime and low-crime neighbourhoods in Chicago, showing how unvarying they were over time. Numerous criminologists have followed this trend, examining spaces producing deviant patterns, while others have kept looking at criminal careers among certain types of individuals perverting the spaces where they lived and operated. But what is more interesting, it seems, is the interaction of the offender, the target and the external/internal control involving political, historical and cultural features of urban governance.

In France, the notion of urban violence received its legitimacy in 1991, when the Department of Cities and Neighbourhoods was created within the General Intelligence Service (Renseignements généraux) of the national police. It collected daily information in 'sensitive' neighbourhoods, information based on urban violence as 'collective, open and provoking: it is both destructive ... emotional ... expressive, sometimes playful, frequently criminal ... always juvenile' (Bui-Trong, 1993, 235–6). This definition was later contested by researchers. Urban violence can indeed be committed by adults; registering crime depends on the number of policemen on the field. The media use urban violence mostly to refer to antisocial behaviours, also called 'incivilities' – that is, behaviours disrupting common norms allowing for public tranquility. They are not necessarily illegal and, if so, not necessarily controlled by the police. Intrusive squatting by youngsters in the entrance halls of public housing estates is illegal in France, yet it is very difficult for the police to enforce the law. Such youth behaviour, frequently associated with drug dealing, is intimidating for older and vulnerable residents and can be described as a low-intensity form of urban violence.

In the United States, debates related to violence in cities were frequent in the 1960s. President Lyndon Johnson appointed a commission on the topic under the auspices of Milton Eisenhower, the president of Johns Hopkins University and the brother of former US president Dwight D. Eisenhower. This 'Violence Commission' and its numerous recommendations are worth remembering. But the societal debate regarding the production of violence in American society disappeared during Republican presidencies of the 1970s, and the term 'crime' came to the forefront. 'Crime' was a way of externalizing the issue, of connecting it to troublemakers in dangerous places who are not part of 'us' (Body-Gendrot, 2000, xxv). The term, 'crime', and the debate related to the violence of American society are at the top of the public agenda when the victims are the middle classes (for example, the shooting of a member of Congress in a public place in Tucson, Arizona, in 2011) or their children (the school massacre at Columbine, Ohio, in 1999).

The principle of precaution

According to the laws of the European Union, it is a duty for public bodies to act to avert serious or irreversible damages. More than a decade ago, Ewald (2002) compared this principle of precaution to risk management. This principle was not just concerned with the anticipation of future harm, he thought, but it also had to do with the pre-emption of disasters and with what could not be calculated. The perfect moment for someone to act is not always predictable. Yet if the idea that a catastrophe is bound to happen is overwhelming, then pre-emption brings the future into the present; any action thus seems better than inaction to prevent the emergence of the threat. This mode of thinking is pervasive in the field of safety and is used to justify pre-emptive governmental intervention, surveillance and identification. Uncertainty constitutes a dominant justification for governmental action before the unknown threat makes itself known (Zedner, 2009, 58). The flaw in this type of reasoning, as pointed out later by Ewald (2010, 10), is that in the management of uncertainty risk becomes correlated to threat. Negative emotions or manipulations prevail over the advice of experts who know that the risk in question is microscopic. 'The recourse to risk...has saturated almost every aspect of our lives and times'(Ibid.). 'Moral panics about dangerous groups, places and behaviours inform policing and community safety policies, and within urban development, unjust fortressing and surveillance strategies clash with rhetoric about inclusive and peopled cities' (Pain and Smith, 2008, 1).

In the case of terrorism, facing an alleged or real danger, precautionary measures are taken by power-holders, and the principle is brought up to justify them and to minimize criticism. Anticipating the questions: 'what might be' or 'what if?' (Crawford, 2010, 13), governing elites claim that it was their duty not to wait for the next act of terrorism which is not 'if' but 'when'. The three powers – scientific, media and political – that could neutralize each other in such circumstances amplify one another.

Organization of the book

To facilitate comparisons of global cities' responses within each category and between categories, this book is organized according to types of threats. It starts with the most lethal one, terrorism, a relatively rare one compared with homicide and violent death; criminal cartels and gangs challenging city power, itself weakened by corruption, in some cases; and it ends with socially destructive urban violence. My cases are chosen both from the North and the South because it is important to compare how mega-cities deal with threats and dangers whatever their location and because, at a time of globalization, research has to create a dialogue between global cities and discern convergences and differences. This research does not attempt however to be comprehensive; the book is not an encyclopaedia, and comparative analysis is privileged.

The book is organized in two parts. The first focuses on the global context leading to new forms of fears and anxieties in cities, and the second focuses on case studies. It looks at cities' leverage and constraints when confronting various types of human-induced threats.

The Part I examines what is new in this (more or less) diffuse urban fear and insecurity linked to globalization. After all, fear has always accompanied the history of cities. In comparison with the past, the destabilizing macro-mutations to which our era is submitted foster, if not fear, at least strong concerns. The perspective is global. Take demographic evolutions: more than half the world population currently lives in urban zones. In mega-cities, in the South, in particular, demography explodes. It has less to do with birth rates, which tend to stabilize, than to massive arrivals of populations pulled to cities by desertification, wars, jobs and hope for a better future. As a consequence, even if global migrations are not massive at the scale of the planet, they dramatically threaten historical arrangements, frames and norms of local societies. Ageing populations, however, particularly in Europe, need more young migrants to fill the services that they need and to pay for their pensions. But the immigration issue usually raises two types of worries in Western countries: the mal-integration of second and third generations from developing countries, on the one hand, and on the other – also the case for the South – the impact of undocumented migrants on local economies and on the transformation of values and cultures. In the United States, 'a nation of nations', the trajectories of Latinos bring some optimism, but in Europe the integration of Muslims proves to be more difficult. The definition of their identities incorporates criteria relative to influential countries of origin, religion and belonging. Incomplete and complex transmissions regarding belonging imply that each generation has to redefine itself here and now and reveal its own vision of the world. This is specifically the case in France, a conservative country where changes foster worries relative to the future and to risks in general. In a society of 'distrust', uncertainty operates against any positive tolerance for differences. The more that these poor populations (born abroad) and their children become part of the mainstream in labour, housing and educational markets, the more fears of downward mobility are felt within established vulnerable groups. Far-right and conservative political parties manipulate such general concerns with a racial lens when advocating national preferences. They create binary visions of "we" – an undefined mainstream society – and "they," – ill-defined, predatory others.

States have a choice between policies of redistribution, allocating subsidies and benefits to people and/or punishment. 'Locking people up or giving them money might be considered alternative ways of handling marginal, poor populations – repressive in one case , generous in the other' (Greenberg, 2001, 70). Liberals usually claim that good social policy is the best criminal policy. Obviously, a selective eligibility diminishes the role welfare states play as buffers against general anxieties relative to the future. Following Lijphart (1999), one should distinguish consensual (or corporatist) democracies (taking as many views as possible into account) such as Switzerland and the Scandinavian countries, and also Austria, Belgium, France, Germany, Italy and the Netherlands, from majoritarian or conflict democracies (the majorities dictate the choices; they are also less corporatist), including Australia, Canada, Ireland, New Zealand, the United Kingdom and the United States. Consensual democracies are more welfare-friendly, more prone to 'trade-offs' and lean toward leniency, while conflict democracy expresses more severity. Moderate penal policies have their roots in consensual and corporatist political cultures. A society with great social distances is more prone to apply punishments to 'others' and to the alleged undeserving than would a society of equals, concerned with general well-being (Lappi-Seppala, 2011). The most difficult question of our time then becomes: how can global cities alleviate social tensions when the sense of solidarity is eroded ? What is possible?

Confronting this diffuse rise of fears – or at least tensions – focussing on the collective experiences of living together within diversity, are states indeed the most competent players, or just among the many? The Chapter 2 questions the changes brought by the 9/11 attacks in the United States and the choices made by the Bush administration, which boosted nationalism to silence its political opposition and take advantage of a 'liberalism of fear'. With this expression, Judith Sklar means that liberalism has abandoned its commitment to rights perceived as too abstract, and moved to a fearful defensive stance against the arbitrary intrusion of governments. The liberalism of fear implies that there is a political mobilization on that theme, and it indicates that the vocabulary of fear has become part of a wide range of discourse (Sklar, 1998). The politicization of fear is a conservative choice. Other options are always possible.

After 9/11, with neoconservative elites in power at the White House, public anxieties were nurtured. An arsenal of technologies of identification, control and surveillance was set in motion both in the public and private sectors. Strong measures of order maintenance buttressed the presidency's powers. The 'punitive turn' already taken years before 9/11 was reinforced.

Is this a new phenomenon? Not really. From the mid-1960s onward, the politicization of the issue of crime in American cities acquired new vigour. Episodes of anxieties during World War I, the Cold War, 'McCarthyism' (or the 'Second Red Scare') and the Vietnam War had distinguished the American past. In the 1980s, the Reagan administration emphasized the idea of 'danger at our doors'. Public questioning regarding the production of violence by American society itself and its root causes was then silenced.

What gives terrorism its specific place in current fears is the idea of an alleged presence of enemies who have infiltrated, ready to commit unpredictable and blind actions. Threats of this type erode the foundation of states' legitimacy, revealing their incapacity to protect citizens and cities adequately. They blur the usual frames of analysis and distinctions between internal and external security.

Currently, political authorities dealing with public anxieties take initiatives translating into constraints on civil liberties. In the scenario anticipating terrorist actions, suspicion does not spare anyone. Intruding into citizens' private lives without warning to counter such potential terrorist actions is thus justified by political authorities. But when both innocent and guilty people are stopped and searched, not necessarily for what they might do but also, as categories, the social contract and trust that ideally links citizens to one another and to their state is betrayed by prevailing suspicion. Trust is the foundation for stable and effective democratic government. Trust is an indicator of social bonds and social solidarity. Declining solidarity implies accepting tougher actions from governmental authorities (Lappi-Seppala, 2011, 313). When suspicion targets a specific category of the population, for instance young Muslim males, this approach then amounts to discrimination.

The Part II of this book presents case studies of global cities confronted with threats. The term 'world city' emerged early in the 1960s to reflect the increasing global influences of economic and financial powers on urban life. It refers to cities concentrating complex transactions and decisions emanating from headquarters of transnational financial corporations, multinationals, stock exchanges, advanced corporate service producers and information-processing centres. In these global cities, fortunes are made and destroyed. Rich and poor live side by side, servicing a global assembly line. That such places would gather wealth, assets and potentialities, and would also attract a widely diverse people from various countries implies social disparities which may translate into social risks and dislocations, and sometimes into crimes and violent events. This is what Chapter 3 is about. Elites in charge of the well-being of such cities cannot tolerate disorder, whatever form they take. In New York City, after the crack epidemics which caused a record number of homicides, Mayor David Dinkins was criticized for not 'doing something'. His successor, Rudolph Giuliani, promised his constituents more secure streets via a 'zero tolerance' approach. He leaned on punitive populism, which had then been a mainstream trend in the country since the 1960s. London aligned itself with this posture[3] approving many ordinances aimed at antisocial behaviour, harassing delinquents, and the distribution of parts to play by market and by citizens in the co-production of security. In one city and another, the implementation of security schemes has been both local and regional. But what is of interest for this current research is how, after 9/11, New York City took the lead in developing a very sophisticated counterterrorist force, in some respects bypassing federal authorities and making New York City a success story.

The argument is more difficult to make for Paris and London because, as capitals with their national governments located in the city, national/local distinctions are not clear-cut in terms of security enforcement. London may have a 'reassuring' police force but in Paris, where the police are national, the omnipotent French state dwarfs whatever leverage the city has in its responses to threats, even in the case of terrorist threats.

Nor is the matter clear for Mumbai, a mega-city that depends greatly on the state of Maharashtra and on India for its protection

The Chapter 4 examines global South cities threatened by organized criminals and gangs. As previously stated, it is important to study North and South metropolises jointly, as they have so much to learn from each another. Here, convergences with North cities come from the private strategies of social and territorial entrenchment. The weakness of state authorities and their lack of legitimacy are very real problems for the South and make it difficult for cities to take the lead in preventing catastrophic takeovers by criminal cartels. Who is responsible, who coordinates efforts and manages funding? There seems to be a plurality of overlapping actors who diffuse the notion of accountability. As a consequence, metropolises frequently choose to privatize services which are no less corrupt than public ones. Gated communities proliferate in Latin America, Asia and Africa. As observed by Bauman, '[I]n an ever more insecure and uncertain world, the withdrawal into the safe haven of territoriality is an intense temptation' (1998, 117). Fear of crime is frequently the reason given by affluent people for such secession, thus continuing the tradition of apartheid in Johannesburg. In São Paulo, the excuse of fear is also invoked by wealthy and established families belonging to the old social order and not ready yet to live side by side with lower classes. When they have to share 'social' (meaning shared) elevators, for instance, they find ways to mark their difference and establish symbolic walls. In these global cities of the South, police and justice which are required to be more efficient in conflict prevention and in order maintenance are rarely up to the task.

Another type of threat targets French and British large cities – which the Chapter 5 is about – and this is a pervasive delinquency of exclusion and numerous incivilities, making precarious populations' daily lives difficult. The general feeling of insecurity and, sometimes, fear that they generate extend beyond problem areas, even though episodes of violent urban unrest, frequently called 'riots', remain geographically circumscribed and unusual. This type of violence does not occur frequently in Europe, but the issue cannot be taken lightly. Among populations, it reinforces a general distrust of authorities that are perceived as inefficient, and this may explain votes for extremist political candidates expressing discontent. Such general disenchantment brings support for repressive policies.

The media are a given, which must be incorporated into the analysis. While it cannot be said that the media directly determine attitudes and the formation of public opinion, one can assume that they have some influence in shaping opinions towards delinquency, recurrent unrest and the justice system which is, usually, accused of 'softness'. By using the same terms and similar images to refer to diversified contexts of violence that should be deconstructed, they tend to weave a unifying narrative that makes sense to the general public. General viewpoints are shaped and diffused from isolated incidents. There are structural convergences explaining urban disorders in France and Britain, but ideological, contextual, interactional and situational factors point at differences. National paths of dependency also modified by globalization play a part in the interpretation of incidents: race and ethnic awareness in the United Kingdom, and protests against the state and its symbols in France.

The argument, according to which certain cities are ahead of states in opting for measures that will handle the causes of disorders, is hard to make. In such cases of urban disorder they depend so much on economic and financial resources from central states, despite more or less enforced decentralization laws. Moreover, the current global context makes the situation of already decaying neighbourhoods and localities worse. That the poor fight other poor is nothing new. In the Western metropolises, as in those of the South, mainstream societies' indifference to life at the margins explains why the philosophy according to which conflict is a recurring element of urban life, continues to prevail and lead to submission to (and approval of) the dominant order. Yet such generalization does not always prove to be true. The last chapter focuses on what works. Democratic forms regarding local institutions – from fair policing to restorative justice and pressures exerted by empowered citizens – may lead to cities that are more just. In marginal localities, not only do people get accustomed to living 'together with their difference' and make life possible via 'mutual exchange and cooperation articulated in the proliferation of hybrid cultural practices that transcend fixed identities and closed community boundaries' (Ang, 2010, 161), but forms of 'insurgent citizenship' (Holston, 2008) or smart tactics for dealing with daily life (de Certeau, 1984) reveal that alternative modes of using disorders to create other orders are also more widespread, especially in the South.

Because cities are always in the making, forming and reforming, the very principle of incompleteness is what makes them alive and boosts their dynamism. In numerous societies, from Israel to Greece, cities as a form of social life are very unlikely to die.

Methodology

Though concentrating on globalization, insecurity and cities, this book is the product of twenty years of comparative research focussed not just on those themes, but on interethnic relations, citizens' participation, power relations and public policies, all undertaken in the context of personal or collective, national and international research programmes. The book has benefited from numerous secondary sources, but also from field work carried out in New York City with the New York Police Department (NYPD) and the justice system, with tenants from public housing projects, schools and various institutions. I was a member of the Eisenhower Foundation for fifteen years, the aim of which was to reproduce what works in disadvantaged American neighbourhoods. Numerous trip fields and debates were organized in various American cities. In London, I was welcomed by the New Scotland Yard anti-terrorist unit and by the police chief from the Metropolitan Police Service at Southwark Police Station, and I had exchanges in matters of security with aides to Mayor Livingston. At the LSE, I also acquired insights from architects and planners and numerous academics. In Paris, my five-year involvement with the Police Complaints Authority allowed me to conduct hearings and listen to conflicting accounts on the part of the police and citizens – most of the citizens from poor neighbourhoods – and to make recommendations. I also carried out research with another scholar on discrimination in the French police, in particular analysing calls made by 'visible minorities' complaining about police via a toll-free number, and the training given in police academies on the topic of racism. A member of an interactive institution Profession Banlieue (a resource centre in Saint-Denis) for fifteen years, I have attended numerous meetings between scholars and administration, police, tenant managers, and so on, involved in the poor neighbourhoods of Seine Saint Denis in attempting to understand what works. In the South, I visited São Paulo, Brazil, several times, including a whole summer at the centre for the study of violence and carried out interviews at the periphery with a graduate student. I also visited Johannesburg several times, walked through its streets, listened to the specialists on violence and its prevention, and was taken into the field by various friends, students or experts.

My method is qualitative, although whenever appropriate, quantitative data is used critically, particularly in the cases of opinion polls, supplemented by qualitative surveys. Academic research, public discourses, media and conversations with residents and colleagues in various global cities have helped me clarify my thoughts .

My approach is also interdisciplinary: economic data and theories, political science, sociology, racial and ethnic studies, urban geography, philosophy, history, law and criminology complement various aspects of the research. It also draws on the abundance of material provided by a rich scholarly tradition of urban research. A city is 'a spatial location, a political entity, an administrative unit, a place of work and play, a collective of dreams and nightmares, a mesh of social relations, an agglomeration of economic activity.... There cannot be a unique theory or discipline to study a city' (Beauregard, 2011, 186–202). Complexity requires interdisciplinary approaches and appropriate categories used after the cases have been introduced. This flexibility prevails in my research, and it would be unrealistic to apply rigid categories similarly to North or and South cities and European or American cities. Each city is unique. The challenge is then to mix specifics and generalizations in order to find the appropriate questions and, if lucky, the answers.

Methodologically, walking through a city – observing, adjusting, listening, talking, remembering previous readings that come to mind – is a first-hand experience. It allows one to fill voids between the inside and the outside, the public and the private, the inner and the outer. The city is both a practiced space and a felt space, an experience and an ideal, an idea and sometimes a utopia (Mongin, 2005, 15). In the dialogue that we – *flâneurs*, users, residents, visitors – weave with the city, we allow the city to build within us, to mould, and to transform us. There are theoretical pitfalls in this method, however, when dealing with the local, and misunderstandings may occur.

And, the book is comparative. A comparison of global cities is possible in matters of fear, insecurity and urban threats, even between cities of the North and the South. I immensely benefited from the Urban Age Program at the LSE. Each conference in a world-city was incredibly rewarding in terms of knowledge and exchanges among very different specialists and residents.

Tocqueville has given legitimacy to comparative work on local democracy. But there is only one Tocqueville. The tradition of comparative studies is strong, allowing the testing of hypotheses and taking a distance from narrowly focussed monographs. However, the treacherous nature of the comparative exercise cannot be underestimated, such as comparing world cities in the North and South under the same headings or categories, or analysing threats for which the same terms are used (like terrorism or violence) but which differ in nature and scope when they take place in New York, Paris, London or Mumbai. Taking the comparison differently, and looking at how the violence problem is constructed and what positions are generated by this construction, makes the comparison more relevant. It shows that debates related to the production of violence by society are currently missing; they have been diverted by a refocusing on offenders, hot spots and control – a focus which externalizes the responsibility of societies and reintroduces a binary vision of 'us' and 'them'. This observation can be extended to all the global cities included in this research.

It has not been possible, at the end of this research, to give a list of good practices or to make recommendations. This is critical academic work. Each of these cities – moulded by its own history, its institutions, its economy, the profile of its social components – has to be taken in context and the time frame. Research tools, abundant in North's cities are less so in the South, and attempting to establish a grid comparing key concepts, terms, practices, data sets, processes, actors and institutions will not meet expectations because such concepts and categories do not convey the same meanings according to time and place. One should resist the temptation of merely translating terms. At best, functional equivalences can be suggested, invalidated or supported. The manner in which tensions are expressed and resolved, for instance, are uneven; how ordinary people interpret and make sense of them, and how their 'structures of feeling' play out differ (Crawford, 2011, 9–11). Some threat perceptions are to be connected to everyday experiences of injustice and inequalities, defying generalizations. A term-to-term comparison is just not possible. Indicators concerning the feeling of insecurity get their meaning only after the at-large organization and singular features of each city are understood. (Lorrain, 2011, 34–5).

Keeping these obstacles in mind, I still defend the cross-fertilization, the awareness of diversity, the clarification of concepts and the theoretical challenges brought by international comparative analysis.

New trends of comparative studies link macro-perspectives and micro-ethnography. But they either omit 'difficult' countries such as France or, if they focus on Europe, ignore the United States, and urban research frequently ignores criminal research and its issues. There is, however, more research linking North and South mega-cities. My focus remains modest. I am interested in threats and democratic poisons that work against cities, formally or informally, but I also attempt to focus on actors, allowing cities to move beyond their difficulties, thanks to their accumulated knowledge, and as reservoirs of action. Some city authorities know better than others how to communicate what works. The elected officials' political will and intelligent vision, combined with those of the private sector and of organized residents, can succeed in making cities resilient places of trust, security and hope. Such success coming from cities' vitality, creativity and incompleteness inspire the search for new paradigms and new tools in order to make sense of the ongoing processes.

Part I

Linking Globalization, Fear and Insecurity

1
Old and New Fears in Cities

Insecurity is linked to the history of cities. While phenomena generating fear are not necessarily new, the short-sightedness of our current era makes us unaware of their long prevalence over time. 'Old processes continue to operate, the past is transformed, it is not obliterated. That a "postmodern" city would have displaced the old or the modern cities is not convincing. Novelty is always a rhetorical move and history ever-present' (Beauregard and Haila, 2000, 23). There may have been a time historically when imaginary or real fears were mostly confined to local communities. The story of a crime would not go further than the limits of the district. But, increasingly, risk and fear are experienced, portrayed and discussed as globalized phenomena, particularly since 9/11 (Pain and Smith, 2008, 1). If current macro-changes alarm people, it may be because of a lack of clues to make sense out of them. This chapter firstly examines urban insecurity and fear in a historical perspective. It conveys voices of thinkers who, along centuries, have analysed fear and insecurity. It shows what continuities with our time are discernable. Secondly, it reviews the fears and feelings of insecurity linked to globalization and characterize our time. They impact on collective urban life in various degrees. This analysis frames the context for further investigation into specific threats addressed in Part II.

1.1 Fear: an ancient phenomenon

In Europe, over the centuries, cities, meant to protect populations behind their high walls, were also the locus of fears. Human concentration in circumscribed spaces and the rapid contagion of rumours have supported the persisting idea that cities were dangerous. French historian Delumeau (1978) explored the role of fear in Catholic societies of

Europe from the late Middle Ages to the eighteenth century. Fear of death and of damnation was strong in a background of anxiety rising from wars, invasions, starvation, epidemics, natural disasters, enemies, criminals and many other fears. Fear was everywhere and persistent. It has accompanied the history of cities since their beginning.

Two anecdotes from historians emphasize continuities with our time.

In an exchange of letters between French King Henry IV and the provost of merchants, François Myron, in 1604, the latter writes that 'it is a poor idea to build neighborhoods exclusively dedicated to craftsmen and workers. In a capital where the Sovereign dwells, it is not appropriate that the little ones are on one side and the big plump ones on the other, it would be best and more secure to mix them together: your poor neighborhoods would become citadels blocking your rich neighborhoods. ... And as the Louvre is in the nice part, it could happen that bullets would bounce off your crown. ... I do not want, your Majesty, to be an accomplice of such measure'. The former replied: 'My fellow, you are quick as a beetle but finally a good and loyal subject. Your will shall be met and the King of France will attend your school of wisdom and conciliation for a long time. ...' (Anonymous source).

English historians found a comparable letter, written to the mayor of London in 1730 by Daniel Defoe, the author of *Robinson Crusoe*: 'All the city, my Lord, is alarmed and confused .... Citizens no longer feel secure within their own walls, or walking through the streets, but they are robbed, insulted, molested .... And such mischief happens within your jurisdiction as never before (at least not to that range) and if it is allowed to persist, it will lead to summon the army – and not the magistrates – to put an end to it.'

Political thinkers and philosophers of the past have expressed ambivalence relative to fear and violence. Machiavelli thought that as men were able to inflict harm on one another, the function of violence was to secure social order via a suitable amount of fear. A well-organized state had to be built on coercion and on a constant threat of violence. There is a good use of violence when one's own security calls for it, he states in *The Prince*, and a bad use of violence if it increases rather than decreases with time (chapter 8, 7). To the question of whether it would be better to be loved or feared, Machiavelli answers that it is much safer to be feared but, nevertheless, a prince ought to inspire fear in such a way that, if he does not win love, he avoids hatred. A ruler who spreads too much fear undermines his legitimacy. The control of fear is the basis for control by the state (chapter 17, 1). Fear is what ultimately secures the prince's power and, thereby, social order: 'The prince is kept alive by the fear of punishment which must always be maintained' (chapter 17, 2; Svendsen, 2008, 104).

Montaigne observed in his *Essays* (1575) that 'fear gives wings to our heels...sometimes it nails down and fetters our feet...t'is a strange passion, and such a one that the physicians say there is no other whatever that sooner dethrones our judgment from its proper seat...it is most certain that it begets a terrible astonishment and confusion during the fit' (Book 1, 17). He thus deduces that our frailty means that we gain more by fleeing than by striving. 'The thing I fear most is fear...it exceeds all other disorders in intensity' (Montaigne, 1955, 53). (Thoreau, 1906, viii; 468) echoes Montaigne when he writes that 'Nothing is so much to be feared as fear'.

For Hobbes in *Leviathan* (1651), fear is a passion that must be taken into account in politics. As the life of man is 'solitary, poor, nasty, brutish and short', a cohesive defense against violence, war and dangers that threaten from all sides calls for a sovereign who will impose collective rules. People choose to abandon their freedom in exchange for safety; they draw up a social pact sanctioned by a sovereign with unlimited power. 'Therefore before the names of Just and Unjust can have a place, there must be some coercive Power to compel men equally to the performance of their Covenants, by the terror of some punishment, greater than the benefit they expect by the breach of their Covenants; and to make good that Propriety, which by mutual Contract men acquire, in recompense of the universal Right they abandon: and such power there is none before the erection of a Common-wealth' (chapter 15, 2). Fear springs from the sense of danger, sometimes exacerbated by the state. Fear is thus an instrument of domination in the hands of the prince and a universal lever of power. It is exploited to maintain some form of social order and although people ask for protection, they also dread the arbitrary use that can be made of the freedoms that they have surrendered.

Giambattista Vico thought that all human civilization had its foundation in fear (1744), arguing that it spurred the development of all with which men surround themselves: houses, cities, weapons, laws, social institutions, art and religion. (Tocqueville [1854], 1992, 849), the most modern among those political thinkers, it seems, laments the fears of his generation and describes the democratic malaise that he observes in America as 'a worry regarding the future and an uncertainty regarding the past'. He analyses the loss of markers of the lonely crowd and of individuals with no bearings.

More contemporary thinkers, from Max Weber to Hannah Arendt have questioned the state monopoly of violence (or force) as dangerous. Such demonstration is made by Robin (2004) for whom fear has been viewed as the enemy of independent selfhood and political decency. Currently, the inability of the modern state to give 'neurotic' citizens the sense that they are protected from violence, terror, war and all kinds of dangers undermines its legitimacy.

Pessimism regarding our current era was outlined by Schlesinger (1949), during the cold war. 'The Western man in the middle of the 20th century is tense, uncertain adrift. The grounds of our civilization, of our certitude, are breaking up under our feet and familiar ideas or institutions vanish as we reach for them, like shadows in the failing dusk.' Closer to us, Ignatieff observes that 'the idea of human universality is less founded on hope than on fear, less on optimism about the human capacity for good than on the dread of human capacity for evil, less on a vision of man as a maker of his history than that of man as a wolf toward his own kind' (1997, 18).

Sociologists Glassner (1999) and Furedi (2002) have focused on the unusual cultures of fear that developed in the United States under the use of emotions by the media. 'Media pandering becomes the key villain of the piece', Stearns (op. cit.) observes. Glassner shows, indeed, that between 1990 and 1998, the murder rate in the United States decreased by 20 per cent, yet during that same period the number of stories about murder on network newscasts in the United States increased by 600 per cent. Viewers could not have the impression that crime was down (Glassner, 2004, 820). A similar observation concerns school shootings, which are very unusual incidents. In 1959–67, 19 such deaths were registered out of 54 million children in schools. Yet the former secretary of education, W. Bennett, proclaimed that 'America's beleaguered cities are about to be victimized by a para-digm-shattering wave of ultra-violent, morally vacuous young people, some call the super-predators' (Ibid., 821). Yet the youth homicide rate continued to decline, and more than three times as many people were killed by lightning than by violence at schools. Repetition, the depiction of isolated incidents as trends and misdirection charac-terize 'fear-mongering'. Glassner takes terrorism, which has a low inci-dence, as an example. In 2001, nearly three times as many Americans died from gun-related homicides than from terrorism (Ibid., 823). But such amplification leads to 'acceptance [by the public] of poli-cies that are frequently as misdirected as the fears themselves – for instance, withdrawing kids from public schools despite their normal and considerable safety' (Ibid., 479). For Furedi, the media are 'fear entrepreneurs'; they generate phobias with little relevance to reality. Fear has become the most pervasive emotion of modern society due to technological and psychological developments which, with knowledge, increase anxieties about death, disasters, harm relative to children and health vulnerabilities. In all this research, one perceives that probably with the revolution of information and communication expanding since the 1970s, new elements induce fear and a sense of vulnerability, but how and why remain elusive (Castells, 1996, 29–65; Bourke, 2006). Are our societies more fearful than they were in the recent or more distant past? How? Certainly the media carry weight, but 'the division between scholars who attribute change simply to the media , and those who find in fear a response to more fundamental features of contemporary life, has to be mediated by more analytical studies' (Stearns, 2006, 482; Scheingold, 1984).

Nevertheless, the manipulation of fear by those in power makes it easier to govern people, and it can be used to mobilize law-abiding citizens through appeals for public order against 'dangerous others'. But such manipulation meets with resistance. Equilibrium is not easy to find. As observed by French philosopher Paul Valéry, 'If the state is too strong, it oppresses us; if it is too weak, we perish' (1948 [1931], 967).

This brief glance at the past may help us understand what globalization has changed in our perceptions.

1.2   The global mutations of our time

The instantaneousness of information and communication has narrowed the linkages between global and local spheres. Local phenomena as well as emotions in everyday life are influenced by what is broadcast all over the planet, such as 9/11, Hollywood mass products, and various catastrophes. Research at the interfaces of geopolitical practice, public discourse and everyday life is relatively unusual. Do events provoking fears in one global space make people fearful at very local levels? Researching this topic implies looking at 'the complexity, situatedness, sociality embodied and – critically – constitutive qualities of emotional life. ... How do global insecurities worm their way into everyday life? Where do they figure in local landscapes of risk? What do people do with them? What are the tangible threats to safety and well-being, outside of those fears of "mainstream" society which grab the headlines, and what are the fears of those who are feared?' wonder Pain and Smith (2008, 2), pointing out that there is no in-depth analysis of the social implications of urban globalization regarding risks for cities at various levels. Problems generating insecurity, particularly in some urban areas, are frequently perceived and defined politically, but the link with how they are understood socially and felt by residents experiencing them on a day-by-day basis is rarely explored. The analysis of disorders in Mumbai, New York, and São Paulo and in British and French cities attempt to fill that gap.

Markers between the two spheres – the global and the micro-local – tend to become blurred. 'There are not two scales which inspire and address fear by variously relating to one another; rather there are assemblages of fear built, trained, embedded, woven, wired, nurtured into the way the specific times, places and events work' (Pain and Smith, 2008, 3). It is this linkage that is explored in this research by looking at cases involving terrorism, organized criminals and urban violence. The scope of disorders reveal the cities' difficulties in coming up with adjusted, multidimensional solutions for the challenges that they face. Eager to keep the upper hand, some of them make radical decisions, such as bulldozing massive public housing projects when they prove to be beyond control, or granting voting powers to long-time foreign residents at local elections to reinforce inclusiveness. Logical and functional propositions made by institutions and bodies in charge of decisions sit, however, in sharp contrast with hazard, disorder and unpredictability characterizing city life.

1.2.1   Demographic tectonics

For centuries, the vast majority of humankind lived in the countryside. For five thousand years or so, however, people have headed to cities in the hope of finding freedom, protection and a better future. Yet while only 10 per cent of the world population lived in cities in 1900, for the first time in history, a majority – 3.2 billion residents, four times more than in 1950 – currently does so. While the world population – 7 billion in 2011 – keeps growing at a fast pace, the amount of land remains the same, it even shrinks, gnawed away by desertification and threatened by floods in the most densely populated areas. Vital resources in water and in energy thus decrease. The UN *2009 World Development Report* states that over half the world population currently lives less than one hour away from a city of over 50,000 inhabitants. In the developed world, this rate is 85 per cent versus 35 per cent in the developing world. With 95 per cent of the world population concentrated on 10 per cent of the planet, in only 10 per cent of that land are at least 48 hours needed by local transportation to reach a large city. Only 2 per cent of the earth's surface is occupied by cities, but 53 per cent of the world's population lives in cities (Burdett and Rode 2011, 9).

Annexing growing portions of the world to support a limited number of industries and cities has gone along with the expansion of the global economy. Under such circumstances, Todorov (2008, 12) remarks, competition between countries cannot be avoided, implying that those with less resources threaten those with more resources. This raises fears and determination to preserve and protect their better position.

The growth of global cities is a feature of our time. Nine per cent of the world population lives in mega-cities of over 10 million inhabitants. The number of cities exceeding one million residents totals 450. Out of 20 regions, 15 regions with mega-cities ranging between 10–20 million inhabitants are currently located in the South. Between 1950 and 2005, the number of metropolises over one million grew from 39 to 308 in Asia, Africa and Latin America; by contrast, in Europe and North America, it increased from 37 to 96 (www.urbanage.com). It is estimated that in the next 23 years, cities of the global South will absorb the net global population growth. According to estimates, every hour, 48 newcomers settle in Dhaka and Kinshasa, 40 in Lagos and 44 in Mumbai (Burdett and Sudjik, 2011, 36–37). These figures are to be taken cautiously. Many people are also leaving these cities, not to mention deaths, natural disasters and epidemics. Mobility, however, characterizes the global South confronted with major demands in terms of infrastructure, housing, services, jobs, health and security. By comparison, European demographic problems seem microscopic.

In each world region, urban galaxies are found around core cities, such as Greater Tokyo, 55 million; Shanghai-Nanjin-Hangzsou, 50 million; Boston-New York-Washington, 55 million; Pittsburg-Chicago-Minneapolis, 46 million; Cologne-Amsterdam-Brussels-Lille, 50 million; London, Manchester-Liverpool, Leeds-Sheffield, Birmingham, 49.1 million; Milan – Rome – Torino, 47 million. Such a method of clustering may be contested. However, one understands the urgency to enlarge the Greater Paris, already at 14.6 million, and to establish clusters with London and the largest Belgian and Dutch cities. Compact urban development seems indeed to be an adequate sustainable answer to uncontrolled sprawl, energy over-consumption and pollution – as cities contribute 75 per cent of the world's CO_2 emissions. The integration of older urban centres into these giant urban developments alleviate problems of urban decay and of desertification.

Numerous typologies are elaborated upon to make sense of these evolutions. Moisi (2007) does not distinguish societies according to their political regimes, geographical location or types of civilizations, but according to their responses to these macro-changes, what he calls 'a clash of emotions'. The Western world displays a culture of fear, he observes; the Arab and Muslim worlds are trapped in a culture of humiliation, and much of Asia displays a culture of hope. Instead of being united by their fears, the United States and Europe are more often divided by how best to transcend them. The culture of humiliation, in contrast, helps unite the Muslim world around its most radical forces. Resentment structures the social life of active and influent minorities in these countries. They hold the Western world as the source of their private misery and public powerlessness. The chief beneficiaries of these antagonisms are the bystanders in the culture of hope who concentrate on creating a better future for themselves. There are obviously variations within each region but, basically, such dynamics and interactions impact on the world for years to come. The West fears the economic strength of Asia and the nuisance capacity of the Muslim world (energetic threats included). Among the fearful, Europeans have two more causes to worry: their ageing populations (demographer Sauvy said that the twenty-first century would be 'the century of demographic ageing') and their difficulties at melding in second and third generations whose parents migrated from countries of 'resentment'.

1.2.2   Ageing societies: Europe at risk

Table 1.1 shows that all the world regions will keep growing in population until 2050, except for Europe.

The birth rate among European women has decreased since 1970, in particular in Eastern Europe, but also in Italy and Spain. By comparison,

Table 1.1   World population ageing

Population (in millions)	2005	2050	Variation (%)
Europe (including Russia)	728	653	–10
Africa	906	1937	+114
Asia	3905	5217	+34
Oceania	33	48	+45
North America	331	438	+32
South and Central America and the Caribbean	561	783	+40

Source: United Nations, 2009, United Nations Population Fund. *World Population Aging*. Department of Economic and Social Affairs, Population Division.

for many years, the United States has balanced deaths and births (with a rate of 2.1 births per woman of childbearing age). Concerns are less pronounced in Ireland and France, where birth rates almost balance deaths. In 2000, the world population aged 60 years or over numbered 600 million, three times the number of 1950. The 2009 UN study of ageing populations reports, however, that in 2050 the proportion of older persons is expected to reach 22 per cent (44 per cent in Japan) (2009, viii), as long as old-age mortality continues to decline and fertility to remain low. In 2009, this population had surpassed 700 million. By 2050, older persons are projected to total 2 billion, implying that their number will once again triple over a span of 50 years (Ibid.).

The social impact of decreasing active populations in European cities cannot be overlooked in any study on urban insecurity. Longevity, divorce rates, single-person and single-parent households are all on the rise, contributing to the weakening of integrative social structures. In the developing world, family structures continue to act as a social cement and constitute the main economic and social organization dimension (Body-Gendrot, Garcia, Mingione, 2012, forthcoming). In the Western world, by contrast, the combination of employment changes and demographic transition is undermining all of the variants of the breadwinner regime with regard to available economic resources and access to social rights and benefits, either directly or indirectly, through the husband-father working career (Mingione, 1996; Esping-Andersen et al., 2002). Therefore, employment no longer provides a fixed point of reference for building job identity and life stability, at least in the case of men.

In one century, the average life expectancy has increased by half. It has consequences on the meagre shares allocated to young cohorts, on their resentment and 'indignation', as will be seen in Chapter 5. That the percentage of the 'fourth age' (over 75) will numerically explode leads to re-examining systems of social protection at a time when the pie is no longer as large as it was after World War II. Social anxieties have a political impact, and the most vulnerable categories violently mark their refusal to adjust to policies of austerity.

The financial impact of increased longevity on health services, housing and pension costs has caused the already high level of social spending in Europe to rise further (Body-Gendrot, Garcia, Mingione, op. cit.). The issue of pensions is a source of massive fear, discontent and urban unrest. But so are the issues of care, health insurance and new occupations to be created to meet seniors' demands. Within societies of Southern Europe, small firms still provide opportunities. But the family is under considerable stress, resulting in falling marriage and birth rates (Mingione, 2005).

The issue of ageing is particularly acute for women. According to a study of senior citizens over 75 in nine European countries (Delbes et al., 2006), in all European countries, ageing with a partner is more frequent for men (two out of three) than for women (one out of five). Living alone after 75 is a characteristic of Northern European women.

Opening the doors of ageing societies and of labour markets to younger immigrants has frequently been conceived as a possible solution. But can societies of fear and societies of resentment mix harmoniously within circumscribed urban spaces?

1.2.3   Migrants as a solution?

There are two major concerns associated with the issue of immigration in Europe. One relates to undocumented migrants in cities, and the other to the integration of second and third generations perceived as 'visible minorities'.

(a)   The issue of undocumented migrants in cities

Regarding undocumented migrants, cities bear the consequences of policies on which they have no leverage. Continuous flows of poor migrants pour into ports of entry located in Spain, Malta, Italy and elsewhere before moving to larger cities in search of jobs. When geopolitical decisions are made, global and national domains tend to ignore the burden of the impact these decisions have on cities and other subnational levels. Including cities from the start in the decision-making process and in the transactions would lessen the dramatic problems, conflicts, tensions and forms of violence that result from such phenomenon. Macro-level frames should be held accountable 'for the types of stress that arise from violence and insecurity in dense spaces in everyday life – the type of issue that global governance discourse and its norms do not quite capture' (Sassen, 2011).

It is important however to de-dramatize the question of migrations and to bring it into a larger perspective. Through the centuries, migration has been an ongoing process. Migration is a key phenomenon in the history of humankind. It should be examined with relativism. According to the UN report on human development already quoted, only 170 million people live in a country where they were not born, that is 2.7 per cent of the world population. The number of internal migrations averages 740 million, a number four times greater than that of international migrations (2009, 9; 23). One third of these migrants are Chinese farmers moving to cities, others are refugees in camps. The average rate of migration from countries with a low level development represents one third or less (1 per cent) of the level of those with a high level of development (5 per cent) (2009, 24; 27). This situation is all the more surprising, as migrants from poor countries would make enormous gains if they did migrate to rich countries. Their income would increase 15 times ($15,000 a year), each individual's level of education would improve from 47 per cent to 95 per cent, and the rate of infant mortality would fall (from 112 per 1,000 to 7 per 1,000) (UN Report, 2009, 26).

Migrating from poor countries, however, remains difficult and limited.[1] After the fall of the Berlin Wall, rumours had predicted a massive exodus from the East to richer Western countries. It did not happen. Fears caused by 'Polish plumbers' did not materialize. While locally the issue of undocumented migrants has an emotional impact, seen globally and from a long-term perspective, undocumented migrants should not be a cause of fear.

(b) American solutions: a model for Europe?

Another perception of immigration as a problem relates to the integration of migrants' children and grandchildren into Western societies. Will they be a cause of disorder or will they benefit the cities that incorporate them? From which point of view and for whom? Schain (2010) produces a stimulating comparison on that issue. In contrast with European policies, American integration policy generally recognizes, and even encourages and protects multiculturalism and diversity. During the past decade, integration policies in both Europe and the United States have converged, with a focus on both civic integration and anti-discrimination policies. Concerns about urban insecurity, which have driven integration policies, have however resulted in different policies with different outcomes. Looking back over the last 25 years, the French policy of integration first arose out of a quest for public order after urban disturbances that have punctuated French urban life since the early 1980s. Other challenges, such as those set by young Muslim girls wearing hijabs in public schools or women with burkas in public places, were met with more laws. As local authorities searched for mediators among 'second generations', they sometimes supported whatever associations of immigrant origin they felt could maintain social order, an issue that will be explored further in Chapter 5.

Integration policies are reinforced and constrained by the development of European integration (Schain, 2010). In March 2006, the interior ministers of the six largest EU countries (the Group of Six, or G6) agreed to pursue the idea of an 'integration contract', using the French model as a starting point. One of the first initiatives of the French presidency in 2008 was to propose a comprehensive, compulsory EU integration program and the 'European Pact on Immigration and Asylum' was passed by the European Council in October 2008. Three criteria were selected: language mastery of the receiving country; knowledge and commitment to its values; and access to employment (www.euractiv.com July 2, 2008). At the same time, anti-discrimination programs in all European countries have increasingly benefited families already settled in the receiving countries. First initiated in Britain in 1965, the anti-discrimination approach was given a major push by the Treaty of Amsterdam in 1997 and by two directives of the European Council in 2000.

Similar to the initial French integration efforts, the British approach has been rooted in a need to maintain public order (Bleich, 2003). Since 2001, it has taken distance from multiculturalism and favoured a stronger sense of collective identity (Home Office report, *Secure Borders, Safe Haven: Integration with Diversity in Modern Britain*, 2002). Immigration is perceived as contingent upon increased civic integration and 'shared values' (Joppke, 2004, 253). The terrorist attacks in London in 2005 accelerated such a process, requiring national cohesion and loyalty to the national community.

The United States knows how to 'metabolize' and integrate its immigrants. The size, the history, the institutions of the country participate in that success story. The issue of undocumented immigrants, however, divides Americans along two considerations, that of jobs and that of culture. The number of undocumented is estimated around 9 million, out of a Latino population officially put at 50 million, which is, 16 per cent of the national population. Opinions regarding undocumented immigrants vary according to the levels of education of those polled. For example, a majority of Whites with a four-year college degree (56 per cent) say that immigrants strengthen the country through their hard work, while just over a third of this group (37 per cent) disapprove and see Latinos as a burden. Not only whole sectors of the economy would be unable to function without them (food, building, fish and forest, agriculture, tourism, and so on.) but these Latinos, in return, consume goods and services and pay taxes which are beneficial to the whole country. They are not the poorest ethnic group in the United States. Whites with less than a high school education split the opposite way, with 63 per cent seeing immigrants as burden and 30 per cent as a strength for the country. Similar but less pronounced differences appear among non-Whites with different levels of education (Pew Hispanic Center, 2006, 15).

The success of immigration in the United States cannot be understood without taking into account the specific conditions of Blacks, whose integration remained slow and difficult after they migrated to industrial cities of the North and East of the country. Their demands as a group were reinforced by the emergence of 'Black neo-ethnicity' in the midst of the civil rights struggle the 1960s. The partial accommodation of their vigorous demands for policies against racism and discrimination and for better working and living conditions allowed the formation of a Black middle class. In this sense, the cooption of Black elites into the mainstream had to do with the civil rights movement followed by the instrumentalization of urban violence by Black militants exerting intimidation and pressures on the political decision-makers. Organized immigrants, ethnic groups and women took advantage of the door which had just opened. These interest groups all lobbied for their specific interests within an American political system receptive to such lobbying (Fuchs, 1990, 18; Zolberg, 2006). Even as an afterthought, it appears that American political leaders were confident enough to promote cultural diversity, a concept that European leaders (especially in countries where the far right is strong) either fear or seek to carefully manage (Schain 2010; Body-Gendrot 2010b).

(c)   The issue of second and third generations in Europe

There has been an increase of state involvement in the integration process during the past 40 years. Some immigrant groups' children (Indians for instance) surpass their British counterparts from similar socio-economic backgrounds in education.

Yet there has been Schain remarks that in the United States, protection for access to employment and housing is available to immigrant populations. Until recently, political parties have generally made a greater effort than have those in either France or Britain to recruit and mobilize immigrant populations and their children.

In France, the neglect of immigrant children's specific problems in education results in inequalities which are worse than in most other countries. The proportion of immigrants' children who drop out of school, or who never get to upper secondary education, is high (also high in the United States, but comparatively low in Britain). Britain has encouraged ethnic identity formation and modes of organization which have proven successful in education and employment, but not in politics. The counterpart has been to legitimize a awareness of separation among ethnic minorities, explaining the new political emphasis on cohesiveness. In the United States, multicultural policies have strengthened a sense of ethnic identities and a well-established trend of ethnic political participation. In France's case, despite some support for multiculturalism (mostly at the local level), the central government has been eager to reinforce republican values, emphasizing French identity.

Regarding discrimination, two directives of the European Council in 2000 required all EU countries to institute commissions that would both monitor and act against patterns of racial discrimination. Such commissions have a fair record in Britain, but in France, the Higher Authority (Haute Autorite de lutte contre les discriminations et pour l'égalité) never had legal and financial resources to investigate properly patterns of discrimination. In 2011, it was merged into a larger administrative body in defense of rights. American integration and anti-discrimination policies have reinforced both minority identity and legitimacy on the one hand and, on the other, political opportunities. For instance, between 1996 and 2007, the political representation of Latinos in the United States increased by more than 50 per cent at the national and state levels, compared with slightly more than 25 per cent at the municipal level (NALEO, 2007). France has consistently had poor records in this area, and the British not much better. In the French case, neither the left nor the right in power have been very responsive to the potential of new ethnic voters whose parents had migrated from North Africa and Africa. The availability of this electorate has been somewhat delayed by French citizenship law (immigrants to Britain are eligible to vote with the establishment of residency in contrast with long-term noncitizen residents). This electorate's geographical concentration in relatively few constituencies in France makes it less attractive politically than comparable voters in the United States and Britain.

This comparison on the integration of second and third generations in three countries yields surprising results. A positive marker of integration in France concerns identity. According to a 2006 Pew Research survey among Muslims in fifteen European countries, 73 per cent of the French see no conflict between being a devout Muslim and living in modern society (versus 35 per cent of British and 42 per cent of Americans). Only 29 per cent of the French admitted to being racist (versus 40 per cent in 1990). By contrast, 81 per cent of British Muslims regard themselves as Muslims first, then British. They construct themselves on differentiation; 69 per cent are hostile to Jews. Conversely, 29 per cent of the French Muslims are hostile to Jews. One Muslim out of two sees him/herself as French first. One should be cautious with these data (also confirmed by Gallup polls), because the term Muslim is elusive and identity is composed of many strands.

It seems easier to integrate a language like Spanish than a religion like Islam, Zolberg and Wong (1999) point out. In the United States, 8 per cent of Latinos of the first generation marry out of their group, compared with 32 per cent of the second generation and 57 per cent of the third generation (Pew Hispanic Center, 2003).

Fundamentally, the impact of the past cannot be neglected. Islam plays on imaginations fed by past religious wars in Europe. Resources easing migrants' mobility are currently less efficient at a time of globalization where the economic, social and political spheres are disembedded. Formerly, trade unions, political parties and churches took care of neighbourhood problems such as schools, housing and leisure and transmitted a sense of trust to their members. The autonomy of the social question reveals needs for cultural differentiation within class cohorts that soon become boundaries and markers for in-groups. In France in particular, a largely rural society until the end of World War II, an obsession with patrimony, and the fear of possible losses, foster a fear of risk and of the future, which reduces a sense of tolerance of difference. Communitarism is demonized and seen as a threat to the unity of the nation. France and its culture of fear, which hitherto appeared as an anomaly in Europe, is felt in other countries experiencing economic and financial hardship. Currently, the competition for the best positions puts solidarity and ethnic succession on the back burner. As aptly described by urban ecology, all social categories struggle for the best jobs, the best homes and the best schools, and those with very little social and cultural capital are left with no possible choice. In a context of uncertainty and indeterminacy, strategies of avoidance exacerbate the social rift. Voting rights for immigrants are denied priority in numerous European local elections. Such rights being ignored, parents do not transmit faith in the ballot box; it may explain why, instead, young generations take to the streets.

The other reasons why the integration of Muslims is made difficult – an important difference in the previous comparison with Latinos in the United States – comes from a correlation between Islam and terrorism, fed by the news coverage of events taking place in 'rogue' countries. It also has to do with the intrusion of Muslim laws (sharia) and norms into domestic European issues: (forced) marriages, divorces, dowry, burials, mosques, inheritance, codes of honour and so on. The loyalty of Muslims is then more in question than that of other migrants from Europe or Asia.

Cohen (2005) listed ten reasons why moderate Muslims in the United States would remain silent regarding radical Islam – solidarity with the Middle East and hostility to American policy towards Israel ranked among the first reasons. In Europe, these reasons also prevail, but so does the influence of extremist political parties holding solid constituencies and allies among dominant groups.

1.2.4 Social and economic vulnerability

The economic crisis hitting developed economies in 2008 has created a reordering of priorities. Networks of information and communication do not let anyone ignore the vulnerability of jobs and benefits. Supply and demand do not match each other, new social risks meet a high variability in territorial distribution and numerous people fear downward mobility for lack of adequate skills in shrinking job markets. A plurality of social and economic factors influence such distribution: class structure, family organization, level of education and available social programs (Ranci, 2010). Prevailing economic vulnerability impacts on a general feeling of insecurity. A few decades ago, essays were written on the end of work, comparing its precarious status with that of the years after World War II, when societies were fully employed (Rifkin, 1995; Meda, 1995). The idea was that there would not be enough service jobs to offer former farmers and workers and their children, and that automation and rapid technological changes would make numerous service jobs obsolete. Castells (1996, 255) vigorously denounced the credibility of such writings as superficial and ideological, and offered counter-examples of job creation in the United States and Japan. Yet such depressing visions persist in numerous countries. France seems particularly hit by despondency. Out of twelve countries participating in a Gallup poll – including the United States, Germany, Britain and Japan – only 15 per cent of the French said that they expected things to be better in 2011 than in 2010, the lowest result of all the countries (see, 'Briefing France', *The Economist*, April 23, 2011). In his report, the national ombudsman described the French as 'psychologically exhausted', suffering from 'burn-out', as if globalization meant decline. He ignored a less-visible France, plugged into the rest of the world, not averse to risk and forward-looking, which explains why the country remains among the top economic powers.

The social question linked to work status is nothing new. The Industrial Revolution dreamt of giving work to everyone and thereby to abolish poverty. By 1848, this dream having proved impossible, welfare institutions were created. The currently relevant issue in the twenty-first century is whether there will be more jobs and more remuneration for more work in western countries.

National contexts obviously interfere with the fate of cities which do not have the upper hand in that issue. A general precariousness of work, the gradual disappearance of automatic protections, the employers' preference for outsourcing (at least in the North), the segmentation of labour: these factors generate social tensions in most countries. But the face-to-face conflicts that formerly characterized the industrial world have currently been replaced by more atomized and side-by-side tensions or by urban violence. National societies seem to disarticulate in a strange movement of de-modernization (Touraine, 1991). All over the world, cities are submitted to new types of conflicts and to forms of violence generated by external forces that they have not initiated.

Few cities have been progressive enough to build or retrofit housing in valorized spaces for the more vulnerable categories. That the city is not equitable is forcefully demonstrated by Fainstein (2010). Public services such as public transportation, when they exist, are not always fairly distributed. Policies of redistribution have benefited protected categories of citizens (corporations, citizens endowed with status and traditional elites). More broadly, if globalization homogenizes modes of thinking via shared knowledge, images and communication (thus creating a form of consensus), then some of the excluded claiming to be the 99 percent, eager to express their dissent, may resort to the dramatization of their plight in the public space. Global cities thus have to mobilize their resource, knowledge and experienced practices to confront social threats of various kinds. Within which parameters they can or cannot act depends on the types of regimes constraining them.

Different types of urban regimes may be observed.[2] Americans usually do not seek solidarity from the state and are reluctant to pay taxes to support state intervention perceived as a form of suspicious collectivism. The American welfare state has been labelled a 'laggard state': less than 2 per cent of housing is subsidized. The persistence of ghettos and barrios is often blamed on racism. But as aptly remarked by Marcuse in a conversation with Fainstein (2010, 68): is mixing races a democratic requirement, implying that by living next to Whites, Blacks will improve their destiny? 'If ghetto residents live in a great working-class neighbourhood, why do we want middle class people there, too?' he asks. To which Fainstein replies that diversity is a lesser value than equity. Relatively homogeneous neighbourhoods with porous boundaries are to be preferred to proportionality in each precinct. In the United States, in the absence of effective welfare programmes and with the destruction of public housing units (Hope, VI, a federal Housing Program initiated in 1972) unmatched by an equal number of newly constructed units (a choice synonymous with policies of poverty dispersion), inequalities loom large. American cities demonstrate forms of efficiency in terms of law and order for majorities, but at the expense of the most vulnerable categories whose rights are frequently bypassed in terms of displacement, unequal treatment, segregation and punitive treatment.

European cities (in which inequalities and segregation are also high but less so) display more processes of historical continuity. Globalization, Europeanization, and de-territorialization exert their influence on cities, however. The decline of stable job opportunities in large cities upsets the uneven balance in the standards of living of national residents, immigrants and naturalized minorities and, in particular, of young people who cannot afford the price of housing rentals. However, until the 2008 recession, poor urban areas where disadvantaged households exist seldom constituted 'ghettos' comparable to those of American cities. The lack of opportunity for mobility in the job market is indeed alleviated by welfare regimes (the welfare budget in France – including health expenditures, pensions, family benefits – has the world record in welfare expenditures –33% of the GIP- and in pension allowances –14% of the GIP vs.8% among OECD countries). Programmes of public housing demolition are frequently matched by important programmes of reconstruction. These absorb most of the funding for urban renewal. By contrast, the social treatment that should accompany such programmes is frequently neglected, particularly in France and in Southern Europe, and remains controversial. The displacement to better areas of poor households of various origins does not offer a solution as long as policies focused on adequate job training and better public transportation remain so difficult to implement. The focus on secure cities may appear as a 'post-comprehensive policy' after comprehensive social treatment has proved to be too limited.

1.3   Trust and distrust

'Winning-losing societies (if you win, I lose) are prone to national depression, social jealousy, withdrawal, aggressive surveillance by one another', two French scholars observe (Agan and Cahuc, 2007). By contrast, 'societies of trust are win-win societies, based on solidarity, common projects, openness, exchange and communication'. Just before the election of President Obama, American society may have been the illustration of such a society. For Fukuyama (1995), trust is a form of social capital: Societies characterized by strong internal trust succeed better economically and socially. Trust is a tool enabling one to face unpredictability.

Currently, however, the loss of trust in institutions, elites, organizations, professions and their transactional costs opens a path to expressions of populism. 'When trust diminishes in a society, this results in greater social disintegration, with isolated and apprehensive individuals. Everyone is a potential danger for everyone else' (Svendsen, 2008, 95).

Surprising surveys reveal, however, how differently countries react to similar external forces – in correlation with their history, their leadership and their imagination. For instance, for 'least trustful in justice', after Turkey and Belgium out of 21 countries, France comes third; it comes fourth for 'no confidence in Parliament' or in unions.[3] Only 22 per cent of the French trust each other. Cheating in public transportation, taxes, public welfare (accepted behaviour in France) illustrates forms of institutional and personal distrust also observed in developing countries (Agan and Cahuc, 2007). In a similar vein, in a 2007 Mori survey on trust in São Paulo compared with London, an equal share of residents – 45 per cent – ranked crime and safety as their first concern (at the national level, 53 per cent of respondents in both countries did so). But 59 per cent of Londoners versus 31 per cent of Paolistanos felt safe walking at night in their neighbourhood (versus, respectively 35 per cent and 69 per cent who felt unsafe). The major difference was that while 57 per cent of the English had trust in their local councillors and 44 per cent in their mayors, only 29 per cent of the Brazilians did.[4] More research is needed to find explanations for such contradictions within one society and between the urban societies of the world.

This chapter reveals that global changes generate restlessness and anxiety encapsulating a larger set of concerns regarding ageing, employment, public policies, trust and so on, which reveal themselves by a focus on cities. Pointing at such ill-defined feelings, noticeable in everyday life, would be incomplete if one ignored the consequences of an event which impacted the whole planet: the attacks on the World Trade Center in New York City on September 11, 2001, and the security turn that was amplified from this moment on in the United States, in Europe and other countries as well. It has had a direct impact on the governance of world cities.

2
The Turning Point of 9/11

In numerous societies, fear is often based on distorted perceptions of 'Otherness'. Fear inspired religious wars in Southern Europe in the second half of the sixteenth century. A 'Great Fear' swept over France in 1789; the British feared invasion by Napoleon; the Japanese developed an extreme fear of crime and overreacted to it, and so on. For its part, American society has historically experienced phobias towards nonconformist 'aliens': American Indians were perceived as incapacitated by mental debasement and in no way could be considered as trustworthy; witches were malefic; bandits in the West were a threat to public order. From 1880 to 1930, discrimination intensified against Southern and Eastern European immigrants 'threatening to destroy' American values, and against labour insurgencies. For King (2001, 143–74) American national identity was, from the country's very beginning, constructed on the exclusion from the polity, and on metaphorical representations, of groups distinguished as savage, racially inferior or non-Protestant. Such a background of racial and ethnic violence has been documented by historians (Stearns, 2006; Lane, 1997; Graham and Gurr, 1979; Monkkonen, 2001). Nineteenth-century cities were perceived as dangerous as well, for all kinds of reasons that will not be enumerated here.

The 1960s should be seen as one aspect of an ongoing series of negotiations through which Americans have attempted to uproot old and stubborn problems of racial discrimination, exclusion and fear (Gerstle and Mollenkopf, 2001, 14). Serious crime problems, concentrated in particular areas, could not be alleviated due to weak or ill-adapted legislation regarding the wide circulation of guns, domestic violence, and later in the century the deinstitutionalization of the mentally ill as well as all kinds of deregulation and public service cuts. Low tolerance for violence is particularly perceptible when unexpected shootings take place in public spaces, schools, hospitals, trains and official buildings, but less so in Black ghettos.

Three strands have emerged since the cold war (Stearns, 2006, 3–5). The increasing importance granted to experts has led to a re-evaluation of personal fear and of risk. Then, the media have made a disproportionate use and promotion of fear to feed their audimat (audience ratings). Last, the collective reactions to danger and to foreign threats were amplified by the development of a bipolar world during the cold war and particularly since the fall of the Berlin Wall (Ibid.). One could add that scientific, technological and psychological developments, fears regarding health, the environment and child-rearing reached a greater number of people receiving information via the media and the Internet.

Increasingly, Americans express a utopian desire for more safety, or protection against risk. Inflated warnings and precautions about hazards characterize American society in the last quarter of the twentieth century. Other societies also experience all kinds of fears, but the power of the American media on opinions cannot be ignored. The media create a picture of society in which crime is overwhelmingly on the increase, where policemen struggle and the justice system is too 'soft'. Yet if they do have an impact on attitudes, there is no determinism that would trigger moral panic due to media bias (Cohen, 1972; Grabe and Drew, 2007) The media observe, correlate and reflect reality, and their interaction with a very heterogeneous and unstable audience is socially filtered (Boda and Szabo, 2011).

This chapter focuses on the United States, where some of the elites' concern with urban safety started early. American policy debates on that issue (for instance, regarding risk management, the precautionary principle, pre-emptive actions, zero tolerance) more or less influenced other countries. Its context is comparative, with states as a focus, and it attempts to provide clues and links to the subsequent case studies related to world cities. It deals mostly with the North, as the states and global cities of the South have not felt the impact of 9/11 as much as did the United States and its closer European allies. States are important actors; they frame debates, make choices and provide policies and resources which impact on cities, but they are also increasingly one among many at tackling global problems.

Studying how they participate and respond to globalization is a challenge. Globalization cannot be reduced to the 'victimhood' of nation states. Globalizing dynamics entail deep imbrications with the national spheres, which are often one of the 'key enablers and enactors of the emergent global scale'. They unsettle 'previous arrangements regarding legitimate claims, existing meanings and systems, rule of law and justice'. We can no longer speak of the state, of the nation state versus the world order. Segmentation is operating inside the state with privatized executive branches of government aligned with global actors (Sassen, 2006).

Being hit as a symbol of global domination by 19 terrorists on 9/11, 2001, American authorities' defensive responses, at various levels of power, displayed continuity. The precautionary principle was applied as early as the mid-1960s. It was not named as such then, but it influenced numerous societies in Europe and in the South as well, whether they were willing to do so, or had to at the United States authorities' demand. The private market of security was prompt to take advantage of the new awareness of risks by authorities and sold them its high technologies of surveillance, control and identification. Gated communities, which were already a widespread phenomenon, proliferated with a consumption demand for safety.

2.1   Why law and order became an issue in the United States in the 1960s

The mobilization of American middle classes on the law and order issue was deliberately launched in the 1960s by political entrepreneurs. Before that time, families would leave the doors of their homes open; children would play on the street and walk home from school without supervision. But during the 1960s, American urban dwellers became alarmed by their unsafe streets (Flamm, 2005). Why is that so? There was more property crime in late modernity societies. Due to affluence, more goods were left without surveillance and therefore became a target for petty thieves (Garland, 2001). Violent crime against persons also increased as internal mechanisms of neighbourhood control and protection were decreasing. Although the FBI statistics are to be taken cautiously, they indicate that violent crime doubled in the United States between 1960 and 1969; the rate of property crime rose by 73 per cent in seven years; in New York City, the number of robberies was multiplied twelvefold, and in Washington, D.C., assaults against persons were four times the national average (Flamm, 2005, 2; 42). If crime per capita was highest in urban centers, it grew faster in small towns and rural areas. Gangs and drug businesses moved to smaller cities.

Conservative politicians – Wallace, Goldwater and later Nixon – eager to turn law and order into a cementing theme, used the elusive issue of law and order to address 'the forgotten American'. They amalgamated fears about racial riots, anti-conformist students' demonstrations and rising urban crime into a powerful denunciation of the 'soft' liberal state. They played on representations and on insecurity caused by major changes occurring in American society and based on racist stereotypes, creating a spontaneous link between Black crime and White victims. Their strategy was successful. Gradually, the optimism that character-ized the beginning of the 1960s, when a man could reach the moon and, poverty was an 'anomaly' meant to disappear in America, was replaced by disenchantment and by the 'twilight of common dreams' (Gitlin, 1995). In 1968, a White father of five expressed his view of the state of the nation in the following terms: 'I am sick of crime every-where. I'm sick of riots. I'm sick of poor people demonstrations (black, white, red, yellow, purple, green or any colour) ... I am sick of the lack of law enforcement ... I am sick of hippies, LSD, drugs and the promo-tion the news media give them. But most of all, I am sick of constantly being kicked in the teeth for staying home, minding my own business, working steadily, paying my bills and taxes, raising my children to be decent citizens, managing my financial affairs so that I won't become a ward of the city, county, or state and footing the bill for all the minuses mentioned herein' (Flamm, 2005, 1). In the conservative politicians' campaign, law and order became a form of racial code.

The Johnson Administration was similarly concerned with that issue and summoned several commissions to find solutions. Crime fighting become the stock in trade of some prominent Democrats, including E. Kefauver and R. Kennedy. In 1964, a memorandum, written by the Department of Justice for President Johnson and entitled *Riots and Crime in the 1960s*, anticipated the kind of political exploitation the context of unrest could lead to. Street crime was a real threat for many, it said, not a political smokescreen. Demographically, the number of young men was increasing at a faster rate than the general population, and anti-crime programs had to be strengthened. It advocated the creation of a Crime Commission (Ibid., 46). The President's Commission on Law Enforcement and the Administration of Justice issued a report in 1967, called *The Change of Crime in a Free Society*. In 1968, the United States Riot Commission produced the famous *Report of the National Advisory Commission on Civil Disorders*, better known as 'The Kerner Report'. Then, in 1969, Milton Eisenhower, the president of the U.S. National Commission on the Causes and Prevention of Violence, handed President Nixon the document *To Establish Justice, to Insure Domestic Tranquillity: Final Report*. Most of these reports linked patterns of crime and violence to structural changes occurring in American society, such as the age distribution, the increasing number of minorities living in large cities, the lack of mobility for number of their youth, cultural transformations and mutations in the criminal justice system. In other words, they pointed at urban life as conducive to crime. Subsequent chapters will examine whether this assumption is valid or not.

The Johnson Administration in early 1965 made the mistake of announcing a 'War on Crime', linked to the 'War on Poverty'. Not only is it difficult to establish a link between reducing poverty and reducing crime, but crime can never be 'banished', despite a presidential pledge. Moreover, such an announcement gave too much importance to the issue and allowed the conservative opposition to play on fears. Their advertisements would show a White woman walking a dark and deserted street, while a voice would give statistics on crime. Yet the possibility for a woman to be raped by a stranger was as likely then as that of being hit by lightning. America was much safer in terms of murders than in the 1930s before the end of Prohibition (the murder rate had decreased by 50 per cent in 1964) (Flamm, op. cit.). Fear however was real in cities. As remarked by Thomas (1928, 571–2), 'if people define their situations as real, they are real in their consequences'.

Because the protection of women and children was frequently portrayed as against a Black mugger, and although race and crime were not identical, in conservatives' campaigns they overlapped. The Eisenhower Commission's report made 200 recommendations which are currently ignored. They show that at the time, American society was concerned with violence and debating how and why such violence occurred. Was America a sick society, glorifying killing on movie and television screens and calling it entertainment, as U.S. Attorney General Robert Kennedy bemoaned? (Flamm, 2005, 142) Was it a civilized nation? Conservative columnist William Buckley asked: 'In civilized nations of the past, it has not been customary for parents to allow their children to do what they feel like, for students to seize their schools and smash the equipment, for police to be ordered to stand by, while looters empty stores and arsonists burn down buildings ... It is not expected that public figures should be considered proper targets for casual gunmen' (Ibid., 153). This speech is worth remembering because the type of societal debate which was reflected in the crime report has currently disappeared in the United States, except when middle classes or their children become collectively victims.

In 1967, riots became the first issue of concern for Americans worrying about their personal protection. As is often the case with the left, liberals were caught in a dilemma: they would not blame Black agitators and criminals; they merely questioned statistics and could not be convincing. The Hubert Humphrey presidential campaign in 1968 reflected such contradictions. Law and order was the decisive factor in Nixon's narrow triumph. The context of riots destabilized the Johnson Administration ('each riot costs me 90 000 votes', the president said) (Ibid., 37). He was blamed for pushing his Great Society programs as an adequate solution to civil unrest (a solution for problem neighbour-hoods also adopted by French social democrats when they returned to power in 2001 and launched a territorial affirmative action policy).Yet this critique by Republicans was hasty. The war on crime,[1] initiated by Democrats in the 1960s, could not substantiate a managerial approach based on accounts and on proofs that good options had indeed been taken and that laws and judicial decisions were enforced. The debates around the law 'Safer Streets', passed in 1968, indicated that Congress controlled by Democrats had also attempted to take hold of the issue of law and order, which until then was a prerogative of states, counties and local governments. This law provided additional resources from the federal government to local police forces and to prison managers on the basis of successful results. FBI eavesdropping was legally allowed in order to stop subversive suspects (meaning Black Panthers or Martin Luther King, for instance), with or without a judge's warrant. Weapons' sales were to be more controlled. Intuitively, Johnson had understood that the issue of civil disorder and crime could make him lose the elec-tions, even if Barry Goldwater's attacks with such a theme in 1964 were premature. The federalization of the crime issue started then.

As a consequence of these political manoeuvres, in the last quarter of the twentieth century a new civil and political order developed in the United States, based on crime and on the fear of crime. The precautionary principle, a powerful ferment for a binary order, unified Americans around their refusal to become the victims of crimes. 'We are crime victims. We are the loved ones of crime victims. Above all, we are those who live in fear that we or those we care for will be victimized by crime' (Simon, 2007, 75; 109). (Victimization surveys launched by N. Katzenbach started in 1965 and were given visibility by the media.) A 'culture of fear' and an imaginary centered on potential victimiza-tion erased differences among people and led them to support punitive forms of populism against alleged or real troublemakers. Judges found themselves under attack for their neutrality, competence and judge-ment. Prosecutors became the champions of victims' cause and of the alleged interests (Ibid., 33). The extension of the definition of crime and the growth in punishment led prosecutors to play a prominent role. A less democratic, more racially polarized and more uncertain America took shape, Simon observes (2007). The arsenal of security measures that proliferated henceforth did not make cities more secure. It fed an endless quest for zero risk.

From this moment on, choices regarding where to live, work, send children to school were made according to the perceptions of risk and to the representation of 'Dangerous Others'. The 'Exile Project' is twofold, Simon observes. It is a 'constellation of commitments that present Americans with the option of obtaining more security for its beleaguered urban cores only by sending the young men of those communities into "exile"' (Simon, 2007, 143). Following his previous work (1993) and in the follow-up of E. Goffman (1961), Simon examines the evolution and growth of American prisons in this process of exile to rural areas. Between 1990 and 1999, a prison opened in rural American every fifteen days (Huq, Miller, 2008, 220). 'Locking out' mirrors the 'locking in' asylum process, that is the choice middle-class Americans make of isolating themselves in gated or secure communities, a process which reinforces that of prison and benefits the administration, the security market and political authorities. Order and regulation replace the idealized solidarity of the New Deal and feed the citizens' 'alienation and rage'. Many citizens seemed to opt out of politics and to fight for their self-interest, ignoring collective commitments. A legitimacy is thus given to the development of high technologies of surveillance, to SUVs with reinforced bumpers, to barriers enclosing properties and to other ways of distancing oneself from others, reinforcing distrust (except inside the security bubble). As, in the later twentieth century, fears were given more visibility by the media, a near 'siege mentality' grasp heavy television viewers. 'The sheer number of frights, exaggerated or not, takes a toll, making it easier to view each succeeding problem as a mortal danger based on the emotions one remembers from the last one – enhanced further, perhaps, by what one's parents conveyed about the one before that. Far from being inexperienced with threats, many Americans may be suffering from threat fatigue' (Stearns, 2006, 195).

2.2   The political exploitation of 9/11

When 9/11 occurred, Americans were already accustomed to the jeopardy of their freedoms for safety purposes. In one generation, mentalities had interiorized suppression, and zero risk had become a sensible expectation, if not a right. Property defence allowed all kinds of populist abuse. The revolution which occurred then was not that of more punishment and less reinsertion for criminals but 'the moulding of citizens spurred by fear and conformism' (Simon, 2007, 39).

The federal government, the legitimacy of which was then questioned by numerous Americans, could have chosen other themes to cement people, such as health or the environment, Simon suggests. It is indeed paradoxical, when citizens are called to get more committed and the central government is seen as a major problem, to observe that the appropriation of threat and risk issues by the state and its response in terms of securitization processes deny citizens any personal choice in confronting risks. The intensification of electronic surveillance in airports, in office buildings, hospitals, universities and residential units and the presence of guards even in classrooms if teachers require them, all express a denial of the citizens' capacity for judgement. Collective confinement and voluntary enclosure in security bubbles appear as the preferred options of the middle classes.

Useful but contradictory debates relative to making sense out of the 9/11 attacks have proliferated, yet the major issue had to do with the vulnerability of Western democracies and with the delegitimization of political and military elites that are unable to anticipate risks. Terrorism inflicts human losses but, most of all, it undermines the legitimacy of states accused of not having protected their citizens. What is at stake here is the governmental response, the pressure 'to do something', namely 'the deepening of oppressive governance, an extension of regulation, the curtailment of liberties and the intensification of the racism that certain groups already experience in everyday life' (Pain and Smith, 2008, 1). With such collateral damage, terrorism has achieved its goal.

The attacks on 9/11 do not mark the dawn of a new era, either in international relations or in everyday life in the way the fall of the Berlin Wall began to put an end to a binary world. To a large extent, there were continuities in the form and function of the national security bureaucracy before and after 2001. There are many parallels between the 'ordinary' politics of pre-9/11 and the 'extraordinary' politics after that event. What emerges, though, is the status given to dissent. Dissent, which is so essential in a democracy, was muffled. One thinks of James Madison's remark when the U.S. Constitution was ratified: 'The great difficulty is this: first, making the government capable of controlling the governed; and then, forcing it to self-control' (Hamilton et al., 1961, No. 51).

Historical examples of executive power abuse abound in American history, as elsewhere. As early as World War I, a thousand Americans were incarcerated for their pacifist speeches, and six thousand German-

Americans were arrested on the basis of their origin. In 1919, raids also based on origin were allowed to be launched by Attorney General Mitchell Palmer. (Palmer had been targeted with a bomb in front of his Washington home. His neighbour, Franklin D. Roosevelt had narrowly escaped injury). Palmer appointed J. Edgar Hoover as head of the General Intelligence division of the Justice Department's Bureau of Investigation. With Hoover in charge, mass arrests began. In December 1919, 249 people of Russian origin were deported. The following month, Hoover and Palmer had four thousand people arrested, with the blessing of public opinion (Dickey, 2009, 45).

In February 1942, seventy thousand Japanese-Americans and forty thousand Japanese immigrants were interned by President Roosevelt, via a manipulation of public fear. Their internment was in part driven by West Coast farming interests which coveted Japanese agricultural holdings. The governmental manipulation of fear was also orchestrated by factions of the public pressuring the government. Roosevelt also created a military commission to try eight Nazi saboteurs who had infiltrated the United States via submarines. The Supreme Court unanimously upheld their convictions. Even today's conservative Justice, Antonin Scalia, remarked that it was not 'this Court's finest hour'. Roosevelt used military commissions to try suspects who admitted their guilt, but the Bush Administration expanded the process to encompass a large universe of 'enemy combatants'. The development of intelligence services led to all kinds of abuse based on formulations (such as fighting 'subversion' to defend 'national security') the vague definition of which was meant to protect those giving orders. According to Schwartz and Huq (2007), secrets linked to presidents' private lives and detained by services constrain the leverage of the latter.[2] A culture of secrecy characterizes intelligence services, and missions are not assigned limits. The passivity of Congress and judges is noteworthy.

2.2.1   What is new?

Policies that followed the attacks on the World Trade Center and the Pentagon on 9/11 2001, question the internal/external security of the United States. Despite the Church Commission's recommendations, no counter-powers have limited the leverage of the executive power. 'The largest disaster in the last fifty years' resulted from this laxity and from the White House lawyers' determination to resist democratic controls, even after massive wiretapping, torture of alleged or real opponents' rendition, and repeated violations of their constitutional rights were denounced.

It cannot be denied that the 2,750 deaths caused by the attacks have been traumatic for the American nation. Taking a hold of this popular emotion, the Bush Administration reacted with belligerent rhetoric a few hours after the events, launching a war on terror,[3] a war unlike any other, displacing the war on crime and the war against drugs, as if following Machiavelli's observation, according to which fear is what secures the prince's power and thus the social order. 'American fear culture opens many people to excessive manipulability' (Stearns, 2006, 217) and they embrace the fears displayed by the White House and exaggerated perceptions of risk.

Another attitude would have been possible in light of European reactions, after the London and Madrid terrorist attacks or the Norwegian rampage by an anti-Islamic extremist who killed 76 young people 'to save' Norway and Western Europe. The consensus then was to reaffirm values that terrorists want to tear down and to rally around the rule of law. When considering American history and presidential reactions to fear, the 1933 inaugural discourse of Franklin Roosevelt comes to mind:

> This is pre-eminently the time to speak the truth, the whole truth, frankly and boldly. Nor need we shrink from honestly facing conditions in our country today. This great Nation will endure as it has endured, will revive and will prosper. So, first of all, let me assert my firm belief that the only thing we have to fear is fear itself – nameless, unreasoning, unjustified terror which paralyzes needed efforts to convert retreat into advance. In every dark hour of our national life a leadership of frankness and vigour has met with that understanding and support of the people themselves which is essential to victory. I am convinced that you will again give that support to leadership in these critical days. (*Roosevelt, 1938–1950*: II, 11)

Roosevelt was eager to reassure his people and to urge them to confront adversity. He came back to this theme in 1941 during his address to Congress presenting the issue of the 'Four Freedoms'. One of these freedoms, he said, is freedom from fear in a world where arms would be so restricted that 'no nation will be in a position to commit an act of physical aggression against any neighbour, anywhere in the world' (*Roosevelt, 1938–1950*: iv, 672). He was referring to hope putting an end to fear.[4] But this was not the option taken by President Bush and his advisors.

One week after the 9/11 attacks, the U.S. attorney general, John Ashcroft, allowed for the deportation of any alien whom, he had reason to believe, would commit or facilitate acts of terrorism. Detention preceding deportation was allowed without a hearing, but once there was a deportation decision, the immigrant was entitled to seek judicial review. But since the immigration system was really being used to detain and not to deport, that was not a problem. All recent male visa applicants from 26 countries, mostly Muslim, were put under special scrutiny. 'For many Americans, the distinction that mattered most was between putatively safe immigrants and dangerous ones, identified as "Arabs," "Muslims" or more diffusely as "Middle Easterners," a designation that often encompassed South Asians' (Zolberg, 2006, 445). Despite injunctions from top officials against discrimination, Muslim and Arab groups became more suspect than others and were submitted to blatant ethnic profiling. Former laws were then enforced by the Justice Department, for instance the 1996 Antiterrorism and Effective Death Penalty Act, allowing the Justice Department to define over 75,000 detained drug offenders as 'aggravated felons'. The rights of 11 million green card holders were jeopardized; they were notified that they would be deported if they committed certain types of offences, after completing their prison sentences. Tougher measures also were introduced at the local level, with more arrests for violation of immigrant laws. The events of 9/11 precipitated sharp critiques of border control practices, revealing careless behaviour on the part of the officers in charge and the infringement of civil liberties (Ibid., 446). Issues of external and internal security became blurred. Similarly restrictive measures, though less extreme, occurred in Europe after the various attacks – measures in which increased selectivity of borders, the internationalization and ex-territorialization of control are currently used.

Invoking danger allows an administration to redirect worries away from questions that it is unable to answer and to refocus attention on security, a state prerogative (Sunstein, 2004; Body-Gendrot, 2008). This makes it easy to divide the voting public into friends and enemies. In the United States, continuous signals urged citizens to be 'alert' and fuelled an undefined feeling of anxiety without an object, which ironically is precisely what terrorists aim to create. Such modes of representation also rely on figures of 'Otherness', the alien and the subversive in the articulation of danger (Borradori, 2003). They also mobilize tropes of 'enlightened catastrophism' (Dupuy, 2002) – an expression meaning that people and bureaucracies are projected into the future at a point in time when another catastrophe has just occurred – in order to minimize or neutralize its recurrence. If other attacks are likely to happen, fate should not be challenged, it is thought, and preventative actions must be pursued. This approach was previously used to assess dangers associated with the cold war and low-intensity conflicts, and it mobilized ideological as well as military defences (Schwartz and Huq, 2007). Since 9/11, three elements mark new trends in Washington: a culture of suspicion, a culture of secrecy and the mobilization of citizens as spies to face "the erasure of the markers of certainty" (Campbell, op. cit., 232, note 12; Lyon, 2003, 41–42).

The Bush Administration regularly injected an anxiety-inducing serum into Americans: differently coloured alerts, the Patriot Act, ethnic profiling and the amalgamation of Saddam Hussein with al-Qaeda. 'The purpose of these manipulations has been twofold: to instil hostility, bellicosity, a fervour for revenge and violent self-protection against external enemies, or "aliens," ethnic, religious or political groups at home, and to get citizens, properly frightened to accept, in the name of the national and personal security, invasions of privacy and reductions of liberties they would not have tolerated if they had not been conditioned to fear' (Hoffmann, 2004, 1029). The imminent dangers President Bush alluded to in his speeches were based on weak evidence or lies. In an address to the nation on 28 January 2003, President Bush asked his audience to imagine the nineteen hijackers from 9/11 equipped with weapons from Saddam Hussein's arsenals: such a vision would anticipate all the horrors the nation had ever known. Due to systematic disinformation, 72 per cent of Americans in January and February of 2003 believed that the Iraqi leader was personally involved in the attacks, with almost a majority thinking that some Iraqis were among the attackers (Svendsen 2008, 113). The subsequent wars made the world a less safe place. Yet, anticipating the question 'what if?' (Mythen and Walklate, 2008; Crawford, 2010), the Bush Administration would claim that it was their duty not to wait for the next bomb, which could take the shape of a mushroom cloud. Continuous signals pushed American citizens to be on alert, thus fostering a diffuse feeling of anxiety, with no object.

The term 'war on terror' was never fully endorsed by all branches of the government in the United Kingdom, and there is substantial evidence that it was not (Greer, 2010, 1,185). D. Blunkett, The Head of the Home Office minister, asked the British people to be on the alert in July 2005, but not to yield to fear and not to exaggerate the terrorist threat. Conversely, the pronouncement of danger by the White House allowed the president to assume almost monarchical powers, to mobilize the army and to force some citizens to abandon part of their rights and freedoms. The call to citizens asking them to report any suspicious movement or person in their neighbourhood was against American civic traditions. Yet it seemed that at that time, the very national survival was at stake and terrorism posed an 'existential' threat. As a member of the military's Joint Chiefs of Staff asserted in 2003, if terrorists could kill just ten thousand people, they could 'do away with our way of life' (Stearns, 2006, 195).

For its part, Europe interpreted terrorist acts that hit the countries as crimes, and the choice of various governments was to launch police investigations to find the culprits and their accomplices in order to have them tried by judges. Whereas the police and justice systems were mobilized in Europe, a military intervention in Afghanistan (and not in Saudi Arabia where terrorists actually came from) was launched in order to search for members of al-Qaeda. The European response displayed defiance over fear, both in principle and in public action, revealing the distinctiveness of public emotion in the United States. The symbolic impact of 9/11 cannot be downplayed, however, and no one knows how Europeans would have reacted if attacks of this magnitude had happened to them. But American distinctiveness does exist, based in part on a lack of experience with terrorism and on being bombed by outsiders for the very first time. Yet Americans had experienced it in their cities during and after World War I and at Pearl Harbor and Oklahoma City. 'They simply chose, in the main, not to cite it. Their suffering was greater [o]n September 11 than that of foreign counterparts, at least in terms of single incidents, but not enough greater to wipe away the more abundant emotionality and its greater durability' (Stearns, 2006, 49).

2.2.2 The Patriot Act

In the context of urban insecurity following the attacks on the World Trade Center and the Pentagon, human rights organizations worried about the erosion of constitutional rights, liberties, due process of law and other protections. The Patriot Act, elaborated by the Bush Administration, passed on October 12, 2001, almost without any amendment by Congress with only one vote of dissent in the Senate and 66 at the House of Representatives.[5] Called the 'Uniting and Strengthening America by Providing Appropriate Tools Required to Intercept and Obstruct Terrorism (USA PATRIOT ACT) Act of 2001', its 342 pages reinforced the merging concepts of national and of domestic security, which had already started. They reveal a deliberate effort to

The Turning Point of 9/11   53

reinforce the executive power, in the spirit of the 1917 law regarding spying, and that of 1918 against sedition.

Fifteen years before 9/11, Cheney and Addington, in their report on the eradication of Contras in Nicaragua and the Iranian threat expressed their vision of an unchecked presidency (Mayer, 2008). The feeling of insecurity generated by 9/11 allowed the lifting of constitutional checks on executive power. A culture of secrecy then developed and opposition was weakened.

Some aspects of the law would have been unthinkable in previous times. Section 218, for instance, lifting the line separating anti-terrorist investigations and criminal investigations allows information and evidence gathered by intelligence services to be shared with police forces in charge of investigations on suspected criminals.[6] With Section 802, demonstrations and protest marches can be carefully monitored by the police. The authorities may also secretly accumulate information on citizens and immigrants and store them in huge databases.

2.2.3   Muslims as favoured suspects?

Mauer, the director of the Sentencing Project, a progressive organization based in Washington, D.C., ironically remarks that things could have been worse. Arabs and Muslims could have been deported into camps as Japanese were during World War II. Petty criminals could have been stripped of their constitutional rights, although if they came from the Middle East, their problems could have been even worse.[7] The war on terrorism depends on ethnic profiling and on the surveillance of high-risk categories based on religion, origins and race. 'Countless potential friends of the United States, including businessmen, students and scholars have been turned away or antagonized as a result. The number includes many moderate Muslims, precisely the group a more balanced, less risk averse national policy ought to be encouraging' (Stearns, 2006, 215).

The belligerent rhetoric used by the Homeland Security Administration addresses not only territorial security but the political and cultural community one belongs to, in an approach of inclusion/exclusion, thus unifying the cultural and emotional dimensions of security against 'them' (Ceyhan, 2001). Some conservative media developed the idea of a silent and infiltrated fifth column correlated to Arab-Muslim populations in the post-9/11 imaginary, despite the fact that Arabs in America are part of the middle classes, two third of them Christians, a third Muslims and African-Americans and most of the other two thirds being affluent immigrants. A vast majority of them disapproved strongly of these attacks. Identifying the profile of who should be under reasonable suspicion among this heterogeneous group marks a change in the criteria of inclusion and exclusion within the American nation. Before September 11, suspects for the police were – and are still – visible historical minorities, young Black and Latino males. A large number of them were incarcerated in the 1980s and 1990s, if they were gang members, dealing drugs or committing violent assaults. After 9/11, male immigrants from the Middle East under 35 years old, or hyphenated Americans from Arab-Muslim countries, were suspected by some police forces or intelligence organizations of being disloyal or leading a double life, put under surveillance and detained whenever they were poorly protected by legal representation. Due to the U.S. attorney general's 'reasonable suspicion', 1,200 men, most of whom had only violated immigration laws, were arrested in the follow-up to 9/11, some of them convicted, others incarcerated without due process of law. Preventing violent acts via incarceration in fact hardly reduced crime and did not alleviate fear of crime.

Ten years after 9/11, a Gallup poll reveals that almost half of Muslim Americans (they are 2.6 million in the United States) experienced religious or racial discrimination in 2010. This was higher than for members of any other religious group. Yet as a religious minority, they were neither alienated nor disaffected; they expressed confidence in the fairness of elections and 60 per cent of them said that they trusted the FBI (versus 75 per cent of other religious groups, who did trust the FBI). On the whole, they were optimistic about the future as loyal Americans (Goodstein, 2011).

2.2.4   Has public opinion any influence?

Regarding threats to civil liberties and the continuous manipulation of fear by the White House at that time, human rights organizations denounced the passivity of American public opinion, which was influenced by the media. In 2003, while 66 per cent of Americans admitted that the missions stipulated in the Patriot Act infringed on liberties, an overwhelming majority (79 per cent) thought that it was more important to confront threats than to respect citizens' privacy. Such poll does not come as a surprise.[8] A majority of respondents seemed convinced that Americans should be the first to strike in a preventive war and massively supported the terms of the Patriot Act: for instance, wiretapping, military tribunals, the incarceration of the homeless, the questioning of Middle East males under 35, and so on. During the fall of 2002 according to some polls, half of Americans found that the First

Amendment protecting freedoms was too constraining. Few stood up against measures restricting immigration.

After 9/11, a report of the National Science and Technological Council via the subcommittee on Social, Behavioural and Economic Science Combating Terrorism wondered about the origins of a 'putative' culture of fear that might be growing among Americans. 'The ongoing contemporary socialization ... leaves too many Americans inexperienced, open both to manipulation and to public contagion when emotion becomes inescapable' (Stearns, 2006, 202). The impact of the media and of experts inflating threats and menaces cannot be overlooked. After 9/11, sales of protection devices, burglar alarms and weapons went up. Increasingly, in the media the line between information and entertainment was blurred.[9]

The American Civil Liberties Union (ACLU, founded to correct abuse to freedoms committed during World War I, saw, however, its membership double after 9/11, 2001. The ACLU underlined that threats to freedoms came from private organizations as well as from the United States administration, and that threats against liberties emanating from technological, legal and political processes were amplified by their joint actions. This perception was confirmed by the Electronic Frontier Foundation, revealing that AT&T had on its own inititative decided to communicate the telephone communcations of millions of Americans to the National Security Agency. The Internet search engine, Google, reports how many times a person has been arrested and for what reasons, how much his/her home cost, and so on. Credit cards, electronic chips, cell phone data, plane tickets, bank ATMs, CCTVs and the Internet are part of Americans' daily life and yield exploitable data for intelligence services. Unlike Europeans, Americans accept that such information should be yielded to public and private agencies. When the airline Jet Blue transmitted passengers' data (without their approval) to the federal government, protest was rapidly stifled. This has become the norm, including for foreigners travelling to the United States.

The quasi-instantaneous transmission of upheavals occurring in the world – the situations in Afghanistan, the Middle East and Africa, terrorist attacks and threats, sensational incidents – feed general feelings of insecurity. Few national leaders resist the temptation to draw a political benefit from the strengthening of public order instead of educating the people to choose solutions protecting liberties. For instance, passengers are not asked for their preferences regarding security measures in airports. As U.S. Supreme Court justice Brennan observed, '[L]iberty is fragile. Just as night does not fall abruptly, it is just the same with oppression. In both cases, first dusk takes place during which nothing seems to change. Yet it is during dusk that one should worry about the changes that take place'.[10]

The Obama Administration experienced difficulties introducing sweeping changes. The Patriot Act has been continuously reconfirmed (between 2003 and 2005, the FBI tapped 140,000 telephone lines). The lack of institutional oversight of the FBI's operations is regularly denounced. Other criticisms of the American response to the terrorist attacks are more grounded. In the follow-up to 9/11, the Pentagon budget has been astronomical, causing a 'financial seism', according to economist Joseph Stiglitz. A Swedish research center on peace estimates that the Pentagon budget has increased by 81 per cent since 2001 ($553 billion). The two wars launched in Iraq and in Afghanistan have cost $1.28 trillion, and the twenty-two agencies of the Homeland Security Department have received $360 billion in additional resources (costofwar.org), not to mention the extra expenditures (e.g., $110 billion allocated to intelligence services)[11] (Stroobants, 2011). Moreover, even if it is fair to assert that the country is undoubtedly safer, a report from the 9/11 Commission ten years after the attacks indicates a slow-moving Congress leaving too many sectors vulnerable to terrorism (regarding cargo imported by air and sea, state drivers' licenses and birth certificates, radio spectrum space allocated to emergency responders, checking foreign nationals leaving the United States, and so on.). Public opinion, divided and uninformed as it is, is unlikely to assert itself in this situation.

The political use made of the slippery precautionary principle remains pernicious, not only in America but in all Western democracies. It was renamed 'pre-emptive action' by the Bush Administration to justify the eradication of weapons of mass destruction in Iraq. Its extension, frequently translated into a punitive turn which is now debated in numerous Western countries, opts for repression rather than for more complex preventative policies.

2.3   A more defensive Europe?

In the ten years following 9/11, numerous Northern European countries responded with a more punitive rhetoric, the development of the precautionary principle, an actuarial approach and tougher criminal decisions. Yet Europeans are not Americans. Differences of scale and of intensity in modes of defence are noteworthy. One should distinguish at which levels politicians waving the red flag operate and according to which culture they are able to do so. 'Suppose we don't act and the intelligence turns out to be right, how forgiving will people be?' Tony Blair exclaimed (quoted in Crawford, 2011, 14). Yet national culture makes a difference. Prime Minister Silvio Berlusconi or President George W. Bush were more often pointing at a dangerous world and at menacing enemies than was the more cautious H. Kohl or Jacques Chirac. In 2009, the French state acted forcefully to stop local conflicts between radical youths of Jewish and Muslim origin fed with images from Gaza, brought by satellite television and the Internet. Meanwhile, despite alarming reports relative to potential terrorist plots in France, J. Barrot, the chair of the section Justice, Liberty and Security at the European Community, took steps to avoid the stigmatization of Muslims in general. Following the positions taken by the French state, his position was that Islam should be seen less as a source of conflict than as a means of integration in Europe. This cautious attitude was not, however, observed for the Romas. Their stigmatization by the French government in 2010 created an embarrassment for France within the European Commission.

In the United Kingdom, at the request of former Prime Minister Gordon Brown (2006), citizens, local communities, institutions and firms were asked to tackle at 'root the evils that risk driving people, particularly vulnerable young people, into the hands of violent extremists'. Measures slowed access to certain sensitive sites, CCTVs[12] proliferated in public spaces, then the security screening in airports and various buildings continuously added more requirements.

The kidnapping and murder of James Bulger in Merseyside in 1993 allowed the government to 'do something', showing citizens that security was taken seriously. It led the private security market to draw a tighter connection with a policy of local regeneration schemes, called 'City Challenge' (1994–99).

The Vigipirate program in France, created in 1974, was reinforced after terrorist attacks hit the country in the 1990s. Armed soldiers patrol railway stations, airports and other sensitive public places. Databases containing files on an increasing number of people have generated controversies.[13] Traceability seems currently more profitable to law enforcers than identity papers with a postal address. 'Everyday landscape is shaped by defensive considerations, boundaries and identities. In fact, fear is seen following form' (Coaffee et al., op. cit., 89).

The British intensification of urban defensive methods is due to a series of terrorist bombs and crime.[14] Until 1998, regulation was minimal. The country lacked constitutional rights to privacy in public spaces. It may explain why the development of cameras was slower at first than in other countries. In the 1990s, new managerial, police-led strategies were launched via public/private partnerships. The 1998 Crime and Disorder Act required local authorities and the police to publish crime audits. Business investment districts hired their own private guards.

But defensive landscaping and the 'design out' of schemes really started after large-scale Provisional Irish Republican Army (PIRA) bombs exploded in April 1992 and April 1993 in the City of London, causing enormous damage, at the core of Greater London. Terrorist threats were then taken seriously. A 'ring of steel' was deployed around the City, one of the command centers of the global financial system, and the number of entrances reduced and made more secure. Defensible space was meant to reassure financial industries. Automatic Number Plate Recognition cameras (ANPR) and large signs at entry points also reinforced the security scheme.

After 2005, three levels of emergency – catastrophic, serious, significant – were matched by directive, coordinated or supportive management planning. The Cabinet Office Briefing Room (COBRA) would intervene at levels two and three, illustrating the centralization of the security management. Unlike French officials' insulated position, the central government sought public cooperation from local authorities, as will be seen in the next chapter.

Coaffee and others provide an excellent detailed account of the long-term strategy of resilience against terrorism (CONTEST), based on four distinct strands: prevent, pursue, protect, prepare.

> 'Prevent' aims at tackling disadvantage and buttressing community cohesion, especially where radicalization might occur. It also focuses on urban generation in continuity with previous urban policies. It is a long-term strategy elaborated in early 2008, in the report *Prevent Violent Extremism: A Strategy for Delivery.* (HM Gvt 2008)

With 'pursue', intelligence and security agencies work together with the Joint Terrorism Analysis Center established in 2003. This collaboration takes advantage of the Terrorist Acts passed in 2000 and 2006. Suspects can be held from 14 to 28 days. (The government would have wanted 90 days, but opposition, emanating in particular from human rights groups limited this endeavour). Assets of terrorist groups can be frozen. The Prevention of Terrorism Act, passed in 2005, allows travel restrictions for suspects, the imposition of curfews and 'house arrest'. These measures comply with the new European Union Counterrorism strategy completed during the UK presidency. Community-based policing approaches involve Muslims under the 'prevent' agenda conflict with the hard-policing methods used for intelligence, surveillance and arrests under the 'pursue' strand, as will be seen in Chapter 3.

'Protect' increases the securitization of borders and of critical national infrastructure (CNI) – mainly energy, water, transport and finance – and that of public 'crowded' places. Advanced biometrics technologies are imposed on visitors to the United Kingdom. This measure is controversial because it can be used for general policing matters and not just for counterterrorism. In the subways, the Intelligence Pedestrian Surveillance System (IPS) alerts operators to suspicious behaviour, unattended packages and potential terrorist attempts. Coaffee and others remark that 'the efficacy of technology-focused counterterrorism policy responses has been called into question and there are here warnings about the danger of seeing science and technology as a panacea to more deep-seated social and cultural challenges' (op. cit, 153).

'Prepare' checks whether the United Kingdom is ready for the consequences of a terrorist attack. More attention is given to prevention, and more demands made on multi-agency, partnerships and stakeholders. This long description of counterterrorist measures emphasizes the challenges raised by governmental cooperation, funding, partnership, innovation, proportionality, liberty, discrimination and public disclosure (Coaffee et al., op. cit.). (The French position justifies silence for this very reason).

The strategy developed after 2005 in France and other European countries follows, in part, the British one. Agencies and intelligence partnerships have been either reactivated or created with this aim in mind (Crawford, 2011), allowing the arrest of suspects before plots of destruction were implemented. It is not my purpose to develop such schemes for each country, but rather to provide a general European framework.

The Europeanization of anti-terrorist policies, although slow to be implemented, is finally taking place.[15] During the last decade, justice and criminal law have been prominent tools of European integration. After 1993 and the enforcement of the Treaty on European Union (TEU), the cooperation of member states in matters of penal policy was made possible and accelerated by the creation of the 'third pillar' of the Union. Its goal was to maintain and develop the EU as an 'area of freedom, security and justice' (AFSJ). While, from the start,[16] the European Court of Justice was supranational, 'that the third pillar remained intergovernmental ensured that Member states were able to retain a high degree of national control over the development of policy and the adoption of implementing instruments' (Baker, 2010, 189). As Baker aptly remarks, this initial stage did not look like 'governing through crime'. The response to perceived threats remained proximate and proportionate (Ibid., 193). The European perspective betrayed a concern for freedoms 'in conditions of security and justice accessible to all' (European Council, 1999, para. 2) and the treatment of *fear* of crime rather than treatment of crime itself. Most of all, human rights perspectives prevailed at the Council of Europe and safeguards were provided, 'giving priority to the rights of suspects and defendants over those of victims and putative victims' (Baker, op. cit., 203). In brief, the Union does not 'govern through crime' but rather governs through 'security', as testified by huge databases and border data-sharing in matters of security.

National histories, institutions, cultures, morals and political choices have led to different options within the Union and to various modes of law enforcement. Penal cultures differ along with population size, duration of Union membership and features of criminal justice systems. 'In the context of this complex set of variables, the influence of penal outlook is unclear' (Baker, op. cit.; 205). Socio-economic and racial disparities in Europe do not currently compare with those of the United States. However, punitive trends come and go. The United States in the 1960s was probably 'softer' than Europe at that time; the death penalty has been banned all over Europe, but when it was still enforced in some European countries in the 1970s, it was banned (briefly by the Supreme Court) at that time in the United States. An important difference may come from non-elected judges and prosecutors retaining their discretionary power in matters of mitigating circumstances regarding sentencing. Another difference concerns voting rights. It does happen in some American counties and states – but not everywhere – that incarcerated persons lose voting rights, while in some European countries, inmates can vote.

The incarceration rate has slightly increased on average in Europe since 2001, yet it currently remains seven to ten times lower than in the United States. Most European countries have stable rates of incarceration, except for Ireland, Scotland, Belgium and Central and Eastern European Countries (higher rates) and the Netherlands, Denmark, Italy (lower rates) (Proband 2008; Krajewski 2010). One cannot claim that there will be an Americanization of prison practices in Europe. More people have entered prisons in the last decade, but they have been rapidly released and mostly in the case of repeat offenders has sentencing been lengthened. One should mention, however, the administrative retention of safety betraying a 'social fear'.[17] At the same time, more alternatives of day-incarceration, electronic bracelets, alternative and intermediary sentencing are made to alleviate the number of incarcerated persons. In many European countries, high-risk populations compose most of the prison population – foreigners violating immigration laws (a small number) or involved in various deals, young jobless males without guarantee of stable jobs and housing to offer the judge. Yet no historical legacy weighs on a specific group, except perhaps the stigmatized Romas, who are less incarcerated, unlike African-American males (13 per cent of the population, 45 per cent of the prison population). Most European states send their juvenile delinquents to juvenile justice courts. The European Convention on Human Rights acts as a watchdog on offenders' constitutional rights. The European Committee on the Prevention of Torture (CPT) is an emanation of that court. Its mission is to control law enforcement's practices where people are detained (police stations, prisons, prison hospitals). Its inspection visits occur without warning. Widely commented-on reports signal the countries tolerating abuse. By contrast, the United States refuses international intervention of this type in its detention practices, as a matter of principle. To our knowledge, the practice of *shaming*, which returned to American criminal justice procedures in the 1990s – for instance, forcing offenders to walk through the streets with their crimes written on a board that they carry – is unusual in Europe[18] but, again, it is not a generalized practice in the United States, either (Karstedt, 2011, 3). Sanctions for antisocial behaviour, though in decline, display however a stunning imagination on the part of British judges (Newburn, 2007).

Finally, it should be emphasized that changes observed in law and order since 9/11 do not just result from politicians, experts and media's calculations. Scheingold warned us to be cautious in our judgment of politicians' behaviour. He admitted that 'national politicians...have strong incentives to politicize street crime. For them, it provides a unifying theme and thus a valence issue. While victimization is experienced differentially according to class, race, gender, and geography, the *threat* it poses to property and person evokes comparable fears throughout the society. National and gubernatorial political leaders can, therefore, deploy the fear of crime to unify the public against the criminal' (1984, 3; 179).Yet, Scheingold was prompt to add that 'it is an interactive process *combining elements of responsiveness with elements of manipulation*. Politicians do not so much "expropriate our consciousness" as take advantage of punitive predispositions about crime that are rooted in American culture. The public engages and disengages from the politicization process for reasons that have at least as much to do with the place of crime in the culture as with the impact of criminal victimization in our lives' (1984, 54). In other words, politicization is a reciprocal process, with political leaders as much taking the initiative as responding to the public. But politicization has only an indirect and unpredictable impact on policy. Power games begin long before demands surface and debates take place. The interplay of interests, ideas and institutions matter a great deal in the comparison of countries' choices of policies.

This chapter has shown that, since the traumatic events of 9/11 2001 and despite diverse frames of social integration marking differences among American and European perceptions, a consensus assessing the risks that societies face has appeared among national and local governments. The so-called precautionary principle (European Commission, 2000) has motivated political decision makers and bureaucrats to construct risks as linked to certain types of 'Others', to their children and to the spaces where they live. Strategies have been developed to protect societies from such 'risks' (Bleich, 2005). In the United States, 9/11 was perceived as being the destructive work of external enemies, whereas the more recent terrorist attacks or potential attacks occurring in Europe are seen as insiders' jobs, some of those insiders being well 'inserted' in the communities where they live.

Regarding security, two favoured types of state strategies are seen to be at work: The first strategy confronts territorial risks and threats without inflaming ethnic and racial differences – it is colour blind. What comes to mind are all kinds of security measures slowing access to certain sensitive places and creating 'defensible spaces'. A second strategy aims at hardening surveillance, identification and the deportation of suspect 'Others', most of all, jihad fundamentalists hostile to democratic principles, but also of hard-core criminals (for example, Dutch bills in 2011 aiming at restricting immigration and at deporting serious foreign criminals). This approach relies heavily on the work of intelligence services and the police. But a third strategy relies on states and on their redistributive measures to strengthen social inclusion (Body-Gendrot 2010b). These principles are currently under attack: austerity policies impose drastic cuts in social budgets. Case studies, focused on world cities confronting threats in various parts of the world, show what use they make of states' strategic decisions and whether their own strategies – consisting of increasing local measures of prevention, organizing events that foreground commonalities out of diversity and differences, and giving more voice to citizens – can be alternatives.

Part II

The Challenges for Cities North and South

Introduction to Part II

This part specifically examines some types of threats experienced by global cities, and their responses to those threats. Not all threats. Some threats, such as pandemics or environmental disasters, do not fit into this analysis. Although some, such as Avian flu and global warming are human-induced, they do not appear as direct social challenges to order, which is what global players, investors, political elites and most city residents and users fear or are anxious about. These threats have also been selected because the stakes regarding order and public tranquillity can be politically exploited, a phenomenon less likely to happen with environmental or health issues. No one is comfortable living in a city in a situation of violence, factionalism or quasi-anarchy as is the case in some regions of the word. The social question is an urban question. Threats to public order, whatever their nature and scale, need therefore to be taken seriously by all decision makers, as these threats are also amplified by 'fear producers'.

This second part of the analysis starts with terrorism, frequently referred to as the most lethal threat for cities, although other risks, such as road accidents, are more deadly. It is followed by an examination of criminal activities taking place on a large scale in some world cities or aspiring to be world cities. This threat, also a cause of fear and insecurity for large segments of populations, is more closely associated with the megapolises of the South: there, criminal gangs may attempt to break down a local government's capacity to exert its functions in a demo-cratic way, and may (temporarily) paralyze local institutions or threaten them more or less permanently. The last section deals with a less lethal form of urban violence, a 'crumbly' violence, in British and French cities.

Yet social outbreaks involving hundreds of young people can be enormously disruptive for a city, region or country; they may be virulent, as seen in 2011, and thus a cause of anxiety for majorities questioning their governments' capacity to anticipate large-scale public disorders.

Cities' authorities cannot, indeed, remain passive. Yet their resources are constrained: their formal powers remain limited and their actions bridled by the need to attract and maintain private investors. Restricting their expenditures makes them particularly vulnerable to large expressions of discontent.

Take New York City, for example. According to the Constitution, American cities are 'creatures of the states', and even though New York has a strong police department, its legal requirements, funding and control come from upper-level institutions. In matters of counter-terrorism, the local struggle with federal agencies is continuous. The justice function is either federal or located at the state level. The city has powers to suspend collaboration with federal programs (i.e., the deportation of undocumented immigrants), but within limits, and it can develop prevention policies.

London and Paris are constitutionally controlled by their national governments. In 1986, the Thatcher government abolished the Greater London Authority, and when it was re-established after fourteen years, it was given limited, albeit significant, functions, in particular regarding policing. The idea of a Greater Paris with more autonomous decision making and electoral legitimacy has not yet taken off. In these cities, when the mayors belong to a political party different from that of the upper echelons, it may either be an asset or a liability.

In the South – India, South Africa and Brazil belonging to the dynamic Brazil, Russia, India, China, South Africa (BRICS) countries – national constitutions allow more local power to be exercised. All three countries are democracies and hold locally organized elections granting legitimacy to representative functions. Granting Mumbai, Johannesburg and São Paulo powers may include letting them pursue global objectives if they fit national schemes. An important constraint on Mumbai's power, however, comes from the state of Maharashtra, which has 100 million residents. The state has to launch policies benefiting the larger numbers and not just the 12 million residents of Mumbai. Constitutionally, the state 'may, by law, endow' municipalities with more powers. But Frug (2011, 352) observes that it has decided not to do so.

In South Africa, there are also three levels of government, national, provincial and local. The 1997 constitution set out a greater degree of equality in the relations between the three spheres of government.

Municipalities are no longer the mere 'hands and feet' of the centre. In the elections of 2000, Johannesburg emerged as a unified metropolitan council led by an executive mayor playing a central role in the city (Mabin, 2007, 52–57). However, constantly threatened by financial crises and with a severely limited budget, the power of the city remains greatly dependent on other levels of government. Johannesburg is run by the African National Congress (ANC) party, which rules with a distinct agenda at all levels in the country. The local government has only limited functions regarding health, safety and policing functions, and no responsibility over education. 'The 200 city councillors conspicuously avoid the violence and crime issues that probably affect poorer groups more severely than anyone else in the city ... A distinct direction of city politics is yet to emerge' (Ibid.).

São Paulo, with the People's Constitution of 1988, has autonomous powers. The state of São Paulo and the national government have equally autonomous powers. As in Mumbai, the local government's limits come from its population, only making half of the state's. It is surrounded by thirty-eight autonomous municipalities. The state of São Paulo, not the city, controls the military and the civilian police and the judicial function. 'This leaves the city without authority to deal either with the street-related or gang-related violence that threatens its development, or with the police force itself exacerbates this violence. Federal power over the city remains considerable' (Frug, op. cit., 353). When successfully achieved, such goals open up possibilities and opportunities for global cities to become part of a larger, multi-scalar governance framing of issues. Cities play an essential role in addressing global problems which almost always have their solutions at the local level.

Finally, (Enrique Peñalosa, 1965), the former mayor of Bogotá, Colombia, rightly points out an important distinction. In metropolises where authorities lack legitimacy, citizens do not feel bound to obey their laws, even less to denounce those who break them ... the poor are too busy surviving to participate much in government decisions and often do not have time to be informed about them[;] it is the role of government to represent them, to ensure that decisions lead to greater equality and justice and not to the contrary (2007, 310; 316).

The challenges that these global cities confront consist in finding their own ways to prevent civil eruptions, to heal wounds and cement their populations in order to retain their democratic legitimacy, while at the same time pursuing their own agendas regarding global parameters.

3
Terrorism

Is terrorism the most lethal threat to global cities? Risks and threats of terrorism are neither similar in nature nor in scope in the cities of the global North and South, as comparisons of New York, London, Paris and Mumbai will show. This chapter reveals that New York City demonstrates an exceptional capacity to respond to the threat of terrorism and, in some respects, with pioneering methods in matters of counterterrorism even surpassing the federal government. The argument that cities can take the lead in innovative solutions to alleviate risks is made with New York. But the other cities studied in this chapter, Paris, London and Mumbai show a lesser capacity and their case is less clear.

Terrorism is a thorny subject. How to define it? It expresses a will to resort to a form of asymmetric war, led by enigmatic enemies who do not respect the conventional rules of war. The attackers represent no state and target individual people who are not state officials. As defined by the U.S. Department of Defense, terrorism is a calculated use of violence or of a threat of illegal violence, meant to provoke fear with the goal of constraining or intimidating governments or civil societies for usually political, religious or ideological goals. Terrorism aims at making a maximum of victims and at destroying symbolic structures, in order to gain from the attention of decision makers and public opinion all over the world. More precisely, what is important is the nature of the act, along with the identity of the perpetrators and the nature of the cause. 'The fear created by terrorists may be intended to cause people to exaggerate the strengths of the terrorist and the importance of the cause, to provoke governmental overreaction, to discourage dissent, or simply to intimidate and thereby enforce compliance with the demands' (Savitch, 2008, xiv). Terrorism is framed as extraordinary, limitless, long-lasting, global, local, and unpredictable

(Tsoukala, 2009). Since 9/11 in the United States, Madrid in 2004, London in 2005, then Mumbai in 2008, terrorist attacks on cities have been carried out by different groups, despite the tendency to rally about the brand name of Al-Qaeda. Such dispersion made responses and their coordination difficult.

Why do three out of four terrorist attacks target cities? Cities' intrinsic features make a certain kind of terrorism effective and possible: they have resources, and they thrive on clustered diversity, unbounded social interactions, fluid and complex interdependence. They provide anonymity. 'If ... cities make and master space, the tactic of terrorism is to undo that supremacy by decontrolling urban territory. The ... objective of the terrorist is to put a halt to city function – preventing it from "crystallizing" its creative energies' (Mumford, 1938), 'breaking down its rich "mosaic"' (Wirth, 1938), 'upsetting its natural "rhythms"' (Lefebvre, 1970), and 'sabotaging its "economic generation"' (Jacobs, 1970), shutting it down abruptly (Savitch, 2008, 95). Terrorists target global and major cities because these offer the best returns: lives, resources and media attention. In some countries, only one city is the target. For instance, in the United States, 92 per cent of terrorist casualties have been located in New York City, and 1 per cent in Los Angeles; in France, 94 per cent are in Paris, but 0 per cent in Marseille. But this proportion does not always hold up. In Italy, Rome, with 55 per cent, is followed closely by Milan, 33 per cent, and in Israel, Jerusalem, 39 per cent, by Tel Aviv, 20 per cent (Ibid., 21). Such data and those which follow depend on specific criteria regarding what constitutes a terrorist incident. Interpol recognized the problem of classification early on, in part because of the difficulty of assessing the sometimes mixed motives of the perpetrators of violence.

Local geography is the building block of religious terrorism, which is all the more lethal as it sanctifies suicide. Savitch explains that in just eight years, twenty-seven cities experienced 1,652 incidents, and that terrorism grew more lethal year after year (from four casualties on average in the early 1970s to eighty in the 1990s), thus confirming Gary LaFree's observations. Lafree's research reveals that, between 1970 and 1993, terrorist acts causing more than ten casualties were unusual and that the probability of being killed in a terrorist attack still remained microscopic. In the distribution of incidents in all the world's regions, North America is proved to be the least targeted (Figure 3.1).

Currently, terrorism mostly targets Iraq, the Pakistan-Afghanistan region, the Horn of Africa, Yemen and North Africa.

From this perspective, the 9/11 attacks on New York and Washington may indeed be perceived as 'the dark horse', the exception (LaFree,

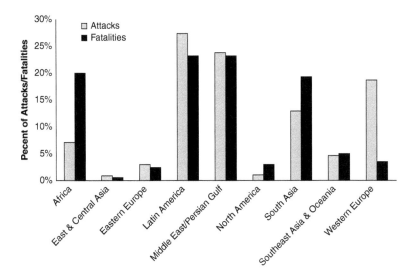

Figure 3.1   Worldwide terrorist attacks by region, 1970–2006 (n = 74,258)

Source: Gary LaFree and Laura Dugan, Research on Terrorism and Countering Terrorism, 2009.

2009). Changes occurring in New York due to terrorist threats (restricted spaces, searches and checks, surveillance, privatization, defensive architecture) are examined in light of the continuation of a period of time, distinguished by the return of law and order and an aim for the 'quality-of-life' put forward by Mayor Rudy Giuliani and his successive police commissioners in the 1990s. Terrorism has to be examined within a context already moulded by crime control and 'war on terror'.

3.1   New York City

3.1.1   New York and crime

The years 1986–92 in New York were plagued by crack cocaine epidemics (Fagan and Wilkinson, 1998). Gangs were fighting for the control of their trade and protected their drugs with guns. Very young boys were involved, either to keep watch, carry the drugs or protect them with guns. Soon some neighbourhoods became war zones (Canada, 1996).

In 1985, 1,384 people were murdered, a figure which in 1990 rose to 2,245. Confronted with such a challenge, the city enforced new policing methods. According to F. Zimring's thesis (2012), in the space of nine years, crime declined by 82 per cent. His argument requires some clarification. He first contests the link established between urban life and crime in America, showing that, despite transformations in the ethnic and racial profile of the city, the homicide rate (30 per 100,000 in 1990) dropped to 5.6 per 100,000 in 2009, a rate lower than that of 1961. Such a crime decline in New York City represents twice the national average. In the five boroughs, all types of serious crimes – robbery, rape, larceny, burglary, auto theft and assault – were in 2010 very low by 1990 standards. Secondly, Zimring explains that the city won this war on crime with little change in the general population, culture, the number of single parent families, the situation of public schools or in economic inequalities. (Only housing improved, but the correlation between housing and crime has not been established). The number of young people committing crimes also declined. Thus, he assumes crime rates can drop without major structural changes such as winning the drug war (the purchase and use of drugs remain stable) or massively incarcerating offenders (the incarceration rate dropped by 28 per cent in the 1990s, while it grew sevenfold at the national level; it dropped for minority males as well) or without any real change in to the pattern of inequality (20 per cent of the New York population were poor in 2005, compared to 25 per cent in 1995). The consequences of this decline are important: if there were 1,600 less homicides during this period, then an estimated 1,000 lives of minority young men who are disproportionately the victims of homicides were spared. As will be seen later, the price to be paid was a 48 per cent increase in the number of arrests for misdemeanours. The intent of this research is to bring a focus on crime, violence and fear of crime and to take into account the interaction of structural ('risk factors') and situational influences (the incidence of new methods of policing in the 1990s), while before trying to keep a balance between the two.

How can such a success in crime decline be explained? Usually, massive imprisonment (but the number of incarcerated Black and non-Black Hispanics increased by 29 per cent in New York City prisons after 1990 versus 65 per cent nationally), a better economy until 2008 and demography (New York's population increased by 12 per cent after 1990) explain some of the variations. But, Zimring explains, potential offenders respond to changing circumstances; modest changes in street environment, drug dealing and use and the surveillance of hot spots had an impact. For him, the meaningful explanation comes from changes occurring in the police: an increase in police numbers (9,000 additional uniformed police in 1990 joined the NYPD), new methods of management and more aggressive and territorially focussed street policing tactics. In the 1990s, Police Commissioner William Bratton, with J. Maple heading the Transit Police Department, deployed a management scheme based on diagnosis, rapid deployment and follow-up. This analytical tool, called CompStat, combines a crime-mapping instrument with management of the police captains who command the city's seventy-six precincts, emphasizing their responses to crime and strategies. Each precinct has 200–400 officers. According to Bratton, then New York Police Commissioner, after two years of this method, felonies were down 27 per cent, murder down 39 per cent, and auto theft down 35 per cent. Robberies were down by a third, burglaries by a quarter (Bratton 1998, 154).

Surveillance and the issue of discriminatory practices

The means of achieving such statistical success are contested. Zimring's thesis praising the police's new management is not convincing for a number of criminologists, in particular regarding the practice of aggressive policing and the stop-and-frisk methods. Indeed, in what he calls 'the indignities of order maintenance policing', Fagan (2011), a professor at Columbia Law School and an expert on police discrimination, points out that a new body of research indicates that in, numerous American cities, police interactions with citizens, especially minority citizens who are stopped, are hostile and aggressive. His argument is that a widespread use of coercive police authority harms citizens' dignity. The U.S, Constitution combines both notions of respect and dignity. The Fourth Amendment protects the fundamentals of human dignity for defendants. Fagan explains that this was much changed after the riots of the 1960s and the subsequent pressure exerted on police by public opinion and the media to respond efficiently to violent crime. The concept of 'reasonable suspicion' led courts to grant more leverage to the police. Deciding whether the alleged criminals' human dignity had been preserved or not during police stops and searches, courts looked more at what harm was done than at what should have been the required procedure according to the law (Harcourt, 2004). As more victims' voices were heard, the enforcement of Fourth Amendment rights changed over time in favour of crime control. The police found suspects, even when the signals of offences being committed were weak. In 2005, police stopped more than one in ten adult citizens over the age of 16, including stops on highways and pedestrian stops (Fagan and Meares, 2008). For Fagan, such police searches without reasonable cause brings up emotions which are detrimental to the trust in institutions. 'Public shaming', and verbal degradation are particularly resented by Black young men who are the most frequently stopped. Moreover, in

New York, until 2010 when a suit was filed, stop records were stored in huge database by the New York Police Department (NYPD), even when there was no evidence that a crime had been committed and any law enforcement officer had access to them.

A March 2010 report issued by the Center on Race, Crime and Justice at John Jay College examines the thorny issue of racial profiling associated with stop-and-frisk policies enforced by the NYPD (Jones-Brown and Gill, 2010). Are such practices efficient? Do they make a substantial contribution both to crime decline and to the arrests of potential terrorists? Tensions between New York police and minorities have always been high, but in the last fifteen years the racial imbalances in policing have been often flashpoints for social tension and conflicts between minority citizens and the police. In many African American communities, the racial breach has prevented police-citizen cooperation. Minorities' distrust of the police has been partly reduced in 2003 after the New York Police Department (NYPD) signed a consent decree prohibiting the practice of racial profiling. An investigation relative to the street crime unit led by U.S. Attorney General M.J. White confirmed the results found by New York State Attorney General Eliot Spitzer: African Americans, 25 per cent of the population, made up half of those stopped; Latinos, 25 per cent of the population, were one third of those stopped, while Whites, 43.4 per cent of the population, were 13 per cent of those stopped. The City of New York then agreed to spend $1.5 million in the creation of files to evaluate the fairness of NYPD procedures; these files are filled in by street officers and processed electronically.

It found that 575,996 New Yorkers were stopped in 2009 (three times the number in 2003, 160,851) (Figure 3.2) and that 473,320 were

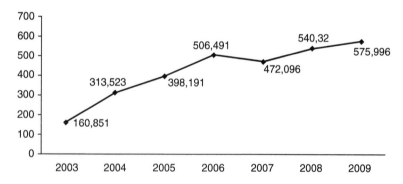

Figure 3.2   Total stops 2003–09

Source: NYPD 2003–07 and Center for Constitutional Rights 2008 and 2009.

what the New York City Liberties Union (NYCLU) calls 'innocent New Yorkers' and showed the importance of the issue, according to J. Travis,[1] president of John Jay College.[2]

Unsurprisingly, the five police precincts where most racial minorities live stand out as having the greatest number of police stops. Four out of five stops are located in Brooklyn and, depending on the year, Harlem or Jamaica, Queens, make the fifth (Ibid., 5). From 2003 to 2009, Blacks and Hispanics combined were stopped nine times more than Whites, and made 85 per cent of all stops (Figure 3.3) (Ibid., 14 and 19).

The most frequent reason given by police officers for initiating a stop is not the suspicion that individuals are carrying guns or their physical appearance but in almost half of the cases, that they were engaged in 'furtive movements'. This is highly ambiguous and ill-defined notion, ignoring the issue of race. According to the report, only 1.24 per cent of all the stops resulted in the discovery of a weapon (gun, knife, and so on) and 1.70 per cent in the possession of some kind of contraband, including illegal drugs. Just 6 per cent of the stops ended with an arrest in 2008 (Ibid., 10). The rationale given by Police Commissioner Bratton in 1994 with regard to the number-one strategy, 'Getting Guns off the streets of New York' and 'Reclaiming the public

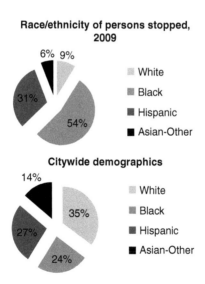

Figure 3.3 Stops by race and ethnicity

Source: Center for Constitutional Rights memorandum, February 24, 2010.

spaces', does not seem justified in light of the following data: 627 guns were recovered in 2003 and 824 in 2008. In raw numbers, 308,101 stops of Blacks yielded only 617 guns; 135,026 stops of Hispanics, 121 guns, and 57,650 stops of Whites, 42 guns (Ibid., 18). Fagan (2011a, 21) adds that about one in four stops in New York City between 2004 and 2009 resulted in the use of force, based on data compiled by the police. Force was about 20 per cent more likely to be used against Black than White suspects, once the characteristics of the stop were controlled. 'From 2004–09, more than 3.2 million stops of citizens were made, with poor arrests rates (less than 10%) (ibid. 13); moreover, since African Americans represented 53 per cent of those stops, while constituting 24 per cent of New York's population and fewer than 35 per cent of known criminal suspects, it is clear that law-abiding African Americans disproportionately endure adversarial contact with the police that produce harm, stigma and, in about one case in four, force or violence' (ibid. 32).

Whether institutions can act efficiently when most citizens think society is unfair remains a basic question. Minorities representatives took New York City to court in 1999 for discriminatory practices (*Daniels, et al. v. The City of New York*) and a settlement was reached. In 2008, the Center for Constitutional Rights, based in New York City, filed a new complaint in federal court accusing the NYPD once more of failing to include essential details on required police forms to show whether the stops were justified. The study carried out by Fagan (2011b) examines police data cataloguing the 2.8 million times from 2004 to 2009 when officers stopped people on the street. He has found that in more than 30 per cent of these stops, the proof of reasonable suspicion necessary to make the stop constitutional was lacking. Minorities were disproportionately targeted for unjustified stops. The challenge to the legitimacy of police action that does not comply with the law has currently led to a class action lawsuit, still pending. During the trial, communities' views on policing practices and the responses given by the police's lawyers are likely to be aired.

3.1.2   New York confronted with terrorism

'Crime and terrorism have to be examined together because they mutate opportunistically and metastasize wherever there is a weakness', remarks journalist Dickey who also studied closely how New York became a secure city (2009, 4). Rascoff, [3] head of the NYPD intelligence division's analytical operation from 2006 to 2008, explained that developing a statistical tool like CompStat gave the NYPD the capacity to preserve important resources and use them instead to undertake counterterrorism strategies. It would have been impossible during the Mayor Dinkins era to do so when so many crimes (due to the crack epidemic) were committed and the police force was fully mobilized. By becoming more professional during those years, the police force gained an intelligence-driven methodology, self-confidence and the budget needed to mobilize adequate resources after 9/11. Rascoff points out that New York was already a global city, with a foreign policy of its own before the 1980s. 'The NYPD acted as an army, with an intelligence capacity and armed men'. Cleaning the streets and putting the city back in order under Giuliani strengthened the counterterrorist approach. The control of crime are global because the threats are.

After the attacks of 9/11, the precautionary principle already described and mobilized as a form catastrophe preparedness, gradually went into effect. Prioritization was given to the safety of neighbourhoods against a range of risks and threats. These priorities were important in New York City because of the vulnerability of its dense population and its global political, economic and cultural assets.

The city opted to give itself adequate tools in matters of policing to protect the city. Police Commissioner Ray Kelly, appointed by Mayor Bloomberg, was convinced that there would never be time to just wait for the FBI (Dickey, 2009, 5). The federal management of security is indeed made difficult by the magnitude of the Homeland Security Department, not to mention the roles of other overlapping agencies. Some police officials, such as Los Angeles County Sheriff Lee Baca, are convinced that 'America's challenge is to act and perform and share information as a single police department. But you just don't know who is in charge anymore or why something was decided which leaves large urban areas to do more and more for themselves, and to try to put smaller jurisdictions into their networks' (Dickey, 2009, 175).

The specific relationship among the federal government, New York City and the state of New York remains complex. The securitization of space and of populations implies a wide diversity of actors and overlapping authorities, some of them being bypassed because of structured impediments, slow processing and professional rivalries. There is nothing new here. Historically, like other local police forces, the NYPD had to fight a sort of a kind of war against the FBI, for every innovative decision at every turn. For instance, sending liaison officers abroad or requesting access to classified documents was made difficult. Politically, demonstrating the strength of the city can embarrasses the federal agents while placing New York ahead in the competition. 'Ray Kelly by improving the capacities of the NYPD acts as a provocateur,' Roscoff observes, and forces national security to improve its methods and its ambition. When Justice Louis Brandeis of the U.S. Supreme Court said that some institutions were the 'laboratories of policy', such a remark would apply to the NYPD.

Richman explains that 'State and local governments must be full partners in any effective strategy for preventing acts of terror: without their participation, the Federal government cannot possibly know what "dots" to connect. But the relationships that local police departments have formed with the communities that they serve can be threatened when these departments are asked to participate in federal intelligence-gathering efforts' (2006, 30).

Historically, local governments gained funds and resources from the 'federalization of the crime issue'. In the 1960s, the COPS (Community Oriented Policing Services) program sent funds directly to big city police departments. Such federal 'intrusion' was looked on with equanimity, allowing local police to boost their anti-crime strategies with more resources. But the Bush administration became reluctant to fund what looked like Democratic strongholds, and federal aid was then transferred to governors rather than to mayors. The federal engagement in the anti-terror strategy requires both state and local assistance. There are 700,000 state and local police officers, compared with 90,000 federal law-enforcement officers (over a quarter of them involved with prisons) who hardly know the field (Ibid., 32). Thanks to a massive increase in resources devoted to the NYPD's own intelligence and counterterrorist divisions, more NYPD detectives have been sent to the Joint Terrorism Task Force (JTTF) dominated by the FBI.[4] From seventeen sent in 2002, the number grew to 100 currently.

The claim made here is that, in its response to fear of crime and to risks of terrorism, New York City chose to be as autonomous as possible. The city then appears as a pioneer, ahead of the federal system, in terms of innovation, savoir-faire and coherence.[5] According to Vallone, responsible for public safety at the New York City Council, 'thirteen terrorist attacks have been avoided since 2001, [the NYPD] is one of the best – if not the best – police forces in the world' (Smith, 2011).

Under Mayor Bloomberg, an $11 million Real Time Crime Center was created at One Police Plaza. It stores data, maps and diagrams, from criminal records to public utility bills. Policemen on the streets have been given Blackberries, and when they report crimes, these are immediately registered. Police officers from the Emergency Service Unit, heavily armed, walk in public spaces (as officers in the French Vigipirate

Program do). Their goal is to check places which could be potential targets, like the Empire State Building. But, for Kelly, the aim is also to make them visible to serve 'as a reminder, to keep the 9/11 story alive, to work against amnesia' (Dickey, op. cit., 107–11). The Hercules forces in the sense of units are heavily armed, more visible in the public space than policemen with backpacks detecting potential radiation among pedestrians, or huge metal boxes with instruments that detect potential chemical weapons. The counterterrorism division is located at Coney Island controls a wide range of concerns, from defence against radiological and nuclear attacks to surviving pandemics. It is assumed that terrorists work with conventional tools and basic explosives.[6]

Under Kelly's leadership, many NYPD police officers are required to speak foreign languages and dialects in order to understand what a foreign suspect tells them and to enable informers and undercover officers can infiltrate immigrant communities. Officers have been recruited from immigrants for this purpose. Currently, more than sixty police officers are fluent in languages, from Arabic to Dari and Gaelic, Bengali to Spanish (Dickey, 2009, 140–42). It remains a very complicated task to extract information from terrorist networks. A small group of ten people may accumulate hundreds different identities and thousands of SIM cards, and so on. It is only by cooperating with communities that information might begin to trickle upwards.[7] Local law enforcement needs to display an 'entrenched realism', to talk to moderate as well as radical community and religious leaders, use cameras and other technical resources, and rely on their know-how. When searching a building or observing street activity, they may confront youth gangs, drug dealers, organized criminals or potential terrorists. Both intelligent counterterrorism and ward policing rely on excellent knowledge of the streets and their social environments. As terrorist networks are indeed globalized, they hit strategic sites, symbols and buildings that are highly localized. It is therefore legitimate to rely as much on local expertise as on new technologies, even if numerous local measures arguably aim at soothing public opinion rather than at impeding further attack. The issue, then, is one of communication – between police patrols operating at street level, intelligence services using surveillance techniques (including customs and immigration services), Internet analysts and other actors. It implies renouncing vertical hierarchies as the sole means of transmission of knowledge, and opting instead for partnerships. Not an easy task.

Police Commissioner Kelly has assigned officers to eleven countries. In London, they work with New Scotland Yard, in Paris with Police

Headquarters, in Lyons with Interpol; they are also based in Amman, Toronto, Hamburg, Santo Domingo, Tel Aviv, Madrid and Singapore. After an attack they may have to conduct investigations in Afghanistan, Egypt, Pakistan, Yemen or the Philippines (Skolnick, 2010, xxv). The greater the national security threat, the more important becomes the local role. Since the Mumbai attacks of 2008, hotel owners in New York are required to report any suspicious client behaviour to the police.

3.1.3   Securing space

From the residents' perspective, however, being protected by the police entails costs. Risk management and the surveillance of public spaces, prestigious streets and parks can mean that taxis can no longer linger along by close to important buildings, that access to towers' promenade space is restricted, that endless searches delay visitors to the Statue of Liberty and other strategic places such as the Brooklyn Bridge, the water reservoirs, the New York Stock Exchange, the United Nations Building, and so on. Inside private buildings, it is no longer possible to enter without showing some form of ID, caterers cannot deliver lunches or parcels to the offices' top floors. In equipped centres, magnetic and biometric screens, or facial identification cameras allow the checking of who gets in and out of a building and denial of entry to unknown faces. This is the price to be paid for a more secure city.

Sociologist P. Marcuse denounces the 'barricading' and 'citadeliza-tion' of the city (2002, 599). He laments the hubris there was at the rebuilding of the 'Freedom Tower', high as the original World Trade Center: it will be again an ideal target for future suicide bombers. The question of surveillance is probably best treated by avoiding hyperbole. New York is neither Belfast nor Jerusalem nor Baghdad. But he rightly denounces the correlation of risk and danger to the very idea of the city. It served as an excuse for a large number of firms, before and after 9/11, to threaten to move elsewhere and cut their costs.

During the cold war, anticipating a possible World War III involving nuclear weapons, Pentagon strategists forcefully recommended that the populations of large American cities should be dispersed.[8] Currently, making space safe is once more a priority, and with sometimes negative consequences: they either shrivel in size, become hazardous for users, or jeopardize the neighbourhoods' quality of life and vibrancy.

Space surveillance affects New Yorkers' daily lives, but it did not start with 9/11. Since the 1960s onwards, urban design and planning have been used to address both the causes of crime, disorder and incivility and their reality. Newman (1973) developed a theory of 'defensible spaces' which became popular among urban planners: the idea was to discourage unwanted behaviour by making delinquent schemes more difficult to carry out, with material devices: fences, lights, walls, and so on. The private security market had worked over two decades on various innovative products and was just waiting for an opportunity to sell its protections and devices to various administrations. The 9/11 attack was very fruitful for that market and for politicians eager to show that they were responding to the fear of crime and of terrorism. More than before, free access to public space became even more limited and mobility more constrained: not everyone wants to have one's face photographed, which would explain why so many youths hide themselves with hoods and bandanas.

As the NYPD priorities restrict citizen's freedom of assembly for safety's sake, it has become more difficult to organize a demonstration or to occupy streets not approved of, as the example of the movement 'Occupy Wall Street' 2011n contained into Zucotti Park shows. It will be seen later that, currently, the preferred option for those in charge of public safety is also to segment a large amount of people in public space and check only strategic points, like bridges or gates. This approach allows law enforcers more leverage and efficiency.

The real estate market investing funds in such valuable locations as Times Square and Ground Zero, has gained more power in the last decade; it defines the architecture of places, the number of CCTVs or private guards, with the blessing of the city. (The same process of privatization for safety's sake is observed in the large cities in the South). The reconstruction of Ground Zero illustrates this development. After architect Daniel Libeskind designed the glass structure, the Freedom Tower, close to West Street, a six-lane highway used continuously by trucks coming from Brooklyn and New Jersey to Lower Manhattan, it appeared just too vulnerable to the head of the Counter-Terrorism Bureau at the NYPD. At his request, experts, engineers and CIA agents convinced the developer, Larry Silverstein, that the tower could not be adequately protected. A firm was hired to design a building which could withstand a bomb carried by a truck. 'They incorporated hugely expensive design features to ensure the safety of the building's inhabitants in a way that no other building in the world did' (Sheehan, 2008, 244–53). It is likely that 'rings of steel' will surround the perimeter, a thousand public closed-circuit television cameras and two thousand private ones will operate within 1.7 square miles. Computerized recorders of licence plates will be either fixed or moving in order to detect radiation equipment and will be connected to bridges and tunnels. On September 11,

2011 a new police command was established at the World Trade Center, the city's largest police precinct with 673 officers. (The police force is currently 34,500 officers) (Robbins, 2011).

An assemblage of, until-then, dispersed processes involving prevention and suppression henceforth form a compact system of protection. The grid of high-risk categories and areas set in place under Bratton as Police Commissioner has been reinforced under the 'War on Terror'. The rise of electronic surveillance and the virtual space of databases has led to a reconfiguration and to a re-territorialization of urban order (Coaffee et al., 2009).

3.1.4   The Muslim issue: federal versus local approaches

The problem of racial discrimination arising via aggressive police has already been identified. After 9/11, the NYPD approach regarding Muslims did not follow that of the FBI. The interesting issue hereafter concerns the kind of cooperation the FBI expected from the NYPD.

Various strands divide police work. As a general rule, local police anti-crime efforts do not overlap much with federal counterterrorism work, but federal counterterrorism efforts overlap with federal immigration enforcement. The latter can threaten to undermine local police anti-crime efforts.

With John Ashcroft was U.S. attorney general, local assistance was needed to interview thousands of Middle Eastern males who had entered the United States on non-immigrant visas (see Chapter 2). The local police were required to arrest them, so that their names could be inserted into the national database of suspects. This request met with enormous local resistance: police agencies typically have a large reserve of discretion. Police chiefs are not generally elected, but in the United States, mayors, county executives and chief prosecutors are, and when police alienate substantial segments of the community, they may lose not only electoral support for material resources but also information about the incidence of crime and the identification of criminals (Lewis, Ramakrishnan, 2007, 880).[9] 'Solicitude for the concerns of ethnic or racial minority groups – which are often majorities within a given city or precinct – has increasingly become a non-negotiable part of a police chief's job description. [T]he police chief whose only desire is to ensure local peace will be prone to give the feds too little help, not too much' (Richman, op. cit., 38). In 2003, the NYPD pulled out of a massive federal deportation sweep aimed at immigrants, and tensions with the FBI simmered even more. New York City passed the consent decree Executive Order 41, issued in 2003, which forbade city employees asking immigrants about their legal status and required employees not to cooperate with federal agents, if undocumented immigrants were to be arrested.

The Terrorist Information and Prevention System (TIPS) set in place in 2002 was suspended after a year. For months after the attacks, however, Muslims who had not hitherto belonged to the category of 'usual suspects' became aware that they could be stopped and frisked for being who they were, if they happened to be close to buildings with a high added value like the UN. On one hand, the intrusive technologies of surveillance, identification and intelligence made such minorities more vulnerable to stop and search. But on the other, supporting immigrants is virtually a job requirement for any New York mayor. New York is a city where illegal immigrants start businesses, raise families and send their children to school with less fear of being deported than they would be, for instance in Arizona.

Mayor Bloomberg and his team are convinced that immigrant neighbourhoods are among the safest in the city. In 2007, in a city of more than 8 million, out of a 500 homicides, only around 100 were committed by foreigners, in a city of more than 8 million. Such data challenges the long-held view that people are vulnerable to random attacks on 'mean streets' (Skolnick, 2010, xxvii). Immigrants are less engaged in crime than is the native population. This perspective can change with the second and third generations.

In 2007, Governor Eliot Spitzer proposed issuing drivers' licences to undocumented immigrants since they were making the city safer. However, after the national program Secure Communities was passed in 2007, federal pressures requiring the cooperation of local police departments to deport undocumented immigrants increased. It seems easier for local police than for correction facilities' managers not to report illegal immigrants until they have committed crimes. At the city jail on Riker's Island, Department of Correction officials had to provide foreign-born inmates' names to federal officers. Since their names are already in the database, and as each inmate costs money to a city eager to reduce its expenditures, the city can be tempted to accommodate the federal demands in that sector. Approximately 3,200 of these inmates are deported each year a fragment of the 780,000 undocumented immigrants, deported by the Obama administration in 2009–2011. The number of criminals deported nationally is more than 50 percent higher (Dolnick, 2011; Hunt, 2011).[10]

On June 2, 2011, however, Governor Andrew Cuomo suspended New York State's participation in the Secure Communities program. Not only did this program fail to deport the most serious immigrant criminals, but it undermined law enforcement and compromised public safety. The New York was the second state after Illinois to do so.

Before examining London, it seems appropriate at this point to include Paris in the comparison. Paris, another global city, was also hit by terrorist attacks. As in New York, measures taken to confront terrorism also buttress order and are used to reduce crime. Yet how each city prepares itself to confront such risks differs. The issue of crime in Greater Paris will be addressed in Chapter 5 and the possible solutions in Chapter 6.

3.2   Paris

3.2.1   Paris confronted with crime

Paris is a case apart.[11] For one thing, the presence of the middle classes in the city, where real estate remains highly valuable (at least in thirteen districts out of twenty), does not fit the sandglass pattern of the global city. Inequalities are high, but in a proportion of one to four, which is less than New York and London. Also, the strong presence of the state and the attachment of the French to the welfare state as a buffer against macro-economic shifts produces a 'soft version' of the polarized city.[12] Among the components of the resilient city, security is seen as a strong requirement contributing to its economic well-being.

'Zero tolerance' for crime is a marketing device in most global cities eager to reassure their investors, businessmen, tourists and residents. In Paris, there are differences between a *concern for* crime shared by a majority of residents living in the city or nearby western and southern suburbs and a *fear of* crime expressed by residents of marginalized areas living at the northern and eastern outskirts of the city (see Zauberman et al., 2012). The majority of those concerned with crime, rarely the victims of serious crimes, are voters who may exert political sanctions; they are patronized by politicians. For two decades, when they were less concerned about the issue, they supported policies of social prevention (*politique de la ville*) meant to restore 'social links', provide affirmative territorial action to deprived neighbourhoods and make society more inclusive (the term exclusion was first coined by the French, the worst fate being cast out of the mainstream matrix). But as the efficacy of these socially comprehensive was not demonstrated over time and as, due to heavy media coverage, the security issue was reaching the top concerns of the public, 'compassion fatigue' was felt. And after 1997 a political shift within the Left favoured domestic security policies, the consequences of which were felt in cities (Body-Gendrot and Duprez, 2002). Paradoxically, even after the terrorist attacks in Paris in 1995 and 1996 and the events of September 11, 2001, terrorism does not appear in the polls as a matter of concern of Parisians in the polls.

3.2.2 Spatial inequalities

The surprising results of the populist vote for Le Pen during the first round of the presidential elections in 2002 revealed latent xenophobia and dislike for 'Arabs'[13] in France. This was less so in Paris, with a smaller turn-out for the far right than at the larger periphery of the city and in other regions. An heterogeneous set of complex attitudes may help explain, however, why mayor can affluent Parisian residents who elected a Left wing mayor and who are at high risk of being victimized, burglarized and assaulted are less xenophobic and punitive, than more secure residents living in the outer suburbs (*Zauberman, op.cit*).

As in other large cities of the world, they experience feelings of insecurity, uncertainty and vulnerability linked to macro-changes (Bauman, 1998). Their malaise comes from a general sense of precariousness and the loss of their bearings in a fast-changing world. As with other French people, they expect the state to provide answers to this type of problems. They are not eager to get involved and co-produce solutions. When the defence of their particular interests is at stake, they take to the streets and go on strike (one out of four Parisians works for the public sector). Currently, the integrating tools of the state have been eroding or collapsing under the weight of a more heterogeneous, self-asserting multicultural society. The Parisian population is estimated to include 14 per cent of immigrants and their children. The rise of persons defining themselves as multiple and hybrid, and of a reinforced individualism, have provoked confusion among national elites as to what they should do to bring back a sense of cohesion and unity to French society. Economic crises have weakened trust in the governing elites.[14]

Although crime and delinquency can tear the social fabric of cities, they are also a social construction. Who the accusers are and who the accused are and what is considered crime and what is not, vary according to time and socio-cultural circumstances. Certain offences are constantly in the socio-political debate, such as those related to marginalized youth, while others, like white-collar crime, are frequently ignored. French governmental elites re-legitimize themselves by mobilizing the threats of crimes correlated to the *banlieues* to maintain an upper hand rather than referring to external threats of terrorism which might endanger their relations with Arab-Muslim countries and with the large Muslim community living in France. The media continuously portray male youth of immigrant origin as 'usual suspects'; policies relying on more visible policing on the streets and on harsher penalties are then easy solutions meant to reassure citizens. The police are to 'contain' undesirable elements in low-income neighbourhoods and at the further periphery. Most of all, they are to maintain order within the city and protect the state, its agents and properties.

3.2.3   Policing affluent Paris

Paris is a well-policed city. Supposedly there are more policemen per capita in Paris than in the French sensitive areas, but the number of policemen by police precinct is difficult to evaluate depending on the kind of policemen (the anti-riot police are usually not included in the Parisian data) and whether or not they are at work (only half of them are on the streets, according to some estimates). Approximately 560,000 crimes were recorded in Paris in 2008, which is two-third of the crimes committed in the region. More than 43 per cent of the criminals arrested in Paris were not Parisians; 20 per cent of them live in the nearby suburbs (French Ministry of Interior, 2009). While there is no municipal police in Paris, the Police Nationale serving in Paris and three nearby departments (6.4 million residents) is composed of 30,200 officers and 8,300 firefighters. Rather than giving citizens a sense of safety with community policing, maintaining order, with the Compagnies Républicaines de Sécurité (CRS) during street demonstrations, for instance, and pursuing organized crime have long been the national police missions rather than giving citizens a sense of safety with community policing. In theory, over 26,000 police officers are dispatched in the various police stations in theory (half of them are actually to be on the streets at any one time, according to a 2010 report); 800 officers are in the intelligence service and over 2,000 police officers are in the investigative branch, analyzing cyber crimes, underworld and organized crime (Ibid.). Policing Paris has, however, undergone changes recently and more leverage has been given to the mayor, although this transformation may only be temporary, for political reasons, policing Paris. The difficulties of implementing reforms in the Parisian police come from the fact that the mayor does not have real police powers, but has to negotiate leverage and resort to various bargaining schemes.

Over 200 sites (5,000–15,000 residents) in Paris benefit from 'proximity' police officers as well as from public employees specialized in social prevention. They are not policing by 'consent' or exerting a reassuring function, as in London. They are asked to be visible. In the most problematic areas – that is, in overcrowded areas where poorer and large immigrant families live – a hundred or so night mediators, in partnership with public housing managers and public transportation employees, signal disorders to the police. However, most of them are not familiar with each other and no one really knows who the commander is. Young street educators are reluctant to be on the streets and would rather work in youth centres. A general lack of leadership to confront police unions' resistance to necessary changes, the inertia of bureaucracies and limited accountability weaken efficiency. The lack of coherence between 'proximity' policing and its 'soft' methods of dialogue during the day and the, occasionally, brutal methods used by police forces in charge of law and order at night or during street demonstrations, is glaring.

3.2.4   Evaluating safety in Paris

Police statistics and surveys reveal that crime, concern and fear of crime declined after 2002. But these figures should be taken cautiously. The debate on the accuracy of police statistics has always vexed researchers. As police chiefs themselves admit, global figures are misleading and should be deconstructed: various types of crime are amalgamated and should belong to different categories or recategorized – preventing long term evaluation.

Approximately 1,100 policemen currently patrol the trains, and thousands of cameras have been added for surveillance and identification in the Parisian region. Most offences occur during the day (and not at night, as Parisians tend to think). While property crimes have decreased in the last ten years, interpersonal violence is up. People feel that it is no use reporting crime to the police, except for insurance requirements. The number of crimes are presumed to be much higher than those reported to the police. In the Parisian region, only 20 per cent of attempted thefts with violence are reported, 24 per cent regarding having received blows, 42 per cent of wounds, 54 per cent of thefts with violence and 81 per cent of, actions incapacitating a person from going to work (see Nevanen et al., 2006). That visible petty crime in Paris is committed by young drifters or prostitutes from Eastern Europe and widely reported by the media is a major issue in representations. While Parisian middle classes complain about thefts and burglaries, in the surveys they do not express fear of crime. They tend to blame crime on non-nationals and especially on youth of immigrant origin, like the Romas, or those who are very visible in the public spaces, in railway stations and in public transportation. Bus drivers complain about youth assaults and some-times go on strike after too many incidents. Such decisions are widely commented upon by the media (16 million French watch the news on the two major channels).

3.2.5   Parisians' expectations relative to safety

Polls on such issues are unusual and rarely made public. They reveal that air pollution and automobile traffic comes first among Parisians' concerns. Security is not even mentioned. A difference with New York, the risk of terrorism does not appear among the Parisians' concerns. Eighty-three per cent of Parisians do not dread an assault.[15]

Eighty-nine per cent of Parisians think that 'it is a good thing that the state is in charge of safety and maintenance [of] order in Paris'. All inter-viewees agree that fighting insecurity and delinquency is an important function of the national police, followed by the repression of sex crimes (60 per cent), organized crime (49 per cent), juvenile delinquency (47 per cent), drug dealing (46 per cent). Eighty-eight per cent of the Parisians polled support CCTV surveillance cameras in the subway; 79 per cent in buses; 66 per cent in public spaces. They are very critical of efforts at social prevention that are not developed enough, especially for drug traf-fickers.[16] Responses vary according to the districts where people live.

In rare, yet spectacular actions, civil society may resort to self-help. Some residents' mobilization against drug dealers, prostitutes and squatters occur now and then in the poorer districts of Paris. Civil rights advocates come forward and talk to the media to denounce police misconduct.

Until it was terminated in 2011 and merged into a larger body of rights defence, a national commission for professional standards in security was established, an external authority investigating complaints against the police and other law enforcers. It could only be summoned by citizens via a parliamentary member or an institution (Children's right authority or the anti-discrimination authority, for instance). The number of cases examined totalled 170 in 2010. While the commission has no power to redress complaints and has been underfunded, it had investigative and hearings powers and also issued recommendations, thus giving visibility to cases of police or prison guards' misconduct (regarding juveniles, intentionally tight handcuffing, discriminatory practices, humiliating strip-searches and deplorable conditions in police custody, for instance) (Anderson, 2011, 397–98).

The core of Paris is a defensible space. Paris has numerous official buildings, public and private mansions and palaces, museums, banks and all kinds of valuable assets. The police are required to protect them as well as provide for the safety of state VIPs. Whenever it is anticipated that disorders could occur (during street demonstrations or massive celebrations, for instance), a strong paramilitary police deployment takes efficient is placed in charge and made responsible for law and order.

Youth violence in the *banlieues* has become a useful metaphor for addressing a cocktail of fears, malaise and tensions in French society. Should a terrorist attack shake Paris and France, the *banlieues* would then either be forgotten in the political and media discourses or, would appear as a sort of fifth column threatening national security.

3.2.6 Paris and terrorism

'The French capacity to fight terrorism [is] the result of hard-won lessons [as] France has always been on the "bleeding edge" of terrorism, confronting terrorism its all its guises' (Shapiro and Suzan, 2003, 68). Anarchist activism at the end of the nineteenth century prompted specific legislation (*lois scélérates*) jeopardizing recently granted civil liberties. It triggered violent opposition. Terrorist attacks as early as 1954–62, during the 'Algerian war', with the case of the Secret Army Organization penetrating security forces also generated specific legislation which was again violently rejected by part of civil society. Cahn (2010, 467) explains that when terrorist attacks hit France again in the mid 1980s, the governing elites showed reluctance to enact special legislation. Domestic terrorism was fought by the agency for international surveillance, by the head of the territorial security (DST) and by the counter-espionage service, (SDECE). In the 1970s, Action Directe undertaken forms of terrorism comparable to those of the Red Brigades in Italy or the Baader-Meinhof Gang in Germany. Then terrorist, Carlos, made the headlines in the 1980s. In 1986, 14 terrorist acts were committed in the names of the Committee of Solidarity with Arabic and Middle East Political Prisoners. The first anti-terrorism statute was passed in 1986. It had taken about 15 years for counterterrorism (Unité de coordination de la lutte anti-terroriste [Anti-Terrorism Fight Coordination Unit] (UCLAT)) to function properly. Resorting to special legislation was excluded for the historical reasons mentioned above. Legislators chose instead to adapt ordinary criminal law and procedures based on the enforcement of specific rules (Cahn, op. cit., 468). (It will be the position defended after 9/11).

Then in 1995 and in 1996, the Algerian radical Islamism Organization (GIA), launched new terrorist attacks. Corsican separatists would be frequent perpetrators of terrorism after 1996. A new anti-terrorism statute adjusted to the evolution of terrorism provided enforcement agencies with the required tools. In 1998, 138 terrorists were indicted for supporting the 'Chababi network' (Body-Gendrot, 2009, 131–32).

Although terrorism became an obsession for French authorities in charge of territorial security, a national silence about terrorist threats and new risks characterized the French approach, at least until 2005, when Minister of Interior Sarkozy marked a break in this French culture of secrecy. He chose to warn the French that the risk of violent action in the country was real, and the threat serious. Europol confirmed in 2008 that France was probably, after Spain, the EU member state most at risk by the terrorist threat (Cahn, op. cit., 468). This new obsession has led to a deep reorganization of state and city security bureaucracies. Four laws were passed concerning anti-terrorism allowing better technological equipment, training, power enhancement granted to police forces and special courts. The term 'war' would certainly be irrelevant in the French context. The context and the NYPD choice, largely communicating its success regarding measures taken to confront threats of terrorism, stands in sharp contrast with the non-communication of the Paris Police Prefect.

3.2.7   Several explanations come to mind

Firstly, the consensus shared by authorities in charge of safety is that information about terrorism is never 100 per cent reliable.[17] Israelis have learned to anticipate what can happen and with what frequency. But in the United States and Europe, risk cannot be realistically predicted, either regarding the nature of the danger, its scale, its likelihood or its targets. Because of the pervasive nature of ambiguity and uncertainty associated with risk, French political authorities are reluctant to overreact or to dramatize risks and create 'moral panic' (public psychosis).

Secondly, traditionally, a culture of secrecy pervades the French higher administration and, within what some call the 'monarchical Republic', important matters like precautionary principles against major risks are just not shared with citizens or the media. As elsewhere, internal security remains one of the last prerogatives of state sovereignty, allowing it to display an autonomous capacity, when so many other sectors have been redefined by the dynamics of globalization. Some scholars call this trend a 'security frenzy' or a 'penal frenzy' (Mucchielli, 2011).

Thirdly, in an age of unrest and indeterminacy, the expertise of the French state in matters of defence and counterterrorism is hardly challenged by third parties. American counterterrorism specialists praise their collaboration with their French counterparts, as was revealed, for instance by Wikileaks, in 2010.

The national strategies developed to respond to risks of terrorism in Paris and New York also diverge.

Four types of national approaches can be distinguished: those applied to space and territories; those securing goods and populations; those protecting critical infrastructures; and those pursuing terrorist networks.

The 2006 anti-terrorist law was passed to reinforce the capacities of intelligence services and improve the services' coordination via UCLAT (the coordinating unit mentioned before, created in 1984). Both the interior and defence ministries exchange information which is subsequently communicated to judges in charge of anti-terrorism. The judges benefit from important resources. The Ministry of Economy also plays its part, researching how terrorist networks are financed, and having freezing their resources, while the Ministry of Transportation protects vital channels of transportation systems. Within NATO and the European Community, the capacity is large but need to be constantly readjusted to match the evolution of threats.

As the capital of the country, the City of Paris's strategies are blurred with those of the state. They could be summarized as depending on reflecting a highly centralized command at the top of a security pyramid which relies more heavily on human resources in the field than on technologies.

The Police Prefect, appointed by the prime minister, commands the established defence zone of Paris and its surroundings. As such, the prefect supervises the actions of other partners who report to him (the army, prefects, firemen who also act as paramedics, anti-nuclear, anti-biological warfare and chemical terrorism experts, utilities officials, public service heads, health authorities, and so on.). The 'red program' coordinating all the activities of protection of sensitive infrastructures (such as water), sites and populations has been legally revised and largely expanded since 9/11, by then the Madrid Atocha station attack and the London attacks on public transportation. Drills are secretly conducted in the Paris subway, airports and railway stations. Information also transits through Interpol and the Ministry of Foreign Affairs.

This territorial strategy which is focussed on individuals. The French intelligence services have a fairly good knowledge and experience of the Arabic-Muslim world, in great part due to the cooperation of the intelligence services in North African countries. With the largest Muslim population in Europe, France experiences a continuous risk. French intelligence services have infiltrate and conduct surveillance on radical extremist groups in the 300 sensitive neighbourhoods around Paris (Body-Gendrot, 2009). Several criteria determine what a sensitive zone is for the intelligence service. Among them are the significant number of immigrants; ethnic shops; non-Western and religious ways of dressing; radical imams, and so on. This is quite a feat for a country which does not officially recognize ethnicity and denies racial profiling! (Ibid., 132). Nevertheless, it is also known that 'cities have a clustering function, pluralism and an uncommon tolerance' for various types of covert action (Savitch, 2008, 93).

From field observations, information trickles up to the Police Prefect, the territorial security direction (DST), the judiciary police and various branches allowing anti-terrorist judges to indict the right people. When suspicion is beyond a 'reasonable doubt', after intelligence services' investigation, under the claim of health and safety checks or of a tax audit, undercover roundups take place. In 2004, 1,200 individuals were stopped and searched after 88 raids targeting radical extremism in the Parisian region; 185 people were indicted and dozens deported, among them, several radical clerics and their followers. During the raids, €1 million in cash was seized. The state agencies, less than the Police Prefect, have the upper hand.

As in New York, agencies in charge of security in Paris display 'entrenched realism' towards risks of terrorism. If terrorist networks are globalized, they do hit strategic sites, symbols and buildings which are (usually) under surveillance. All recent attacks including in Toulouse in 2012, the murders of soldiers and Jewish children by a lonely home-grown Jihadist were undertaken with conventional tools on specific urban territories. It is thus legitimate for local police forces to rely as much on evolving experienced approaches as on new technologies. This is more the case in New York City than in Paris, where the idea of community policing is loathed by many police chiefs.[18]

3.3   London

3.3.1   London confronted with crime

A series of laws against disorder and antisocial behaviour, associated in media coverage and the public mind with minority youth groups, Youth characterize London's experience of crime. One of the choices the Thatcher, Major and Blair governments made was to take a tough stance to confront low-intensity violence which made residents' daily life insecure. They chose to reinforce police control (and the performance of their central management) and to increase incarceration for both offenders – and young offenders. Muggings causing 'moral panic' decreased following the Street Crime Initiative in 2002.

As in Paris, it is difficult to disentangle measures emanating from the city and measures taken by the government, since they target the same territorial entities in the city. The security schemes elaborated by Scotland Yard experts aim at making public spaces safer.

A comparison (excluding homicides) carried out by F. Zimring (2012) indicates that in 2007 serious crime was more prevalent in London than in New York City (Table 3.1).

As elsewhere, the fear of being mugged and the sight of young people occupying public space are the major reasons given by Londoners fear of crime.

According to the Crime and Disorder Act of 1998, the apex of the strategy elaborated by the Home Office to make neighbourhoods safer aims at deploying a global, multi-partnership effort to strengthen a 'culture of control' (Garland, 2001) that is, to anticipate the transgression of norms and the development of 'hot spots' by enticing residents, communities and the private sector to get involved in preventative measures. It is a conception of urban governance, different from France where the actors involved in the production of security are mostly those of the public sector helped by private agencies but without citizens' involvement. Neighbourhood watch, popular in British and American middle-class neighbourhoods, are perceived with suspicion in France. British crime-prevention schemes attempt to make criminal acts more difficult. They operate along a dispersed, pluralist, problem-solving approach. Home Office audits regularly take place, measuring policing improvements in various neighbourhoods of the city. Audits are a remarkable tool, showing that local authorities – which have a statutory duty to reduce crime along with police – can resort to myriad ordinances to discourage antisocial acts, domestic violence and drug dealing, and publicize the names of delinquent families, while the government carries more general audits on what works and why. In 1997–2005, crime went down 40 per cent. People are more interested in these local measures that reflect their everyday life concerns than in policing, per

Table 3.1   Crime rates in 2007 (per 100,000) in New York and in London

	Rape	Robbery	Burglary	Auto theft
New York	10.6	26.5	25.4	16.1
London	30.7	61.0	12.9	50.1

Source: Zimring, 2012, p.45.

se. In 2009, 3.5 million antisocial incidents were reported to the police. Yet Her Majesty's Inspectorate Constabulary report, *Stop the Rot*, in 2010 denounced police inaction, illustrated by the Ms Pilkington case. Over seven years, the mother of a handicapped child vainly tried to stop systematic harassment and verbal abuse by local youths. She called the police of Leicestershire no less than thirty times. Out of despair, in 2007, she burnt herself and her child alive and died (Loveday, 2011). The anti-social agenda within the Respect national program can be placed in a global perspective. In the face of 'apparently uncontrolled flows of capital, goods, people and risks, both municipal and national governments have re-sighted their energies on the management of public displays of behaviour' in a context of 'hyper-politicization' (Crawford, 2011a, 486). Such a return to politics explains reforms requiring more accountability from 41 police and crime commissioners (PCCs) and enabling the public to judge their effectiveness at the ballot box, who are to be elected, and putting the public back in as a referee.

According to a 2005 poll from the MORI institute, 60 per cent of Londoners reported that fear of crime had an impact on the quality of daily life. Not surprisingly, this feeling was more acute among women, isolated individuals (single mothers especially), the elderly and tenants in public housing estates. After housing, crime was their first concern and in some areas of London, crime ranked before housing. Whatever the social class, age and origins, all of them said they experienced fear of crime. More recently, in 2009, 48 per cent of the English say they avoid certain streets and 41 per cent avoid going out at night.

In Elephant and Castle, one of London's thirty-two boroughs. This poor inner-city immigrant neighbourhood of 56 000 residents, located in South London, is ten minutes from the Tate Modern museum, the treatment and character of the public space involves the issue of security, along with retaining the liveliness and attractiveness of the area. Elephant and Castle has a reputation for crime, drugs and antisocial behaviour. According to I. Thomas,[19] the chief superintendent of the Southwark district (including Elephant and Castle), muggings and phone-snatching are frequent on the poorly lit streets.

Elephant and Castle is a space contested, broadly speaking, used by two very different social groups. On the one hand, it has very large estates of social-rented accommodation in poor condition, are home to disadvantaged households – 60 per cent of Southwark accounts for 10 per cent of the most deprived wards in England – and on the other hand, fashionable riverside flats and converted Victorian terraces with new opportunities for 'yuppies'. At least 90 dialects are spoken in the district (the population is 41.7 per cent minorities versus 28.8 per cent in London and 9.1 per cent in England). The neighbourhood experiences high in crime rates due to the presence of gangs and to potential racial conflicts. Any event is dramatically blown up by the media and exploited by politicians. It may defeat months of effort to establish trust and collective well-being. Yet a 'Beacon' status has been awarded to the local police. Their innovative approach to community safety has been praised.

3.3.2 London confronted with terrorism

On July 7, 2005, three near-simultaneous suicide attacks were launched on the London Underground by British Muslims from Leeds, and one hour later, on a double-decker bus. The offenders were carrying backpacks loaded with five to twelve pounds of explosives. Including the terrorists themselves, 56 people were killed, and 450 persons wounded. Home-grown terrorists were targeting the core of the capital city.

The fear of new terrorist attacks legitimated territorial surveillance as a primary strategy. The use of new technologies of surveillance and identification, and a policy meant to secure public spaces in London, were developed via new schemes by Metropolitan Police Service. Many of the CCTVs are located across London as well. In the case of '7/7', the cameras identified terrorists who lived in Leeds and led 'quiet' lives there (making an understanding of their motivations at that time difficult). The cameras were used again after the 2011 disorders, and with the same purpose

3.3.3 The 'suspect community' issue

The notion of Muslim suspects in the United States has already been described in Chapter 2. A rigorous demonstration by S. Greer (2010) seeks to ban banning the expression 'suspect community' as applied to Muslims in the United Kingdom, illustrating clear differences, from a legal standpoint, between the United Kingdom and the United States.

Greer takes issue with an article by Pantazis and Pemberton defining a suspect community as 'a sub-group of the population that is singled out for state attention as being "problematic". Specifically, in terms of policing, individuals may be targeted, not necessarily as a result of suspected wrong doing, but simply because of their presumed membership to (sic) that sub-group. Race, ethnicity, religion, class, gender, language, accent, dress, political ideology or any combination of these factors may serve to delineate the sub-group'. (2009, 649). For these authors, the Terrorism Act 2000 has 'largely facilitated the designation of Muslims as the principal suspect community'[20] (Ibid., 652), allowing the police to stop and search at random (sections 44 and 45). The number of those stopped in 2001–02 rose from 10,200 to 256, 026 in 2008–09, after the attacks. The Metropolitan carried out 72 per cent of the stops (Home Office Statistical Bulletin, 2009: 43–44). Greer established a distinction between 'feeling under suspicion', 'being under official suspicion' and 'being under unjustified suspicion'. If young middle-class British Pakistanis from Leeds, carrying backpacks in a railway station, are suspected by the police of being trouble-makers, such 'official' suspicion is justified. Greer contests, however, the reference to Muslims, who themselves are divided by race, ethnicity, national origin and demographic factors. Out of 2 million, 70 per cent live in London, Birmingham, Manchester and Bradford-Leeds (Peach 2006, 631; 650). Salafism and Islamism are ideologies, not communities. When the British police stop Blacks and Asians, their religion is not recorded and no one knows (as in France) how many among them are Muslims. If there is suspicion in some areas, suspected plots are closely monitored by the Office of Security and Counterterrorism, more because they contain critical infrastructures or places of national significance than because they are Muslim neighbourhoods. In Greater London, at risk of terrorism, police powers are legally restrained. Community impact assessment is a vital part of the police authorization process, officers required to keep careful records. With such tight monitoring, and despite racial unbalance in the stops and searches, there is no evidence that racial profiling is an effective counterterrorist strategy (Greer, Ibid., 1182).

The European Convention on Human Rights (ECHR) does not support the suspect community thesis either, yet it admits that Blacks and Asians are four times more likely than their White counterparts to be stopped and searched. In the case *Gillan v. Commissioner of Police for the Metropolis and Secretary of State for the Home*, the House of Lords unanimously held that provided stops and searches are not based on racial profiling alone and that Section 44 complies with the ECHR. To put an end to this debate, Home Secretary, T. May announced that Section 44 would no longer be used by the police against individuals (but not cars). Likewise, the Prevent Program was terminated in July 2010. It was indeed criticized for its mixture of *trust* and *suspicion*, in particular when over 150 automatic number plate recognition cameras were about to be installed in two predominantly Muslim neighbourhoods of Birmingham as part of counterterrorism strategies. That the neighbourhoods were Muslim had less to do with race and ethnicity than with a specific plot aiming at, killing a British soldier in the area, Greer explains. The Prevent Program was investigated by the House of Commons Select Committee on Communities and Local Government.

The report published in March 2010 questions methods of 'spying', 'surveillance' and 'intelligence-gathering', which hide a variety of questionable interpretations.

Finally, Greer examines civil society suspicion. Pantazis and Pemberton claim that high profile police raids, arrests and detention of Muslim terrorist suspects generate fear, allowing non-Muslims 'permission to hate' them (2009, 661). But for Greer, while Muslim communities as a whole are not systematically represented as suspect: extremist sections within them are. The Racial and Religious Hatred Act of 2006 seeks to protect Muslims from hate crimes. Most Muslims and their leaders support official policies fighting terrorism. But mainstream attitudes frequently mix a distrust of economically disadvantaged groups and also racial and ethnic bias. In 2007, 84 per cent of Muslims affirmed being treated fairly by British society (Mirza et al., 2007).

The debate regarding Muslims as suspect minorities applies in other cities as well, as is clearly seen in New York and Paris. It highlights the contradictions of current public policies and the 'rotten' compromises that they have to find: on the one hand, society has to be protected against Islamist terrorism and the harm that it may causes and, on the other, protection must be offered 'against the potentially arbitrary and unjust effects of anti-terrorist laws' (Ibid., 1185) and their impact on human rights. That the British police are subject to close scrutiny and can pay the price for their excesses has been illustrated by the Menendez case, in which a Brazilian electrician was wrongly killed on a subway train by the Metropolitan police service, after the London attacks. Such a mistake ultimately cost the London Metropolitan Police Commissioner, Ian Blair, his job.

3.3.4   Securing space

Finally, the London landscape, as that of New York and Paris, has been changed by security architecture. '... Walls and defences are social order, written into material form, a key feature for the understanding of human territoriality, Coaffee and others remark (op. cit,, 21). Gates delineates territories', inside and out; they are pinch-points and filters, a spatial location for social sorting. Exclusion zones are provided to protect at-risk sites, while managerial measures regulate public spaces. Discipline is imposed by required passwords and electronic cards to enter certain areas and socially confined worlds. Reinforced steel barriers surround London's Houses of Parliament. The American embassy at Grosvenor Square in Mayfair first required that protective bollards be replaced by bomb-blast barriers, but a new embassy, 'a crystalline cube' surrounded by a moat a hundred feet wide and a park, is currently being built at a cost of $1 billion in a gentrified area. The famous remark made by Information Commissioner, R. Thomas, in 2004, that 'we are sleep-walking into a surveillance society', comes to mind (Murakami, Wood et al., 2006). Technological options prevail in such strategies and threaten the very essence of what a city is, that is 'making society'.

Do the responses of the three city cases brought up here – New York, London, Paris, all located in the Western hemisphere – differ from those of South metropolises, which are also confronted by terrorism? The case of Mumbai flags up convergences with London and Paris: the state remains very much in charge and holds ultimate control, especially when matters of defence are at stake. The city plays a secondary role, healing its wounds.

3.4   Mumbai

3.4.1   Mumbai confronted with crime

The pervasive atmosphere of lawlessness in some no-go urban areas in the global South, where 40–65 per cent of big-city populations live in substandard conditions, offers a context which obviously does not determine terrorism but 'does create desperate conditions and mounting chaos – both of which may be precursors for recruiting' (Savitch 2008, 42). Megalopolises, with a minority part of the population living in gated or highly secure communities while massively excluded majorities experience very hard conditions of living, generate confrontational identities, caste tensions and ethnic hatred, especially among youths exasperated by their lack of a future. It may lead some of them to act out, to use violence as a tool and for a handful of them, to accept martyrdom for a cause that they have embraced.

Mumbai has a low rate of crime. This may result, as in Jacobs's vision, from the proximity of rich and poor residents in this very dense city. 'This proximity provides security to pedestrians because the roads are never empty; urban violence and crime à la São Paulo are absent. There is symbiosis: the homeless provide maids, drivers and the like to their more fortunate neighbors', D'Monte remarks (2011, 100). Yet the city has experienced recurring episodes of inter-communal violence, and communal tensions arising after provocation characterize neighbourhood life. After the destruction of a mosque in the early 1990s in northern India, the city experienced traumatic riots. These were attributed to the presence of Bangladeshi, labelled Muslims by residents who were afraid of having their jobs stolen by outsiders; but D'Monte (Ibid., 96), then Mumbai editor of *The Times of India*, dispelled such rumours. Mumbai's ethnic and religious diversity, added to that of the 19 million of people in the region, makes it a cosmopolitan world city, exuding vibrancy and energy. But how to manage everyday life tensions, also arising from the control of the state authorities and of powerful interest groups?

Governance is difficult in Mumbai, due to a lack of strong executive authority and to pervasive corruption. The mayor, elected by city councillors, has less leverage than the municipal commissioner and the state's chief minister who, via the Mumbai Metropolitan Region Development Authority (MMRDA), defends other interests. The city, contributing 37 per cent of all taxes paid in India, only gets a small fraction of it back (Mehta, 2011, 104). The national and state governments are not eager to grant more leverage to Mumbai, at a time of global challenges, and 'even the largest city with all its resources cannot superimpose as a substitute for the state. Power sharing between the centre and the state has been a difficult process in India' (Sivaramakrishnan, 2011, 93).

Greater Mumbai, the city peninsula proper, is not to be confused with the Mumbai Metropolitan region, closer to 19 million, with no elected government. The fragmentation of institutions is a problem for urban governance and encourages a lack of accountability (Zehra, 2011, 150). Public interest is not defended per se, but submitted to a pluralistic game among very diverse and competitive actors. 'Colliding interests, informal mechanisms, brokers and mediators playing their parts in the neighbourhoods, pressures of local elected officials, bargaining and a local capacity for mobilizing space users change the rules of the games and procedures once clearly set' (Ibid., 161). Stakes relative to the identity of Mumbai (a cosmopolitan city or the capital of Maharashtra?) and to attitudes relative to migrants are prominent on the city's political agenda.

The number of migrants pouring into the city may give the impression of a fast-growing metropolis, but the reality is different. Migrants, attracted to the city for jobs, are less numerous than in the past. 'Now there is a saturation even of rag and scrap pickers, which are right at the bottom of the employment ladder', D'Monte remarks, and this is the situation in Mumbai (as well as in Johannesburg and São Paulo, next to be studied). The reason why the city does not explode due to the sheer pressure of urban growth comes from the humanity and tolerance of its ordinary people (Ibid., 2001, 96; 98).

The high density of Indian cities is actually deceptive, symbolized 'through an extraordinary high occupancy per room. It may happen that seven out of every ten Mumbaikars live in a single room which includes the 54 per cent who live in slums' (D'Monte 2011, 96). This notion of the slum is also to be deconstructed. What appears as slums to the middle classes is what slum residents call *basti*, which means community. There, hundreds of little shops service every human need. This space provides a shelter against floods, riots and terror attacks, and gives a sense of community (Mehta, 2011, 105).

3.4.2 The globalization of criminal activities

A vignette from Mumbai[21] by Weinstein (2008) displays how much the globalization of criminal activities transforms cities and what forms of responses they and their residents deploy in their everyday life to counter negative changes.

In the 1990s, the reputation of Mumbai was that of a violent, gang-ridden city. 'Hundreds of people were dying every year in wars between rival gangs and in extrajudicial killing by the police. The city was convinced of its own menace' and fear prevailed (Ibid., 107).

Mumbai's organized criminal groups have long had connections outside India. With new forms of capital, they established new sources of power in the 1990s. 'Extended now from the Persian gulf to Malaysia and with links identified in London, Johannesburg and New York, the strength of the city's large organized crime organizations result not only from their ties to political parties and embeddedness in antagonistic religious communities but also in their increasingly global reach' (Ibid., 29).

Their move into land development was a result of the local state's decision to make certain valued land plots available through a series of conversions, slum clearance schemes and deregulation of public lands. With speculation, land prices rose quickly in the mid-1990s. Resorting to violence, threats and bribes, criminal organizations then purchased numerous properties directly or indirectly. Meanwhile, substandard housing and health conditions and deteriorating urban safety characterized life for 6.5 million (about half of the city's population) in the slums of Greater Mumbai. Attempts, like those of Bombay First, a 1993 initiative, were made to turn Mumbai into a world-class city after 2013. Coalitions of the *growth machine* type (Logan and Molotch, 2007) aimed at improving the quality of life for middle classes and stimulating the economy while clearing the slums (GOM, 2004). The World Bank experts inspired by this 'Vision Mumbai' recommended that the 'city finances the city' and maximizes its autonomy. It implied deregulating the real estate market and raising development charges. Such a vision for business looks more like a road map than projects about to be enforced (Zehra, 2011, 200). Charles Correa, the architect, is even more negative: 'There's very little vision. They're more like hallucinations'.

3.4.3 Mumbai confronted with terrorism

Globalization and the 2008 terrorist attacks are connected. A series of ten coordinated assaults took place between November 26–29, 2008. They caused 173 deaths, including 26 foreigners, and left 312 people wounded. The terrorists were ten fundamentalist Muslims, trained in Pakistan. Hit by the Laskar-e-Taiba terrorists based in Lahore, Pakistan, Mumbai is closer to New York City and Paris, also targeted by outsiders, than to London (home-grown terrorism). It experienced thirteen terrorist attacks in 1993, two in 2003 (a bomb blast outside a tourist spot); seven in 2006 (coordinated bomb attacks on commuter trains, killing more than 200 people) and three on July 13, 2011 (at least 20 people killed and 141 injured) (Faleiro, 2011; Mehra, 2011).

Regarding the most lethal 2008 violence, 'The available evidence thus far suggests that the masterminds of the attack exploited the fact of a long-standing, mostly low-intensity conventional conflict to achieve their own, perhaps separate concerns' (Sassen, 2010). The attacks have been attributed to inter-communal antagonisms, as well as to Muslim and Hindu hatreds (the term *atankwadi* (terrorist) is associated with Muslims in the Indian imaginary) or to a geopolitical rivalry between Pakistan and India. But, as pointed out by Sassen (2010), the context is also linked to the segmented condition of the modern statehood's authority. The terrorists exploited a weak state and made use of highly visible and symbolic urban sites to destabilize the elites and the world alike. Mumbai is a militarized, well-guarded city, yet its openness and complex interconnectedness in an array of key places make the city (or any large city) vulnerable to such attacks.

The attacks have been perceived and judged differently: on a daily basis, the average Mumbaikar is probably more concerned with the ten commuters or so who are killed each day as a consequence of falling from trains, or with crime and burglaries. The local and national elites as well as the Hindu and Muslim leaders and traders are worried about the implications. The impact of an attack on Mumbai is considered 'to give a psychological blow on India's rising stock in business, commerce and industry globally, as an attack on Delhi is considered giving a blow on its political nose' (Mehra, 2011).

Terrorists repeatedly target Mumbai – four attacks in seven years (see Table 3.2). Yet nothing much is done, except rhetorically. After the 2008 attacks, all the political parties and leaders, as well as the leadership of India's security establishment, were criticized for not doing anything substantial to protect the nation and its citizens from terrorist attacks. Soon after, the government faced strong criticism for its failure

Table 3.2 Terrorist attacks in Mumbai since 1993

Date	Place	Killed	Injured
July 13, 2011	Serial blasts in Mumbai	18	131
November 26, 2008	Multiple terrorist attacks across the city	166	300
July 11, 2006	7 blasts at 7 locations in local trains across the city	181	890
August 25, 2003	Gateway of India and Zaveri Bazaar	50	150
July 29, 2003	Ghatkopar	3	34
April 14, 2003	Bandra	1	0
March 13, 2003	Mulund Railway Station	11	80
January 27, 2003	Vile Parle	1	25
December 6, 2002	Mumbai Central railway station	0	25
December 2, 2002	Ghatkopar	3	31
February 27, 1998	Virar	9	0
January 24, 1998	Malad	0	1
August 28, 1997	Near Jama Masjid	0	3
March 12, 1993	13 blasts across the city	257	713

Source: http://www.satp.org/satporgtp/countries/india/database/mumbai_blast.htm (Accessed on July 15, 2011).

to pre-empt a terror attack in which ten terrorists could sneak in the country, unnoticed. The Union Home Minister and the Maharashtra Chief Minister were sanctioned and lost their jobs. The Government of India moved with alacrity to set up a National Investigation Agency in 2009, as a credible counterterrorism apparatus. But coordinating with the plethora of organizations proved difficult. Setting up a National Counterterrorism Centre (NCTC), Mehra (2011) reports, was also discussed, as well as a 'National Network Security Architecture' to address a wide range of shortcomings that plague the internal security structure of the country. Two years (over 700 days!) have gone by since, he states, and the NCTC has yet to come into existence. A Task Force 5 (TF5) report on 'Criminal Justice, National Security and Centre-State Cooperation' has been completely ignored. It asserted that the war on terror cannot be won just by enacting more and more specialised anti-terror laws. The NCTC has to seek the support of the police, which it noted, was 'overworked, overstretched, ill-recruited, ill-trained, ill-equipped, ill-paid and ill-motivated'. The boosting of a National Counterterrorism Agency, which should have countrywide jurisdiction to collect intelligence in cooperation with the state police and take pre-emptive measures, was strongly advocated. But, currently, bipartisan political quarrels seem to occupy national politicians more than efficiency at the local level.

Suketu (Mehta, 2004)[22] explains that civic actions that alleviated the effects of terrorist attacks prevented the elites from extreme decisions for retaliation. The testimony of Sonia Faleiro, a writer on Mumbai, gives substance to that argument: 'In the immediate aftermath of the attack (of 2011), as with every previous attack, people took to the street – not simply to commiserate with the victims' families, or to denounce the terrorists, or to demand that their leaders explain why the violence had not been prevented – but to go on living. Life did not stop... Indians have accepted that the city is in the frontline of terrorist attacks on their country. And, like Mumbai, the rest of India is getting on with life' (2011). Faleiro explains that terrorists repeatedly target Mumbai (four attacks in seven years) (see Table 3.2) because this is the city where people move to, in order to experience freedom, and fulfil their dreams more than in any other large Indian city. The term *jaan* means vitality, vibrancy, essence and love. It is associated with the 'maximum city' and its capacity to contain and resist violence (Kandar 2009). But healing cannot take place, since mourning and emotions are not publicly expressed.

New York, Paris, London and Mumbai have all been hit by terrorism. Such risks persist, forcing cities to protect themselves. In the most avant-garde way, New York has established material and symbolic rings of steel around sensitive assets and developed a powerful counterterrorism force and sophisticated intelligence networks that spread outside the country. Paris depends on vertical chains of command for their protection. The London Metropolitan Police may be rid of their omnipotent role, if the National Crime Agency, modelled on the FBI, takes care of serious threats and organized crime, as it is envisioned. At the time of this writing (2011), such reform has not yet been passed. It would allow local police and crime commissions more leverage to refocus on city safety.

In the South, anti-terrorist efforts are less advanced, as shown by Mumbai and by the state of Maharashtra. Yet 'wherever we live, we all have a stake in helping the people of mega-cities like Mumbai. The desperation of slum-dwellers[23] ... directly affects the economic fortunes of people in New York or Los Angeles. It's as important for London to understand Mumbai as it is for Mumbai to understand London, if for no other reason than the next generation of Londoners is being born in Mumbai' (Faleiro, 2011, 107).

The next chapter focuses exclusively on mega-cities of the South, which are confronted by other types of challenges. Chapter 6 shows that global cities' cultures play a tremendous preventative role, cementing segmented populations with common goals for survival.

4
Criminals and Gangs in Global Cities of the South

The two metropolises of the South studied here (Johannesburg and São Paulo), just as Mumbai presented before, share the impact of a colonial past which left an important imprint on their cityscapes and early economic patterns (Segbers, 2007, 340). Johannesburg, initially founded as a mining town, soon evolved into the economic centre of South Africa; with the rapid growth of the coffee plantations at the periphery, São Paulo rapidly became the economic heart of Brazil. Such world regions, due to rapid industrialization, became the industrial engines of their nations. As pointed out by Sassen (2001), with global processes fast developing, the dispersal of production sites has created a need for centralized command, planning and decision-making functions. The sites of these nodes and hubs are located in world cities which provide sophisticated services to multinational and world financial institutions. They are consequently the key sites for advanced information and communication technologies, media and cultural services, and politics. The mega-cities of the South studied here represent 'the frontier of globalization', due to their linkages with core economies and financial institutions (Segbers, 2007). However, important inequalities and wealth assets make them targets for discontented or challenging contenders.

This chapter concentrates less on terrorist attacks, which also occur more in the global cities of the South, than on fears and feelings of insecurity generated by organized violent criminals. After mapping the demographic and economic context, I introduce problems and their perceptions, along with significant crime trends. I analyze the presence or the absence of the police, as well as the role of private security agencies and their influence on people's everyday lives. I conclude with public policy formulation and implementation.

A word of caution is necessary here, as aptly formulated by Parnell (2007, 140): 'Our understanding of who holds power in South African cities is crude, dated, and generally ill-informed, even in a relatively well-researched city like Johannesburg'. The same remark applies for São Paulo. Each case has to be understood within its own specificities, and differences cannot be easily levelled, as will be seen in this chapter.

4.1   Johannesburg

4.1.1   Demography and economy

According to some discourses, 'Johannesburg is a prism through which to view the world (but in order to do so, much work is needed!)' (Mabin, 2007, 59). It is an African city. Africa is a continent expected to mark a huge imprint on the twenty-first century. To the question of whether or not Johannesburg belongs to the global cities, a mixed answer might be the most appropriate. There is no doubt that the influence of global organizations on a restricted number of influential players in the city, along with the effects of global and political change, has an impact at the top. It may also be the case that the authorities' public communications on investments in the new spheres of finance and in key sectors hides away the mounting poverty and exclusion characterizing vast sections of townships and inner cities (Benit and Gervais-Lambony, 2004). A city of 9 million residents stretched over the Gauteng province, Johannesburg (3.2 million) is the key point of global economic transactions for South Africa and the surrounding region and it facilitates the exchange of considerable wealth (Segbers, 2007, 28). Multinationals use the city as a springboard for their African operations. Traders from North Africa sell and buy goods that they resell in West African markets. Cross-border shoppers circulate in cycles of various durations from one capital city to the other. Others flee persecution or impoverishment and seek asylum in the open-border city of Johannesburg which attracts people from all over the planet. For A. Mabin, it could be argued that the entire continuous polycentric urban region to which Johannesburg is central is indeed in the process of becoming a 'mega-urban region' equivalent to some of the larger world cities (2007, 43). It concentrates a large middle-class and an unusually large elite, both of which total over 250,000 residents. There are lots of similarities with São Paulo regarding the development of new business areas close to the business centre or their connection to distant metropolises.

There are approximately 290,000 formal sector business enterprises that employ about 900,000 people. Located in the city are 74 per cent of corporate head offices and 70 per cent of bank headquarters (Ibid.). Growth in the economy of culture, tourism and technology and the thriving informal sector makes it 'a creative city'.

Politically, while the city enjoys forms of autonomy, it still depends greatly on the regional and national strata of power, as is the case with other large South cities studied here. As in Mumbai, the city tries to pursue its own strategic agenda in order to establish itself as a world-class city. Yet its powers regarding health, education, safety and policing functions, of interest here, remain limited (Ibid., 56).

The level of inequality is high, but this does not automatically correlate to a high number of homicides. The general context of African cities is violent, Mabin observes. High criminality may be explained by a lack of hope.[1]

Persisting poverty and social exclusion for an important part of the population comes from a type of economy that does not lift all the boats. 'About one-third of the households in Johannesburg are so poor that they cannot afford to pay for water and electricity, live in decent housing or (if owning a home) pay for rates' (Beauregard and Tomlinson, 2007, 244). In Alexandra, a nearby neighbourhood, 60 per cent of the residents are unemployed; young people make up the largest jobless category; 48 per cent of Soweto children do not go to school. Children whose mothers have AIDS do not go to school. All these factors result from poverty, with its cohort of broken families, domestic violence, drug trafficking, predatory gangs, racism and machismo.

Johannesburg is spatially a dual city divided between wealthy suburbs and poor townships or squatter settlements where the uprooted poor do not have access to proper housing. Thus, the sandglass economy symbolizing that of numerous global cities applies here.

4.1.2   Problems and how they are perceived

Images and representations of fear associated with the most 'crime-prone South African city' come to mind when the name Johannesburg is evoked, even if this reputation is not always and everywhere sustained.

In Johannesburg, the anti-urban discourse linking the city with risk, danger, insecurity – whatever meaning is given to these words – is the daily talk of most residents, and the country's history explains why this is so. The legacy of a brutal apartheid regime which deployed its police against vulnerable Black populations, imposed spatial and social segregation and restricted access to quality-of-life standards by forbidding shared public spaces and transportation. Urban density at the core is low (2,203 people per km^2) compared with Mumbai (45,021 and Dharavi 80,000) and São Paulo (10,376) (Burdett and Sudjik, 2007, 293). The apartheid regime intentionally left space vacant downtown, in order to avoid mixing populations. With the democratization of public life since 1994, the situation of millions of people has improved. However, fear and the status quo maintained by implicit social and racial hierarchies remain and bring the excuse for – or the wish of – 'not living together', not sharing the same public spaces and not encouraging a fluid mobility via public transportation in the city (Johannesburg has no subway). While intellectually the end of the apartheid regime was accepted, practices resist the democratic transition, as is the case in Brazil. As observed by Murray (2011: 332), 'apartheid is not dead; it constantly reemerges, to intrude upon the present and shape the future'. A set of social anxieties revolving around race and criminality legitimize social-control mechanisms. 'An ideology based on fear and avoidance is then founded in a complex relationship between domination and submission' (Boisteau, 2003, 9). White, Black and mixed affluent categories are afraid to lose their power, their wealth, the property on which their identity is based. Their commitment to 'one city' remains elusive. Economic uncertainty, the world financial crisis, the fragile service economy, corruption, and homicide rates are invoked for the defence of a lifestyle benefiting the affluent categories.

Fear of crime comes from the fear of victimization. But the difference between the two notions hides class and race differences. There is hardly any public debate when violence hits the poor. The discourse is coded. Moreover, the post-apartheid regime has not led dominant categories to express their fears, to select them and to think of solutions to alleviate them besides the locking-up solution. According to a victimization survey from the city's Economic Development Unit (EDU) in 2003, 69 per cent of those surveyed said that they were very scared when they walked outside their home at night. They avoided at-risk neighbourhoods such as Hillbrow, Braamfontein, Alexandra, Berea and Yeoville. Three out of four asserted that they had changed their behaviour after they became aware of risks – attitudes also found in other cities of the global South. City Hall has, however, strengthened the police patrols in areas reinvested with private funding. But the media's continuous reporting on crime and the public authorities' insufficient communications may explain why fear of crime persists.

As in the United States, the right to self-protection justifies high walls, electronic checkpoints and all the symbolic enclosures protecting exclusiveness and privilege. 'This logic of defensiveness reinforces apartheid geographies and defers the possibility of anything remotely resembling a coherent city emerging' (Bremner, 2007, 211). The notion of property is also different from that found in Europe and close to that of the United States. Johannesburg is a city in which the malls and gated communities look like those of Southern California. Such gated settlements are virtually recreations of medieval walled cities and can be seen as predictions for what American suburbs may one day be like (Sudjik, 2007, 201). Self-defence and shooting without warning, implying killing a trespasser on one's property, are accepted by popular juries: property is seen as the extension of the owner's body.[2] Johannesburg brings both hopes for the future (as testified by the successful 2010 World Cup Football tournament, in which the city was one of the centrepieces) and despair.

4.1.3   Significant crime trends

Who could be blamed for fearing to venture into an unknown public space or township or even to walk outside one's home after sunset in Johannesburg? Even if homicides disproportionately hit the poor in the townships, and if police data are notoriously dubious since they exclude large sections of the metropolis (Palmary et al., 2003, 105), the 18,148 homicides committed from April 2008 to March 2009, that is fifty homicides a day, is associated with South Africa (Hervieu, 2009). Such data must be considered from a long perspective. The curve of homicides is indeed decreasing: 20,000 murders were registered in 2004–05 compared with 26,000 during 1994–95, in the time of apartheid (Leggett 2005, 583). In 2000, the homicide rate in South Africa was 51.4 per 100,000, ranking the country second after Colombia for the highest homicide rate in the world (Mabin, Harrison, 2006). While numerous victims do not report crimes to the police, murders rarely go unnoticed. In Johannesburg, a very conservative figure indicates 15.7 per 100,000 in 2007 (versus 3 per 100,000 in Mumbai) (Burdett and Sudjik, 2011, 301).

Property crimes do not just target affluent neighbourhoods. Firms' burglaries make up 41.5 per cent of such crimes versus 27 per cent for homes (Hervieu, 2009). That anything can happen, everywhere, at any moment is an idea haunting middle classes. Table 4.1 shows the levels of reported crime in Johannesburg compared with South Africa's average.

Fear of crime leads the affluent classes to transform their neighbourhoods into bunkers with 'impregnable zones of razor-wire, snapping guard dogs, manned sentry boxes and electronic security systems'

Table 4.1 Levels of reported crime in Johannesburg versus the RSA average – 2001

Incidence in Johannesburg	Incidence per 100,000 in South Africa	Selected crime types per 100,000
Residential house-breaking	1986.8	688.1
Theft of motor vehicles	1989.0	228.7
Murder	124.8	49.3
Robbery with aggravating circumstances	1855.6	251.3
Rape	213.4	120.1
Assault with intent to do grievous bodily harm	1005.6	624

Source: South African Police Services, 2003.

(Lippman and Harris 1991, 727), although the affluent are largely spared from crime, since a lot of them avoid walking outside their homes and limit their car trips to the workplace, the club, church and the mall. In the polls, however, residents of gated communities (totalling 600 and most of them illegal) say that they prefer to restrict visits to their friends, stay without their former community and remain alive (Beau et al., 2002, 184; 192).

Crime, however, disproportionately hits poor areas. In the inner cities occupied by Black households, in 2001, the homicide rate was 603 per 100,000, twelve times the national rate and five times that of Johannesburg (Mabin and Harrison, 2006). Who would blame poor households then for also locking themselves up and moving around with Metro Mall, an inner-city transportation service, providing private taxis and mini-buses and carrying around 100,000 commuters per day (Bremner, 2007, 207)? Black South Africans are twenty times more at risk of being killed than Whites (Dawson, 2006, 131).

Women experience high rates of rape, either while taking trains, walking to their workplaces or sleeping in township shelters which are overcrowded. In 2008, 27,715 rapes were reported to the police, a number underestimated according to researchers, putting the number of daily rapes at 1,500 (Hervieu, 2009). Currently, as in numerous African cities, with copious migration flows (from neighbouring countries that are at war) to economically stable South Africa, with illegal land and housing appropriation processes going on, taxi wars and conflicts between street sellers and squatters, public spaces are danger zones, especially after sunset. With the end of apartheid, 'urban violence has been de-territorialized and public space has become the space of insecurity', Boisteau observes (2003, 32). Institutions – the city council, the mayor – are not much involved in the problem of safety. As elsewhere, they are reluctant to enforce poor citizens' rights. The strongest, the most cunning, the most determined thus take the law into their own hands and impose their domination on more vulnerable residents.

Several reasons explain the prevailing collective fear of crime in Johannesburg. Physically, large barren spaces and abandoned lots at the core of the city operate as boundaries between socio-racial settlements. It would be difficult to change them. Residents from various enclosed areas lack the ability to develop reciprocity and a common civic commitment because strong continuities link the apartheid regime and the one that followed with regard to the control of access to public spaces by poor minorities (Brenner, 2007).

As pointed out by sociologist G. Simpson (2001) it has also been difficult for the young shock troops fighting apartheid with idealism to insert themselves into the new democratic regime of transition, which has ignored them. Many are used to carrying arms, drinking alcohol and using drugs. Like veterans back from war, after the transition, a significant number of them became street criminals for survival's sake.

McKendrick and Hoffman (1990), for their part, suggest that frequently in societies in transition, men cannot fulfil stereotypical roles (such as being economic providers). Their frustration is turned on women, whom they regard as their object. 'Men drink excessively and may even use excessive violence to demonstrate their power and position of control. Such men ultimately join street gangs in which violence forms part and parcel of everyday life with, for instance, rape serving as an initiation ritual' confirms a report from the South African police (Crime Information Analysis Centre, 2001, 14). That homeless women, cleaners, street vendors and prostitutes are more often raped than are other women in public spaces has been well documented. South Africa has one of the worst records in the world for that crime (Dawson, 2006, 134). For poor women, the danger comes both from outside and inside. An ethnographic study revealed that 'suburbs where women seek work during the day were labelled as unsafe, because they were deserted during the day ... The women thought that ... they would not be helped by anyone, because the houses are walled off and there are very few people on the streets' (Dladla, 2002). The criminal justice system seems more concerned with punishing property crime than domestic or gang violence. As long as there is a middle-class toleration for such practices, it remains difficult to defend poor women's rights.

4.1.4   Role of police: presence/absence

'The Metro Police Dept does not have the power to investigate crime, and has little control over what the South African Police Services (SAPS) do to combat crime,' a report stated (City of Johannesburg Metropolitan Municipality, 2006, 225). In recent years, however, a new Johannesburg Metropolitan Police Department (JMPD) has moved beyond its mere function of traffic control and taken the responsibility of crime prevention. By mid-2003, it was composed of 2,500 men and 1,630 uniformed officers, distributed among special sectors within a number of precincts in eleven regions. Since 2005, a safety team is responsible for the program and for the coordination of the concerned agencies. For their part, 10,000 policemen from the SAPS investigate crimes in the city and its suburbs.

Four Geographic Focus Areas (GFAs) have been defined to alleviate the sense of insecurity. These are located in the inner city, in Soweto, Alexandra and the northern suburbs.

These areas benefit from highly visible forces patrolling key access routes, and from CCTVs. A series of measures intend to secure space: environmental-design improvements in mixed-income residential accommodations with retail businesses and entertainment facilities; community policing with a zero tolerance attitude toward all 'crime and grime', fighting illegal traders, squatters, illegal dumping, high-jacking, clandestine liquor outlets, crack houses and other places housing criminal activities. An active strategy against the illegal possession of firearms (operation Sethunya) is reinforced by the creation of gun-free zones.

Organized crime is specifically targeted as are crimes affecting the well-being of business activity (kidnappings, carjackings, armed robbery, thefts, crimes affecting tourists in pubs, *shebeens* and clubs, and so on). It should be mentioned that a new Municipal Court hands down fines to illegal traders, businesses and owners of defective buildings, and to those guilty of quality-of-life crimes (disturbing the peace, pollution, vandalism) but its efficiency is a matter of debate.

In general, there is awareness that better community–police relations, lower levels of police corruption and improved distribution of police resources across the centre and the periphery are profoundly needed.

4.1.5   Private security in Johannesburg

More than 20 per cent of South Africans are said to own weapons in order to protect themselves. Vigilante groups have a long tradition in South Africa, and they regard violence and corporal punishment as legitimate. The post-apartheid state institutions have not eradicated them. 'This lack of action against vigilante activity undermines public willingness to adhere to the rule of law and sends the message that taking law in your own hands can be tolerated' (Sekhonyane and Louw, 2002). In the past, the Muslim organization, People Against Guns and Violence (PAGAD), fought gangs violently and did not represent any alternative method of justice. It mutated into a revolutionary fringe of bomb-throwing Islamists who murdered prosecution witnesses and state officials alike (Gervais-Lambony, 1995, ix; Leggett, 2005 581).

Because trust in police and justice is low, the privatization of security by third parties is thriving. Yet the distinction public/private is not always clear, and many policemen also spend their off-duty time as private security guards. 'The result seems to be something in the nature of a public/private security continuum rather than two clear and distinct categories of "private security" and "public security"' (Shearing and Stenning, 1987). South Africans appear to trust the protection provided by private security organizations more than the police.[3] More survey respondents (79.3 per cent) also feel that it is a good development that security services expand their policing functions (Naudé et al., 2001). The pervasive presence of private security agencies in the public space takes place without significant public debate.

The conclusions are easy to draw. As a very successful sector,[4] the private security industry can impose its decrees and refuse to protect homes insufficiently monitored, for instance. Alarms and panic buttons are not linked to police stations (thus losing their public monopoly) but to private companies with names like 'Terminators' or 'Stallion'. There is a wide gap between a social minority of residents able to pay for their security and to secede from the rest of the city, and poor majorities who can only resort to self-policing and vigilantism for their protection because they do not trust a pervasively corrupt police force. Social separatism based on insecurity is supported by the powerful market of private security.

In 1996, as a response to Nelson Mandela's requiring private partners to be involved in crime prevention, the organization Business Against Crime (BAC) formed a partnership to enforce prevention in high-crime areas and to assist under-resourced police and courts. The BAC's decision to reclaim parts of the central business district in recent years has had visible effects in terms of improved lighting, high technology, CCTVs, cleanliness, private patrol units, renovation of buildings, green spaces and so on. However, the occupation of public spaces by masses of mixed populations, as can be seen in Latin American cities or even the nonchalant *flânerie* of affluent Whites in the public streets downtown are not frequent.[5] Social inclusion, density and diversity in public space may take several generations before the apartheid's legacy vanishes from attitudes and behaviour.

Yet efforts are made at both ends of the social spectrum. For example, the city council fights against the pervasive privatization of space. Public road access restriction has been made more difficult, Mabin and Harrison observe (2006, 28). Given the diversity of positions within the ruling African National Congress party (ANC) in Johannesburg and also the pressures from other groups, it would be very difficult for the local council to ban restriction. The boundary between public and private spheres and the right to closure need continuously to be renegotiated. By 2003, despite the council's opposition to gating, 556 barriers were still illegally in place before the council began removing them and forms of compromise could be reached.

4.1.6   Policy formulation and implementation

Looking at central Johannesburg, Kihato remarks that, for a majority of those living in the city, efforts from bulldozing slum areas and the removal of street hawkers to more sustained state interventions to make everyday urban life sustainable have seemed like 'rearranging the deckchairs of the *Titanic* while it is sinking' (2007, 215).

Can the city and the state be vehicles for maintaining public tranquillity and safety? One of the problems to be dealt with concerns the overlapping of institutional decision making. The municipality does not have autonomous power over many of the functions that promote improved community safety. The plan, 'Johannesburg 2030', makes crime prevention one of the five-star priorities that the city needs to address. It is acknowledged that crime prevention would improve the local business climate and tourism. But the state, tied to class interests, seems unwilling to change a narrowly defined private vision of the city.

Z. Bauman remarked that 'if too much state is a catastrophe, so is too little'. It may be then that with a minimal state, the language of rights needs to be strong. In an illuminating study, Lazarus (2006) establishes a distinction between 'the right to security' as a political aspiration and security as 'the right to life'.

That everyone has the right to life, liberty and security of person, is stipulated in Article 3 of the United Nations *Universal Declaration on Human Rights*, and in Article 143 of the UN General Assembly 2005 'World Summit Outcome': 'We stress the right of people to live in freedom and dignity, free from poverty and despair.'

How much is this 'right to life' a legal right? A distinction should be established between the right to security and the right to life. In Western countries, security has been socialized, implying that one's security depends on others. But in the case of South Africa, is the right to security included within human rights or is it distinctive or derived? Is it a negative right, prohibiting the state from infringement, or a positive right, enjoining the state to protect individual security (verging then toward the 'right to life')? Lazarus asks, is it a duty of the state alone or does it bind other parties (2006, 4)?

In South Africa, the 1996 constitution delineates a notion of security as distinct from liberty in a number of ways (Ibid., 11). The right to security of a person is specified as the right to be free from all forms of violence from either public or private sources (section 12(1) c), which is both a positive and a negative right. Is this right enforced? A few legal cases offer an interesting perspective on the interpretation of this right, implying the right to stay alive: the state is held accountable by the courts to protect its citizens from violence.[6] A few cases[7] indicate the progressive definition of state accountability in protecting citizens from violence, but also in creating the conditions so that they stay alive – for instance, when using public transportation.

In the case of *Rail Commuters*, 2005 a lobby was formed after a student was stabbed and killed on his way home on the train. The lobby called for safety and security services on rail commuter facilities 'in order to protect those rights of rail commuters as are enshrined in the Constitution, right to life, to freedom from all forms of violence from private sources and to human dignity'.[8]

Struggles occur over rights because institutions are unable to secure them. The judgment held that the transporters, a public monopoly, bore a constitutional obligation to rail commuters. 'The spatial planning of our cities means that those most in need of subsidized public transport services are those who often have the greatest distances to travel. Those people are also often the poorest members of our communities who have little choice in deciding whether to use rail services or not... Boarding a train renders commuters intensely vulnerable to violent criminals who target them' (*Rail Commuters*, 2005, paragraph 82). The principle of accountability and the constitutional right to protection make it impossible for the state to justify its inaction, Lazarus underlines. A minimal state in terms of protection of the poor has to be reminded by the courts that it is its duty to safeguard the lives of those within its jurisdiction, an ancient principle established in medieval Europe and reaffirmed by Article 2 of the European Convention on Human Rights, requiring authorities 'to take preventive operational measures to protect an individual whose life is at risk from the criminal acts of another individual'.[9]

Without consistent analytical rigor, 'there is strong danger that the rhetoric of a "right to security" has the potential to displace a "right to life", hard-won, carefully reasoned, marking a fragile consensus around the foundation of fundamental rights' (Lazarus, op. cit., 20). Such a fragile victory, however, justifies a strong interest for the evolution of Johannesburg and South Africa in the years to come.

4.2 São Paulo

While governments continue to play an important role in matters of threats to security, in an era of globalization cities need to find their own responses. The case of São Paulo is worth analyzing in that respect, as crime hitting major cities Latin America reaches very high rates. In 2000, the World Health Organization for Latin America and Caribbean countries showed a median of 23 homicides per 100, 000 (LaFree et al., 2010, 622).

Historically, Brazil was created from the encounter of nomadic Indian nations with a small number of Portuguese and other European settlers. 'Anyone (could) eventually be a landowner, get rich and enter the elite ruling class in Brazil' (Wilheim, 2007). São Paulo was established as a base for the conquest of the hinterland. At the end of the nineteenth century, it attracted numerous, mostly Italian, immigrants who were endowed with an entrepreneurial spirit. They merged into the city without making enclaves of their own, and the second generation married outside its group of origin (Ibid.). The wealth of the city came from coffee growing in the hinterland and generating commerce. The city grew from 65,000 residents in 1890 to 265,000 ten years later. Currently a metropolitan area of 19 million people, São Paulo is 'a classic second city that became a first city' (Sudjik, 2011).

Another major element distinguishes São Paulo, related to its past. If cities have historically been the locus of the citizenry's development, global urbanization creates specially volatile conditions: cities become more crowded with marginalized citizens and non-citizens contesting their exclusion. In these contexts, citizenship is both unsettled and unsettling.

Brazil has two entangled notions of citizenship.[10] The Brazilian regime, inheriting Portuguese rules of domination and its bureaucratic approaches, has never denied inequalities (Holston, 2008, 38). Neither the state nor society felt the responsibility to equalize opportunities or to provide social justice. Brazilian citizenship is 'a combination of two considerations: one is formal membership, based on principles of incorporation into the nation-state, the other is the substantive distribution of the rights, meanings, institutions, and practices that membership entails to those considered citizens. Since the inception of the Brazilian nation-state 200 years ago, the formulation of citizenship has used social differences of education, property, race, gender, occupation, and the like to create legal inequalities and differential rights among citizens, it may be seen as the "Brazilian legal paradox"'.[11] By requesting, for instance, that voting rights be based on literacy and as half the Brazilian population was illiterate in 1950, the capacity of exclusion was effective. As in Johannesburg, the rich categories expelled the poor from the centre, with an elaborate justification of social management and of slum removal (Ibid., 158). Developing an out-of-sight-out-of-mind tranquillity, they let construction spread at the periphery: as long as this took place at the margins, it allowed distance from the poor to be maintained. Due to uncertain property ownership twisted along for centuries, workers used the law legally, paid for their lots, and 'insoluble procedural complexity' followed, generating significant conflicts. The legal and the illegal thus maintained a porous intimacy. The law was then used to legalize the illegal, the unjust and the unequal. It forced most Brazilians into illegal conditions of settlement, alienating them from law. This estrangement from law is reflected in the classic Brazilian adage, 'for friends, everything; for enemies, the law'. Due to politicization fostered by a feeling of injustice, by 1970, Holston asserts, a majority of São Paulo residents had obtained political rights. People wanted to vote for mayor, governor, president: they taught themselves literacy and, after getting their voting rights, attempted to get property rights, as homeowners. Workers seized the land to construct shelters for themselves and their kin. Consequently, homeownership in São Paulo is currently high, reaching 69 per cent (Ibid., 183). In the 1970s, two types of citizenry started to coexist and confront each other in the same social space of the city (Ibid., 249). The former poor understood that fundamental socio-economic needs could be rethought in terms of the universal human rights of citizenship.

4.2.1   Demography and economy

A study by Mastercard among 75 cities reveals that in the global South, cities like Mumbai and São Paulo are in the top group for financial and economic services, but are brought down by their low rankings regarding 'the ease of doing business' and the lack of well-being for vast sectors of the population. São Paulo ranks sixteenth on the 'financial centre' indicator and twenty-sixth as a business centre. It jumps to the top ten on some indicators, such as commercial real estate development and derivatives and commodities contracts (Sassen, 2011). It has the most active stock exchange in Latin America (Bovespa is the sixth in the world for the volume of negotiated contracts). The city is the site of 70 per cent of Brazil's national and regional headquarters, 100 per cent of the headquarters of international banks and finance corporations, 85 per cent of the largest banks and 90 per cent of the most important publishers (Municipality of São Paulo, 2002). The concentration of multinational companies, the presence of Latin America's most important stock exchange and the rapid development of a knowledge economy make São Paulo a global city with multiple circuits that connect it firmly to other parts of the world. The vision of the city government is to rejuvenate neighbourhood centres and to strengthen São Paulo's image as a global city (Jacobi, 2007, 284).

But, as in most globalized cities, inequalities are an important issue. It is as if two cities coexisted in the same space, one participating in globalized economic transactions, the other sheltering low-skilled labourers at the margins of the city economy (Ibid., 280). The Gini index of inequality in 2008 was high (61) in São Paulo,[12] and the polarization of the labour market has increased in recent years.

But there is little relation between the city's spectacular access to global circuits of power and its level of social inclusion. Many of the wealthy categories have moved away from the centre and yielded to the temptation of gated communities in the suburbs. Although only 10–15 per cent of the poor live in *favelas* (Caldeira, 2011), more than 60 per cent of the population live in substandard housing. For a majority of the city's residents, education, of mobility and altering one's life prospects are slim.[13] Such ambiguities help explain the intricacies of the crime issue.

4.2.2 Problems and how they are perceived

Fear has always played an important part in the imaginaries of Paulistanos, all the more so as the city absorbed wave after wave of poor migrants and as territorial inequalities have, over time, become highly visible. After Brazil's transition to a democratic government, fear of crime became an excuse for the most affluent to lock themselves away. 'Fear, the talk of crime, and the adoption of walls and separations all transform the character of public space. Privatization, enclosures, policing of boundaries and distancing devices create a fragmented public space in which inequality is an organizing value.' It is 'a process which in turn moulds reputations, reinforces stigma and influences the future trajectory of the area' (Caldeira, 2011, 174). Fear is indeed widespread: in the 2008 Urban Age survey, 67.9 per cent of residents were very worried about crime and they had good reason to be: 28 per cent of them had been assaulted, almost half had a close relationship with someone who had been killed; 57.3 per cent reported that either they or a close family member had been robbed (www.urban-age.net). Due to fear, all the features of urban life that usually bring people together – public space, public transportation, market places, street entertainment – now keep people apart (www.urbanage.org). As in Johannesburg, 'entire blocks are sealed off and private armed guards sit in bullet-proof cabins to restrict entry' to residences (Tulchin, 2010, 306). Despite democratization, invisible walls separate the rich and the poor whenever they have to share spaces, such as elevators. Yet violent deaths, assaults and rapes largely spare the upper and middle classes; the burden of violent crime is heavily impacting on the least-protected populations (in shantytowns or slums) and committed by the poor on the poor. But inaction seems to prevail in the highest spheres of power. 'The exclusionary nature of urban policies to combat crime are acceptable to most citizens because the vast majority of them believes that crime is a matter of "us" versus "them", of an invading "other". If we believe that crime is committed by someone unknown, it is reasonable to impose policies to keep that someone out. But who is the outsider in a city? And who determines who is to be kept outside?' (Ibid., 307). The answers to these rhetorical questions lie in the inter-subjectivity of those who live in gated/protected communities.

4.2.3   Significant crime trends

The trends in violence reveal that the poorest categories are hit disproportionately. The 2006 murder rate, estimated at 21 per 100,000 (versus 3 per 100,000 in Istanbul and Mumbai), distinguishes São Paulo from other mega-cities of the South. (It had reached 60 per 100,000 in the late 1990s). The incidents are distributed unevenly. 'Many of the neighbourhoods in the peripheries had a murder rate of more than 110 per 100,000 people, compared with less than five in the city's central districts' (Caldeira, 2011, 171). If limited to the young, it reached 57.3 per 100,000 in 2000, then decreased to 11.3 in 2009, a low figure compared with Medellin, Colombia (110 per 100, 000 in 2009).[14] The presence of the *'Comando'*, (a fraternity of organized criminals) in São Paulo, and its regulatory power in some neighbourhoods called *quebradas* contributes to such decrease.

The intellectual challenge is therefore to understand what singular circumstances cause such violence, ruling out terrorist attacks, which have spared the city. Is a certain type of globalization or a specific local culture responsible for the high levels of violence? Or could it be the inefficiency of law enforcement organizations and the lack of political will to alleviate inequalities of treatment? Or all these dimensions combined?

4.2.4 The specific issue of criminal gangs

Gangs are a main source of social involvement among young people in South American cities (Jones, 2011). As shown a long time ago by F. Thrasher (1927), who allegedly counted 25,000 young men belonging to gangs in Chicago at the beginning of the 1920s, they congregate on boundaries dividing two urban zones, at the margins of the city core. 'There are cracks and fractures in the social organization structure. Gangs can be seen as interstitial elements in the social fabric and their territory as an interstitial zone in the sprawled city,' he wrote (1927, 20). Gangs organize and participate in various types of illegal trafficking. They interact with community leaders, politicians, magistrates, small businessmen, bankers, the police and other gangs. Most of all, they know what is going on in their neighbourhoods: domestic violence, alcoholism, drug addiction, child abuse, disputes, thefts, lethal contracts. Consequently, they play an important regulatory role in conflict resolution. 'A drug gang's decision is final and non-compliance is not recommended ... People have less reason to believe that a gang's verdict will be any less just than a judge's and their decision will be arrived at more quickly and cheaply. In Rio, it costs less to have someone killed than to arrange an illegal hook up to the electricity supply' (Jones, 2011, 158). Bosses and gang leaders offer reciprocity; for instance they alleviate problems of water and drainage in a neighbourhood, may start a kindergarten or take care of the older people when the presence of the state is weak. They are mediators, sometimes engaging in these kinds of good work and some have not avoided romanticizing a usually squalid social reality.[15]

In São Paulo, a major crime syndicate, Primeiro Comando da Capital (PCC), imposed its power over weak local institutions. The PCC is a sort of 'fraternity of thieves', according to Adalton Marques, the official goal of which has been to check oppression in prisons (it has a chart valuing truth and solidarity). Amazingly, it delivers a human rights rhetoric

(Holston, 2008). It may provide large drug and arms supplies but it is not essentially a drugs/arms trafficking enterprise as are the syndicates of Rio. Its leader, Marcos Williams Herbas Camacho, nicknamed Marcola, who was in a maximum security detention centre, 800 kilometres from São Paulo in May 2006, then launched the operation 'Fear in the City' to demonstrate to local authorities the power of his organization. Most leaders of the PCC have been murdered in prison; he is a survivor. On May 14, Mothers' Day, when numerous visitors, mothers, spouses and children visit prisons, 150 attacks took place, by the PCC's command, in the penitentiaries of the state of São Paulo. In fifty-five of them, hundreds of hostages were held by inmates. thirty-six buses were set on fire, four banks attacked by assault weapons. Seventy-four people lost their lives, including fourteen inmates, thirty-six prison guards, and some army Rangers and a prison chief were burnt alive. Because the fire-power of the organization exceeded that of the local police, the federal government felt compelled to call out the armed forces and the federal police to cope with this takeover of the city. Vice-governor Lembo, eager not to jeopardize his sovereignty, refused to do so. More deaths occurred the following day, and schools started to close as well as public transportation, stores and shopping malls. Panic spread, fuelled by the media. The PCC rebellion turned São Paulo into a ghost city. Then the prisons became quiet again. It is very likely that a secret negotiation had taken place between the state secretary in charge of prisons and the PCC leader's lawyer.[16] In the days following the attacks, heavy repression took place, both in prisons and in the *favelas*. It is estimated that fifty-seven people died. Among the thirty-one policemen indicted by the prosecutor, only three were eventually condemned for their acts of violence (Ibid.). But no PCC member was transferred to the new federal prison in the state of Parana.

Ninety per cent of the 147 prisons of São Paulo are under PCC control, even if no inmate is a member (also called 'brother').[17] Around 2,000 PCC brothers contribute a monthly payment (within a racket) which bring the syndicate substantial resources. The PCC's power extends beyond the state's limits. On August 7, 2006, sixty-three violent attacks on banks, buses, public buildings, supermarkets and even on the parking space of the police investigating organized crime, followed an incident related to a planned transfer of prisoners to maximum security prisons. This transfer did not occur.

It was not the first time that the organization demonstrated its strength.[18] The origin of the PCC is actually related to a massacre in Carandiru, then the largest prison in South America. The nine buildings of the prison, with 220 guards, was meant to hold 4,000 inmates, but in 1992, it held 7,000. The latter complained of continuous abuse from guards. In October 1992, a massive rebellion started and 500 riot police were called to the prison. At least 111 inmates were killed. Yet, after this brutal intervention, no policeman was indicted and only eight prisoner families received financial support.[19] The social democratic party, at the head of the State of Sao Paulo since 1994, then increased the number of prisons from 60 to 144 in the next 12 years, while the number of incarcerated tripled, from 55,000 to 143, 500; totalling 40 per cent of Brazil's inmates (Gasnier, 2006).

Gangs, distributed in six large organizations in São Paulo, are influential in the public space. 'Besides their local criminal activities, ... they are also increasingly taking over "government" functions: "policing", providing social services and welfare assistance, offering jobs and new elements of rights and authority in the areas they control' (Sassen, 2010). They exhibit the gross failures of the state and of its justice system to enforce the law, protect citizens, respect the rights of prisoners and develop policies of security. Organized crime receives the support of corrupted elected politicians and the *commandos*. They all use the language of rights, Holston remarks.

In-depth ethnographic research (Telles, 2011) points at a new trend, however. Much has changed in the Comando's arrangements. No similar attack on the city has taken place, and the rate of homicides decreased from 43 per 100,000 in 1999 to 22 in 2005.

A neighbourhood which registered figures comparable to those of a time of war, Cidade Tiradentes, with a population over 190, 000, half White and half Black residents, has experienced a fivefold decrease in homicides, from 106 per 100,000 to 22 in 2005 (Telles, op. cit.). For one thing, drug trafficking has become better organized. The PCC has imposed a protocol on the production and distribution of the merchandise. This process has taken place at a time when, thanks to President Lula's welfare schemes, poverty was decreasing in São Paulo and the informal sector was providing more jobs. The PCC has set decrees against the settling of scores by murder. If a dispute is serious, a committee will make a decision, including other criminal organizations' leaders (via cell phone) in the discussions. Then a form of restorative justice will take place or, on the contrary, a decision made on the offenders' deportation or possibly lethal punishment. The PCC operates less as a pyramidal chain of command, mafia-style, Telles observes, and more on a reticular, rhizome pattern, although *torres* (tower controls) exert supervision from a distance. In the 'bandit world', conflicts occur all the time, involving teenagers, property owners and all kinds of residents. The PCC pacifies the neighbourhoods, resorting to dialogue and discussion, but punishing offenders as well. The PCC has reached its goal of symbolically consolidating its hegemonic power, therefore no longer needing to demonstrate its threatening organizational capability on the city at large.

4.2.5 Role of police: presence/absence

Until 1999, violence and crime kept rising steadily in Greater São Paulo, but the police remained very little involved in the neighbourhoods where they occurred and, as will be shown below, there are reasons for this situation. In 2000, the conviction rate was 2 per cent, according to the University of São Paulo's Centre for Violence Studies. Both the military police and the civil police, a detective force, were prone to corruption and violence. They exerted extortion in exchange for protection or noncommitment. There is more rivalry than cooperation between the two forces. The residents buy police protection in order to be left alone.

The key to the understanding of São Paolo's violence is to grasp the nature of illicit business – in particular, of drug deals (Misse, 2006). These form 'dangerous liaisons' and power relations, requesting police protection which, in return, exerts extortion, in what Misse calls the 'market of protection' fuelled by criminal practices as well as legal ones. Policemen intervene mostly when private agreements between authorities and powerful people and clients have been broken for one reason or another. Telles (2011) rightly shows, as in her previous research focussed on trajectories of urban mobility at the periphery (2007, 207–8), that as the state apparatus is so much incorporated in dubious practices and part of the illegal sector, it allows São Paulo to grow as a 'metropolitan bazaar', where order and disorder, formality and informality, legal and illegal practices overlap. What the global city requires in order to thrive at the top – deregulation, financial freedom, the extension of legal and illegal markets – is mirrored at the bottom in civil society itself. The gap between the legal city and the illegal city is blurred (Body-Gendrot, 2007a). Take a young man, portrayed by Telles: he is a respected resident with a wife and child in one place and a drug dealer in another. His pragmatic cleverness allows him to manage his different lives and to avoid difficult hurdles. 'Poor families, community leaders, local dealers, shopkeepers and bus drivers all share the same neighbourhood history and all know each other's disputes and moments of unhappiness...People move, cross over, commute, change their positions, according to the spaces where they find themselves. Microscopic life stories "meant to leave no trail", according to Foucault's expression (2003), transit in a permanent state of exception, making things work' (2007).

4.2.6 Policy formulation and implementation

It has been argued that in São Paulo, coherent plans have been abandoned in favour of fragmented 'strategic plans' developed at the level of municipalities and below them. The lack of an institutionalized administrative structure hampers the development of the metropolitan level (Lorrain, 2011, 347). While São Paulo has much to lose by an image which remains synonymous with danger, addressing inequalities and the segmented nature of public services appears to be a low priority for city officials. Participatory budgeting and the introduction of subadministrations reveal, however, that there is some local autonomy from the national government and that an important change has taken place in recent years. But can such a change gradually overthrow the entrenched power structures of Brazilian society? The example of insurgent citizenship and the role of entrepreneurs at the periphery, as studied by Holston (2008), yield some optimism.

The city's Strategic Master Plan issued in 2003 includes both global visions and local ones. According to Wilheim (2007), it hopefully ensures that private resources are funnelled through public-interest solutions. Public space and the environment have to be improved as well as infrastructures. But, he remarks that 'the public interest is not the same as the interest of all'. The city needs to regulate the building industry and the real estate interests, which are powerful lobbies, in order to pursue a policy of social inclusion, in particular for the marginalized households at the periphery. Law-enforcement institutions are in great need of reform and need important resources and savoir-faire to confront criminal gangs efficiently.

To summarize, these two cities, Johannesburg and São Paulo, are challenged by visible threats emanating from criminal and organized gangs. Taming such cities is a daunting task. They seem to be torn by their aspirations to become world-class cities, and by a reluctance to reduce corruption and make institutions more trustworthy. Transparency in terms of democratic processes does not seem a goal that can be reached in the near future. While in São Paulo the insurgency of newly empowered citizens coexists with the entrenched powerful families that cling to privileges inherited from the past, this entanglement may not be alleviated by globalization. In Johannesburg, also a dual city, the choice of city planners to bring it into conformity with its world-class aspirations – sequestering places through security devices, excluding offensive behaviour and opting for punishment – also yields the image of a city 'at war' with itself. 'Urban stakeholders are actively engaged in a zero-sum competition over access to scarce resources, and ... the victorious haves are willing to go to great lengths to defend their privilege, such as it is , and have become increasingly vicious in keeping the have-nots at bay' (Murray, op. cit., 234). Criminalizing and blaming the poor, pushing out the victims of changing economies, does not augur well for the development of more inclusive, democratic societies in the South. Formal citizenship does not translate into equal treatment.

The last type of threats to be examined appears at first sight far less dramatic. What is called urban violence in Europe does not translate into a huge number of murders or the takeover of local governments by criminal cartels. Yet, the importance given by the media and politicians to these disorders, and the measures taken by various bureaucracies to quell them, reveal that much more is happening below this tip of the iceberg. Indeed, global circumstances play a role in a general context of fear, insecurity and frustration. Any spark can set such social tinder-boxes on fire.

5
Disorders in British and French Cities

Western cities have a long history of civil unrest. Currently, the causes, triggers and nature of urban conflict and disorder have evolved under the impact of globalization, which transforms cities, which creates new centralities and new marginalities, transforms cities, and the scope and leverage of welfare states. Economic mismatch, spatial entrapment, the disruption of traditional arrangements, of values and of collective efficacy – all weigh on the mechanisms of social control that have been best cases exerted in low-income, working-class neighbourhoods in the most salient cases. More specifically, the irresponsible acquiescence of central governments to budget deficits and mounting debt has translated into major crises entailing austere fiscal policies and drastic cuts in social services in many countries. These choices have generated more dependency in households at the bottom of the social ladder, more broken homes and moral disenchantment, which in 2010–11 have now and then translated into public protests by 'indignant' citizens in Latin American, Israeli, European and American cities.

The degree to which individuals feel concern, malaise or fear depends on the capacity one has to avoid victimization. The media launch campaigns, public demands are expressed to and pressures exerted on public authorities and, all urban authorities need to respond to popular 'voices', in particular regarding collective violence conducted in public space and defined as an action that 'immediately inflicts physical damage on persons and objects, involves at least two perpetrators and results in part from coordination among those who perform the damaging acts' (Tilly, 2003, 3). In the representations of many people, such violence indeed causes incapacitation, hospitalization or death, but this is a distorted vision of how officially violence is categorized (In France, 50 per cent of violent acts are verbal).

Few analyses look at how violence erupts and with what consequences. A comparative approach enables us to look at contexts of social and economic forces at work, at dynamic trends of low-intensity violence (will be studied) and at its management.

Two European countries, the United Kingdom and France, have been selected, because they experienced recurrent forms of urban disorder in the last quarter of the twentieth century and continue to do so. Historically, their political experiences have been central to the development of enlightenment, democratic ideas and rules of law, but also to social insurgency, confrontations and protest, in which the poor are driven to violence to express their emotions and their claims in modes of 'violent bargaining'. The nature, development and dynamics of such disorders reveal variations, both within cities and from one country to another throughout the three decades studied here. Analyzing them allows us to understand how they fit within a whole set of theories and practices, and also what continuities or ruptures they introduce. In the first section of this chapter, a conceptual framework related to public disorder defines the context and dynamics that are evoked in the second section. Some misunderstandings generated by terminology which hides more than it reveals are also clarified. Thereafter, the types of protesters, locations of unrest and the different logics from one decade to the another demonstrate that they have their own dynamics, according to circumstances, external forces and scales of interactions, and also show that there is hardly any transmission from one type generation of protesters to another, even in the same neighbourhoods. Differences and convergences in British and French cases are both underscored.

An increasing awareness of diversification in the nature and forms of disorder generates a reconceptualization of police intervention and of law enforcement's response to such situations. Yet public-order policing is not simply reactive. The second section of this chapter examines the forms of adjustment by police forces to various types of disorder in the two countries over the last thirty years. Modes of policing usually distinguish Britain and France, but does this distinction hold for the policing of public disorder? In both countries, when disorders occur, the discretionary power of police officers in the field – what Monjardet called 'a hierarchical inversion' (1966, 88), and Her Majesty's Inspectorate Constabulary termed 'flexible options' in defusing tensions (HMIC, 1999, 59) – cannot be overlooked. A demonstration of this was made again during the disorders that recently hit British cities in 2011.

The third and fourth sections of this chapter attempt to make sense of disorders, reviewing various modes of analysis and examining the weight of national *paths of dependency* in the interpretations and choices made to quell local outbreaks of disorder.

5.1 Conceptualizing public disorders

Although researchers have learned to develop a 'cautious ignorance' regarding the spatial location of disorder, some assumptions appear to hold. Theories on public disorder in Europe have been influenced by American theories that analysed the race riots in American cities the 1960s. The Kerner Commission in 1968 discarded 'riff-raff' explanation which emphasized the role of agitators and socially deviant, irresponsible individuals. It showed, instead, that rioters were quite similar to the residents in the neighbourhoods where agitation took place. The commission pointed out that urban disorder occurred in places with a 'reservoir of grievances' regarding police harassment, poor housing and lack of jobs. Other commentators insisted on the lack of official channels for grievances aggravated by racial segregation, on generalized hostile beliefs shared by such communities and on the importance of rumour. British criminologists D. Waddington (2007, 41) rightly remarks, however, that societies do not divide clearly into law abiders and deviants, that subcultures distinguish police and civil society and that although certain types of intervention in certain circumstances may do so, police intervention does not necessarily escalate disorder, although certain types of intervention in certain circumstances may do so.

Looking at clashes between police and young Blacks in England, Benyon (1987) coined a 'tinder and spark' metaphor distinguishing between contexts with structural handicaps and immediate *precipitants* related to police abuse or intervention. Other theories gave importance to street counter-cultures prone to interpersonal violence in the absence of channels defending young minorities' interests. Pernicious 'military' police strategies were highlighted. Other explanations have brought forward the role of the media in transforming victims of recession into 'folk devils' and creating 'moral panics' (Cohen, 1972, 28; Hall et al. 1978, 16).

Some explanations have been criticized because they only incorporated processes and ignored the past history of a place. It is essential, however, to look at history and geography, at 'locales at which resentment of power relations [is] transformed into resistance of power relations' (Keith, 1993, 59), a position shared here, which argues that the logic of context has to be grasped to make sense of incidents.

The challenging 'flashpoint frame of public disorder' elaborated by Waddington and his colleagues defines six interdependent levels of analysis. It is 'flexible enough to encompass a variety of types of disorders, while allowing for the uniqueness of each situation' (2007, 51). The *structural* level refers to material inequalities, life-chances and political powerlessness. The *political/ideological* level looks at responses offered by institutions like police and justice and the media to the demands of the concerned group. The *cultural* level examines sub-cultural groups' shared conditions and experiences and their views, when the salience of conflicts occur on the merit of accommodation or of confrontation. The *contextual* level pays attention to the circulation of rumour, to the history of the place and to media coverage of issues in these localities. The *situational* level analyses the profile of the territory and who 'owns' public space, whether turf wars occur, and what surveillance is exercised by the police. Finally, the *interactional* level focuses on the nature of encounters between the police and the public. 'In highly charged situations, a particular incident (the throwing of a brick, an arrest or police charge) may spark off disorder. Such "flashpoints" are interpreted symbolically as indicating the underlying attitude of the other side. Particularly important are intensifiers...' allowing disorders to take place in some communities and not in others (Ibid.). This theoretical framework is tested by case studies in the third section. A caveat is needed, however, regarding the terms used, which illustrates differences in the comparison of Britain and France. Such words have been socially constructed and their use and meaning differ. For instance, in the United Kingdom, race and ethnicity differentiate individuals and place them into official categories according to the colour of their skin or to their religious, cultural or linguistic backgrounds (ethnic minorities make up 8 per cent of the population). By contrast, the use of ethnic and racial categories is officially banned in France, where only nationals and foreigners are distinguished. (Immigrants and their offspring are estimated to make 14 per cent of the population). It is not easy for non-French observers to understand this position.[1]

The United Kingdom distinguishes Afro-Caribbeans (West Indians also called Blacks) and Asians (Pakistani and Bangladeshi) from Chinese, who are in a specific category. In France, Asian refers to Chinese, Vietnamese, Thai and Cambodians. The notion of *community* also has a different significance in both countries. *Community* refers to the cohesion of a neighbourhood, to a sense of common belonging, which can be ethnic and racial, which can be, but not necessarily, ethnic and racia. In Britain,[2] it is also, regarding security, an administrative tool of management – for instance, regarding security. Other forms of social bonding and commonalities have more recently appeared beyond territorial communities. Institutions, such as the police, have had to adapt their practices as such (Bartkowiak and Crehan, 2010). By contrast, the term *community* is handled with mistrust in France, except to refer to the nation or to Europe.[3] In other words, a differentialist 'model', built on group boundaries and on the *e pluribus* in the United Kingdom, contrasts with an assimilationist 'model' focused on the *unum* in France. ('Model' does not imply that it translates into practice.)

The term *disorder* is here preferred to *riot*. As suggested by Tilly (2003, 18), *riot* expresses a political judgement rather than reflects an analytical distinction. For historian Hobsbawn (1959) riots must be understood as a prelude to negotiation, as was the case in 1968 when 'Black Power' leaders in the United States opted for a ten-point programme, a chart, and an organization before engaging in negotiations with the White establishment.

There are, for example, worries about the impact of the 2011 disorders on the Olympic games taking place in the summer of 2012 in London. The disorders studied here have little to do with the 'riots' experienced in India or China, or even in Los Angeles in 1992. Moreover, it is not the number of deaths and colossal damages by which they are characterized, nor did they trigger negotiations. By comparison, urban violence examined here is a very disturbing and sometimes devastating form of violence for, yet it is very disturbing and sometimes devastating for the neighbourhoods concerned where it occurs. It should thus be taken seriously in our study of the security challenges faced by cities.[4] The position adopted here is that, although this urban violence does not translate into numerous deaths and collateral damage, it may be lethal for the image and reputations of the localities and their neighbourhoods. Those who can may move out. A stigmatized locality may be abandoned by investors, employees, deserted by tourists, students and potential residents. There are serious concerns about the appropriate training of policemen in charge of public order, regarding the Olympic games taking place in the summer of 2012 in London. The interchangeable use of terms like *violence, disorders, outbreaks, disturbances,* intends mostly refers to a rupture of order. Yet it goes without saying that social order and disorder are deeply intertwined.

A chronological division helps focus on the most visible events occurring in the two countries decade after decade, allowing cross-national comparisons of both convergence and divergence.

5.2 Urban disorders in the last thirty years in the United Kingdom and France

Mobilized actors in recent disorders in the United Kingdom, as in France, share similar characteristics: they tend to be young males wearing indistinct, hooded sweatshirts, living in disadvantaged areas and reflecting a diversity of cultures. In the United Kingdom, in the 1980s, public attention was caught by young Whites confronting Blacks; then the focuss was directed at Blacks clashing with the police. In the 1990s, the media reported clashes between young White delinquents acting collectively to confront the police; in the 2000s, White 'nationalists' confronted young Asians over issues of drug dealing in the industrial cities of the North, before 42 per cent whites and 46 per cent blacks, 7 per cent Asian people ransacked streets in various British cities during the summer of 2011 (Singh et al., 2012, 29). In France, public disorder that attracted public attention also appear to be structured in the same manner. Those of the 1980s involved French youths of North African origin, referred to as *beurs*, many them living in public housing projects at the periphery of large cities. Then the 1990s were distinguished by clashes, occurring each year, and opposing a diversity of youths who were experiencing hardship and disrespect, to symbols of the state: namely the police but also depending on contexts bus drivers, fire fighters, teachers. The year 2005 represented an apex, with three weeks of unrest throughout three hundred urban locations in France. Smaller but violent urban disorders in marginalized neighbourhoods were to follow in subsequent years.

5.2.1 The urban disorders of the 1980s

In the United Kingdom, as in France, public disorder was widespread all through the nineteenth century. Urban violence was a mode of expression by the masses, deprived of political representation, and a form of 'violent collective bargaining' (Hobsbawn, 1959; Chevalier, 1984). At the beginning of the twentieth century, however, public and private elites perceived working-class disorders as a threat to their political, social and economic order; they reacted by criminalizing collective protest, on one hand and, on the other, by praising the virtue of public tranquillity. In England, the famous remark of Sir Robert Peel that 'The police are the public and the public are the police' was characterized by a peaceful form of police intervention which later was interpreted as policing by 'consent'. In fact, street patrols were highly contested at that time. Strong opposition to the police in a deeply class-divided society forced the police to adopt a low profile with a minimum use of force when intervening in working-class neighbourhoods (Taylor, 1997, 99). The lack of brutal repression during working-class demonstrations was thus a tactical choice. By contrast, a militaristic approach prevailed in France when the police or the army were required to put down working-class disorders. In Britain, the decline of civil disorder after serious riots in the nineteenth-century riots (related about the price of bread, religious strife and industrialization) could be attributed to, the repeal of the Combination Acts, which allowed the growth of working-class organizations, the integration of religious minorities, reform movements and improvements, emigration of the poor, the spread of literacy, and better welfare provisions (Anderson, 2011).

Despite persistent socio-economic and cultural inequalities, significant class conflict came to an end in the 1950s. Bargaining techniques replaced modes of violent face-to-face conflicts and, in working-class neighbourhoods, a relative calm accompanied three prosperous decades after World War II.

In the United Kingdom, the first widely publicized and incidents were those of Nottingham and of Notting Hill in London in 1958, which immediately were identified by the government as 'race riots'. The violent and complex dimensions of these incidents forced political actors to question perceptions and accepted ideas about social cohesion and diversity. Hundreds of young Whites, with stones and bottles confronted Blacks. The political elite, in particular the Party then in power, warned that a serious 'race problem' threatened the country, the solution to which was immigration control.

Other signs of looming social tension in multicultural cities (for instance, in Leeds in 1972, 1974 and 1975) appeared before the widely publicized incidents in Bristol and Brixton in 1980–81, the latter resulting in a long and highly critical report (Scarman, 1985).

(a) Bristol and Sheffield

In the early and mid-1980s, recurring confrontations occurred in inner cities between African-Caribbean youths and the police. These disorders are illustrated by those of St Paul's in Bristol and in Sheffield, which are less well-known. We refer here to the research led by conducted Waddington and Critcher (1989). In these two cities, the youths those engaged were second-generation black residents. On April 2, 1980, in the St Paul neighbourhood of Bristol, a police raid during a private party at a bar led to the arrest of the owner, a well-known African-Caribbean individual. The police intervention attracted a hostile crowd. As they left the place, the police were assaulted with bricks and bottles and, despite backup and two hours of military-style tactics, they had to withdraw, greatly outnumbered and also unable either to protect themselves or their area; they were to be booed at looted store' owners. Twenty-three policemen were injured (Muncie, 1984, 85). For the elites, this incident was a 'social aberration' (Benyon and Solomos, 1987). Yet it will reoccur the following April year in Brixton, after a after the use of a major police tactics, called 'Swamp 81', that consisted in saturating the locality, stopping and searching suspects and raiding homes to eliminate 'muggings' was undertaken. Serious clashes then occurred, as 200 people were arrested, 145 buildings damaged, over 200 vehicles destroyed and 450 reported injuries (Waddington and King, 2004, 14).

Hundreds of smaller disorders followed: Southall in London between skinheads and Asians; then Toxteth in Liverpool, Moss Side in Manchester, Handsworth in Birmingham and Chapeltown in Leeds.

In August 1981, the Sheffield disorders involved a large number of people. Interest in these disorders derives from the local police know-how, which avoided a contagion of such incidents in nearby localities. As is often the case, these disorders should not have allowed to occur. Young West Indians were used to sitting on the stairs of The Haymarket, a commercial mall. They were noisy, listening to music, smoking and drinking, and as a result customers avoided this spot. But with time, the local police admitted that these youths had a right to be there, while the latter acknowledged that the police did their work in responding to complaints and in regulating their behaviour (ibid.).

Sheffield, by contrast to Brixton, has only a small West Indian population. Youth–police relations were not good but, by comparison, they are not tense. According to Waddington and Crichter (1989), the local police had mediators in the public housing estates where West Indian families were concentrated, and left it to residents to settle disputes. Yet in August 1981, with the Brixton incidents occurring a few months before, the police were on guard and the usual arrangements were suspended. New police, unfamiliar with the routine behaviour at The Haymarket, were sent to the mall. The head of the unit ordered the youths to leave. As they refused, two of them, seen as leaders, were handcuffed to the stairs' railings. The youths retaliated, targeting a female police officer. Police honour was challenged. The context and the nature of the incident had, however, limited importance: The crowd was eventually dispersed and a compromise reached. After seventeen young people were arrested and twelve convicted for obstruction and assault against the police, the matter was closed. This urban confrontation was not seen as an expression of any wider racial conflict.

Other disorders followed in 1985 in Brixton, at Handsworth in Birmingham (122 injured, a majority of them policemen), at Broadwater Farm in London (a policeman stabbed, 233 policemen wounded), in Tottenham and Toxteth in Liverpool (Body-Gendrot, 1993).

(b) Les Minguettes in Lyons

Meanwhile, in France, in 1981, a number of youths, most of them French of Arabic origin, started joyriding with stolen cars around rather new housing projects (*cités*) named Les Minguettes in the outskirts (*banlieue*) of Lyon, in a locality called Venissieux. They burnt cars in front of TV cameras crews and threw rocks and other heavy objects at the police. This *cité* has 40 high-rise buildings housing 35,000 people, a majority of them immigrants (Jazouli, 1992; Body-Gendrot 1993; 2010b). This 'hot' summer started what was labelled by the media as the *banlieue* crisis. At the end of that summer, around 250 cars had been burnt out. Clashes between youths and the police in *banlieues* located near Paris, Lyon and Strasbourg continued during the 1980s.

At first sight, in both countries, the 1980s after disorders appeared to confirm the flashpoint model. In marginalized areas that concentrate many of immigrant families with numerous children and structural handicaps, small incidents become flashpoints for youths who share similar profiles. The media acted as a magnifying glass. Youth marginalization and their isolation steer them into confrontations with the police.

5.2.2 The disorders of the 1990s

In the United Kingdom, groups of disenfranchised young men became visible via four incidents in 1991. These were White working-class youths, in areas characterized by high levels of unemployment, living in public housing estates in Cardiff, Coventry and Newcastle and perceived as petty delinquents in areas heavily distinguished by unemployment. As with youths in Les Minguettes, they were, out of boredom they were also joyriding with stolen cars. Their activities were covered by the media and they clashed with the police. In Oxford, in the area of Meadow Well, car thefts, and arson became until one night in September 1991, after a police chase, two youths died driving a stolen car. Rumours blamed the police as the cause of their deaths, and for four days the neighbourhood was vandalized, subject to arson attacks and looting (Power and Turnstall, 1997).

Then, in June 1995, in the neighbourhood of Manningham and in Bradford, two policemen attempted to stop a noisy soccer game taking place on the street involving many of young Asians. According to rumour, policemen entered a home and attacked a woman before arresting three youngsters. The area was already a tinderbox, with the police were accused of doing nothing to stop prostitution and drug trafficking (Webster, 2007, 103). For the first time, the media were to cover disorder which involved Asians rather than West Indians or White youths (Garbaye, 2011, 64).

Vaulx-en-Velin

In France, at the beginning of this decade, disorder and arson shook Vaulx-en-Velin, a *banlieue* of Lyons close to Les Minguettes, after a youth was killed during a police chase, for three nights in 1990. In the public mind, large public housing projects became associated once more with youth violence and immigrant families. There were no less than 250 reports of the event by French media which, in a spiral of amplification, broadcast the idea that rampant and wild violence, emanating from those very visible young males, threatened the peace of local communities and of French society in general. They associated the issue with immigrant families' lack of social integration. As in Britain, it also drew many comparisons with the American ghettos, emphasizing the dangers of the Americanization of French society (no-go areas, drugs, gangs, communitarianism and so on.).

In the first half of the 1990s, each year between ten to fifteen clashes between youths and the police occurred in such sensitive areas, usually after a claim of police abuse by the youths (Lagrange, 2006, 44): Mantes-la-Jolie, 1991; Sartrouville, 1992; Melun, 1993; Dammarie-les-Lys, 1997; Toulouse, 1998; Lille, 2001 and Clichy-sous-bois, 2004, saw deadly encounters with the police that generated unrest (Jobard, 2009, 29). What was particular about these forms of collective violence was that their targets were frequently symbols or agents of the state. Such attacks made up for around 40 per cent of the cases between 1992 and 1996 (Lagrange 2006). Yet, after 1997, as in other countries (Norway, the Netherlands, the United States, for instance), for much the time, turf wars or quarrels about girls or family feuds caused the disorders. Police shootings or police chases became in fact less often the sparks for these disorders. Whether the turf areas controlled by drug dealers remained quieter than others or not, remains a matter of debate.

5.2.3 The disorders of the 2000s

The disorders which took place in the United Kingdom in Oldham, Burnley and Bradford in the spring and summer of 2001 reflect the antagonisms of the two previously identified types of groups: on one they are disenfranchised young Whites (petty criminals, some of them close to the far right), and on the other, young marginalized and resentful Asians. The media coverage of disorders shaped the context, they crystallized extreme emotions and increased speculation among Whites, Asians and the White local police. The outbreaks in Oldham, in May, involved 500 people; police officers were wounded and the damage estimated at £1.4 million. In Bradford, in July, the same number of people participated, 326 policemen were injured and the damage went up to £10 million (Denham, 2001). The Burnley disorders analysed below have been documented by the Denham (2001) and Cantle reports (2001) and by research carried out by King and Waddington (2006).

(a) The Burnley disorders

Burnley is a locality of 91,000 residents. In June of 2001, rumours of imminent attacks by racist Whites mobilized young Asians. In Burnley, immigrant neighbourhoods represented about 5,000 people, almost 5 per cent of the population, concentrated in three public housing estates which are 60 per cent Pakistani. During the election of 2001, the National Front caught 11 per cent of the votes. The usual scenario – tensions, ascent, climax and decrease – was predictable in a conflict-ridden context. Numerous fights over drug trafficking involved drunk youths – either White or Asian. Pakistani cab drivers regularly complained of racist harassment and intimidation by Whites. Tensions went one stage further after two young Pakistanis were stabbed by two others. Then conflicts between White and Pakistani drug dealers translated into vandalism and cars were set on fire. The escalation came from an attack targeting a Pakistani cab driver. Soon, a rumour was that the driver had dead after being hit with a hammer by Whites who were not detained by the police. The police tried to give their own version of the facts but due to their communication channels remained limited, due to heightened tensions. Angry Asians walked to a bar where many nationalist hooligans Whites met regularly. With cab drivers circulating the information on their radios, they armed themselves with knives and baseball bats and confronted Whites who were 'fuelled with drink, singing songs and hurling racial abuse' (Taylor, 1997). The local police managed to keep them apart and avoided a potential 'bloodbath' (Ibid.). After three nights of tension, calm progressively returned.

(b) The 2011 disorders in British cities

After a peaceful demonstration on August 4, 2011, following police shooting of West Indian, Mark Duggan, in Tottenham, a poor neighbourhood in north London, violent local protest followed two evenings later, and rapidly reached five London boroughs, such as Shepherd's Bush and Enfield, Islington, Brixton and Croydon. Tottenham is a multi-ethnic neighbourhood. That the August disorders kicked off in an iconic site in London – Broadwater Farm, where a police officer was killed in 1985 – was a key event for the police as for the community. In 2011, a range motivations pushed drove heterogeneous individuals and groups to 'act out', from an opportunity to experience a 'happening' adding to the thrill of playing hide and seek with law enforcers, and the opportunity to commit arson to loot (Singh et al., 2011).

What was new was the use made of the Blackberry's encrypted instant message service and other social networks by hooded and masked youths directing speedily to the right places. The police were ill-equipped to monitor those connections. On the first night, youths employed to their usual repertoire: police cars were burnt, stores looted and several buildings set on fire. On the following night, two officers were hit by a speeding car, and the rampage continued. The outbreaks reached Hackney, various other London neighbourhoods and extended to Birmingham. The murder of a twenty-six-year-old man took place in Croydon, in south of London. Because the disorder kicked off in a different way on the third day (spreading to other parts of the country as well as across London), the police were able to 'protect' some locations in London (Oxford Street, Westfield shopping centres, for instance) but local high streets felt the brunt of the disorder (Clapham Junction, Ealing, Hackney, for instance). On the fourth night, about 700 people were arrested in London and 100 in the center of Manchester. Leeds and Liverpool experienced similar unrest. Damage estimates exceed £250 million. Independent communities and victims panels may pressure the state to deliver exceptional emergency funds to compensate the losses experienced by uninsured store and home owners. The seriousness of the damage is explained by another trigger during these chaotic four nights: violent aggressors, some of them gang members, made use of the disruption, and coordinated violence for personal benefit. They orchestrated looting with some efficiency, intending to resell stolen goods at a profit. Three Pakistanis in Birmingham were run over and killed trying to defend their stores. Including a sixty-eight-year-old retiree, five people died during the unrest. What the participants had in common, it seems, was an unfocussed hostility, a detachment from their communities that allowed them to act spontaneously and without remorse with hardly any guilt (also possibly boosted by the use of alcohol).

Regarding the police, the police response was slow and inappropriate on the first night (the parents of Mark Duggan were not personally informed of his death by police and filed a complaint). Also at first, strategic errors were made. Once in control, with backup arriving from nearby regions (overall the whole 16,000 officers were on the streets of London four days after the start of the outbreaks) and the courts' active support, the police arrested around 4,000 individuals, and 2,420 of them were charged for a number of offences. While the courts' tough approach (two thirds were sentenced to between ten and sixteen weeks of imprisonment or transferred to high courts 9 out of 10 arrestees had previous criminal records (Singh et al. 2012:29)) was overtly supported by the public. However governmental measures on zero tolerance (advocating the suppression of family benefits and the eviction of delinquent families from public housing units), meant that political parties in opposition (including former prime minister Tony Blair) and human rights groups criticized such a punitive posture: toughness is not meant to hide the lack of welfare services.

(c)   The 2005 unrest in France

What happened in France in 2005 is worth comparing with the 2011 events in the UK: in no locality was there more than four nights of unrest (Cincelli et al., 2006, 3). What made these disorders the largest in Europe since World War II was the contagion that spread from the north of Paris to three hundred neighbourhoods in the country, the length of the unrest – roughly 21 days – and the new locations where it occurred.

The trigger event is well-established: a group of boys in Clichy-sous-bois,[5] after playing soccer, headed to their homes to break the day's fast during Ramadan. Three boys, one of Turkish origin, the other two of African heritage, took a shortcut across a locked construction site. An employee called the police. A patrol car from the Brigade Anti-Criminalité (the BAC, France's anti-crime unit) arrived on the spot.

In Clichy-sous-bois, like much of the Seine-Saint Denis, confrontations are common between the police and boys from public housing projects. As the police car approached, the boys fled, since they were not carrying their identity cards.[6] They hid in an electricity substation. A pursuing officer from the BAC unit reported over his radio that the boys were seen climbing into the installation. But when he did not notice any movement inside the property, the police patrol returned to their station.[7]

In the meanwhile, two of the youths had trodden on live wires and died instantaneously. The survivor stumbled upon older boys and immediately a rumour spread that police had caused the deaths of the two boys. Later that day, Interior Minister Sarkozy suggested that if the boys had not been guilty, they would not have run.[8] Within two hours, in an explosion of rage that appeared to be spontaneous, around a hundred young men descended onto the streets of Clichy-sous-bois, chanting 'Dead for nothing!'. Hiding their faces, they threw rocks at city buses and the police and set over twenty cars ablaze. In usual circumstances, the disorders would have stopped after three or four days: the youths express their pain and anger after an incident with the police, they torch cars and garbage cans, break windows and vandalize public property. The police and youths clash and after a climax, the disorder recedes.

But a second unanticipated event then occurred. On the evening of October 30, a tear gas canister, similar to those used by the police those belonging to the police, rolled into the entrance of a store-front mosque, causing those inside – parents, family elders – to rush out, angry and humiliated. Once again, rumours circulated rapidly. Some youths claimed that the police had thrown it on purpose and that Islam had been disrespected; the police denied being involved of the act. But as a consequence, disorders started again, now spreading to seven localities.

Then, a strategic error was made within police headquarters in Paris. Despite local mayors' despite urgent warnings from the police headquarters decision was to heavily protect the National Stadium in Saint-Denis, where a high-risk soccer game was to take place on November 2. Eight hundred experienced policemen were sent there rather than to localities near Clichy-sous-bois, where insufficient and uncoordinated police forces confronted angry youths. The four-day weekend prevented mayors from mobilizing their usual resources. The disorders then spread to provincial cities. In Toulouse, a public library and a shopping mall were damaged. On November 7, marking the apex of the disturbances, after the prime minister had delivered a speech on television, about 1,200 cars were burnt in 300 localities around the country. Then a decrease in activity occurred and, after November 14, the number of torched cars averaged a hundred a night. The weather had turned cold, the actors were tired, numerous arrests were followed by simultaneous judicial processes and the declaration of a state of emergency had been imposed on November 9.

Over 10,000 vehicles were burnt (4,207 in the Parisian region), and damaged or burnt were 233 public and private buildings, 7 bus depots, 22 buses or trains and 18 religious sites. Overall, 4,770 persons had been stopped (2,808 during the crisis), 4,400 taken into custody and 800 incarcerated (including over 100 juveniles). Approximately 11,500 civil servants, including 4,500 police officers and gendarmes (60 units per night) were mobilized on November 13 and 14. Over 200 of them were injured during the outbursts (Waddington et al., 2009, 5). More than half of the violent actions took place in three regions: the Paris region (35 per cent), the Lyons region (10.7 per cent), the North (7 per cent); in 40 per cent of the urban problem zones.[9] Damage has been estimated at €200–250 million, according to insurance companies. Limited copycat attacks occurred in neighbouring countries. As in London in 2011, world-wide media coverage was given to the incidents.

5.3 Interactions between police and violent contenders

5.3.1 The nature of the interaction

In English debates from the early nineteenth century, 'the French "model" of police was held to exemplify the unacceptable face of policing – centralised, at the bidding of government ministers, used to spy on and harass political opponents and sometimes ordinary people, and little concerned about the welfare of citizens; yet the practice of policing in Britain and France is not as different as this simplification suggests. They have become even closer in recent decades' (Anderson, 2011). In both countries, in the last thirty years, with a few exceptions which are considered here, major changes have impacted on the style of public-order policing and evolved towards a more 'negotiated management approach', more benign control tactics restoring, maintaining or enhancing police legitimacy, with a few exceptions which are studied here. Public-order policing is indeed not simply reactive, it entails a dynamic interaction between police and offenders which can pre-empt potential disorder or trigger a mutual spiral of conflict (King and Waddington, op. cit, 119). The issue at stake is whether a lack of experience and confidence in dealing with disorder on an intense scale can be tolerated (Metropolitan Police 2012:120). When there are too few positive signals of government legitimacy within a community to encourage compliance, it is possible that 'rioters' and looters could overwhelm an untrained police force which has weak powers?

In each context of disorder identified above, the role of the police has played a major factor. The dynamics of disorder unfold on two levels: firstly, the organization of the police, the configuration of power, the role of public opinion, police culture and the interaction with protesters are influential (della Porta and Reiter, 1998, 2). For instance, it is likely that the top management level of the Metropolitan Police in London, suspected of corruption after the phone-hacking scandal and having lost their chiefs, initially hesitated as to what course to follow. Also, many police officers and commanders were on leave at this time. Police were blamed for reacting insufficiently at the beginning of the unrest. That the police were understaffed and lacked appropriate equipment may have been also due to cuts in public services. When public emotion was at its peak, 80 per cent of Londoners actually wanted the army to intervene, criticizing police handling of the social agitation. It would appear that British police are currently not need to be retrained for 'the immense challenge' of order-maintenance during intense disorder (Metropolitan Police 2012:116). (Only 5 per cent of policemen, for example, carry weapons.) Yet certain units, using paramilitary tactics, are so trained. On the whole, the tradition of order-maintenance in England is, on the whole, different from that of France.

Secondly, police knowledge which embraces the perception of their role and of the environment that shape their own strategy and tactics on the ground. At every stage, an event can turn one way or another, according to interactional dynamics between police and protesters. Is it possible that particular (militaristic) forms of police behaviour may have the unintended effect of contributing to disorders instead of stifling them (Marx, 1970)?

5.3.2   Police organization

Local police maintain a long memory of events in which they are involved, and the previous interactions with specific groups enable them to elaborate their operational strategies. During the Bristol and other disorders in the United Kingdom, the local police were poorly protected and unable to avoid the bricks and bottles thrown by hostile youths. Many policemen were wounded. Gradually, riot gear consisting of fireproof overalls, visor helmets and shields were introduced (Joshua et al., 1983). Later, tear gas canisters, water canons and flashball guns were provided as additional protection. For Marx (1970), such equipment exacerbate tensions. The relative anonymity afforded the police by their visors, shields and weapons, and the collective dimension of the charge allow possible excesses against antagonistic, similarly undifferentiated groups. During the summer of 2011 in Britain, there was however debate regarding the use of force, of attenuating energy projectiles (AEP), baton rounds and water canons (Metropolitan Police 2012: 120). While it makes sense to use them when the police confront opponents, such as student demonstrators, who march in line, water canons cannot be used easily to reach very mobile individuals who resorting to guerrilla-style strategies. It has also been pointed out that allowing cars to circulate and bystanders to cross effective handling of police lines was not appropriate. Further investigation is necessary, as the events are as yet very recent.

Controlling disorders may generate contradictory emotions among policemen: fear, anger and frustration at the idea of losing control, but also positive feelings. Commanders may experience problems controlling their men and, in the general chaos, the chain of command and communication can sometimes be broken. Some policemen may then be tempted to teach a lesson and retaliate against provocateurs rather than strictly abide by ruled law. It is difficult for the police to isolate and neutralize small, violent groups moving inside relatively moderate crowds.

5.3.3   Police and context

It is common view that policemen better manage public disorder if they are familiar with the context of intervention. Information can be provided by intelligence services or by officers policing by 'consent' in the communities and getting citizens' cooperation because they are respectful, fair and trusted (Tyler, 1990). Then police action can be properly targeted. The nature of the relationship between protesters participants and police in specific contexts may explain why disorders either persist or rapidly stop. Regarding the British cases, Sheffield illustrates this perception. Disorders ended rapidly, in part because the routine context of interaction between West Indian youths and the local police was not tense. By contrast, in Burnley, according to Home Office reports, the police ignored the climate of racist hostility existing prior to the Burnley riots, as well as Asian fear and mistrust. They did not connect the stabbing of two young Asians from racial motivations. Instead they emphasized the criminal nature of the act. Likewise, they made no links with a subsequent assault on an Asian cab driver. They remained passive when Asians complained about no-go areas where antisocial behaviour led to drug trafficking, prostitution and racial harassment (Webster, 2007). 'While the principal blame ... undoubtedly rests with the White racist youths intent on attacking and intimidating the town's Asian residents, specific police practices further ripped apart the social fabric of Burnley' (King and Waddington, op. cit., 131; 135).

In the United Kingdom in usual circumstances, importance is attached to police leadership, legitimacy, trust and respect of procedural rules – consequently, to the nature of the relations that the police have with the local population among whom they work. The Beetham model (1991), according to which the governed give consent to authorities to exercise their power if they do so in a way consistent with their moral beliefs, prevails. But in a situation of public disorder described here, is the 'militarization' of the police, provoking rather than quelling public unrest 'without public debate or accountability' (Waddington, 1992, 185)? Both French and British approaches then begin to look alike.[10]

Concerning the French police's approach to disorder, several features distinguish it from that adopted by the British. According to the Weberian model (1922/1991), a centralized authority to which policemen are accountable controls the national police of 260,000 personnel recruited nationwide. France is usually silent on potential issues of institutional racism, and this situation prevails because public institutions generally deny that discrimination based on race, ethnicity, age or gender actually exist, or that in certain areas abusive practices may do occur. General interest is provided by the state and, unlike in pluralistic systems, does not result from bargaining between various interests groups followed by negotiations and, at the end, by a compromise after which a common interest is supposed to prevail for the good of all. Generally, in France, it is taken for granted that citizens are expected to obey the law and police officers to follow established rules. It implies that policemen look at themselves as professional outsiders, particularly so if they belong to the anti-riot squad (Compagnie Républicaine de Sécurité – CRS).

Increasing tensions confront young rank-and-file police sent to troubled areas, where live a minority of contentious youths belonging to visible ethnic minorities (Roux et al., 2011). The police are indeed required to keep these zones under control and they do so by massively saturating public space with officers, creating a 'siege-like' presence. They have no knowledge of the context of the area in which they operate. 'Negotiation, mediation and prevention are alien, some might say, forbidden, practices' (Mouhanna, 2008, 175). As a consequence, the national police patrolling such problem zones operate in a wholly hostile context. In Seine-Saint-Denis, the most deprived administrative unit (department), 41 per cent of those polled in a Euro-Justis survey do not trust the police (Roux et al., 2011). When disorders occur, however, French police demonstrate a real know-how, arresting protesters without hurting them. In 2005, they were praised for their efficacy and became models for a number of police forces abroad. Yet, in 2005 (as in 2011, in the United Kingdom), the French police did not anticipate the virulence of disorder. Inappropriate responses, misjudgement of the situation, too few police officers deployed in the beginning have characterized these strategic errors, allowing disorder to spread to many localities in both countries. Different units converged at the same places without knowing each other or having their mutual roles defined. The advantage of a centralized police system was offset by its drawbacks (Roché, de Maillard, 2009, 40). In both countries, the resentment and hatred that some youth felt at the very sight of the police exacerbate emotions (Body-Gendrot, 2008; 2012, forthcoming).

5.4   Making sense of the disorders

Numerous explanations have been offered for the civil unrest and the destruction that happened in specific British and French cities. It is now time to test the structural, political/ideological, cultural, contextual, situational and interactional variables as conceptualized by Waddington in his flashpoint model, and find out how or if they apply to the British and French cases. According to this model, an incident becomes a catalyst, in the interpretation of it on the spot. Due to interaction, the situation, its context, and so on, all kinds of variables then begin to overlap.

In both countries, at the start, undoubtedly, a *flashpoint*, a *trigger event* 'sparks' the disorder. The underlying social conditions provide the tinder required for a conflagration. The *immediate precipitants*, or trigger events, involve youths and the police[11] (Benyon, 1987, 33).

Crowd formation expands along as soon as an incident takes place in an area distinguished by tensions and hostility; then the rapid circulation of rumours, the contagion of behaviours, the fluctuation of collective emotions and finally the media coverage of events structure the dynamics of unrest. This description fits the cases above and so does the scenario of normality, high tension, disorder, de-escalation, normality. The transition from one stage of seriousness to the next is rapid, and a climax is reached usually after three or four nights. Then, tensions linger for a while and the police have to contain them to prevent disturbances from starting anew. The time it takes to return to normality depends on context, the efficiency of repressive measures taken, the residents' responses and many include also, ironically, the change of weather, and so on.

5.4.1   The structural level

This approach incorporates the relative deprivation thesis, patterns of discrimination, police harassment and political powerlessness experienced by youth protesters.

In the 1980s, disorders occurred at a time when major transformations hit the labour force, reinforcing the exclusion of working-class households severed from affluent societies that are focussed on consumption and on social mobility. The economic crises translated into violent outbursts in localities experiencing the transition from a Fordist to a service economy one, along with a decrease in welfare protection, the effects of which are 'deleterious' (Gurr, 1981, 338–40).

Not all minority households experienced the same treatment, however, but many alienated Whites did. Consequently, the relations of these groups of citizens to institutions and to the police were frequently tense.[12] Racial disadvantage and discrimination, high unemployment (especially among young males whose families came from former colonies territories), widespread deprivation (substandard housing, environmental decay, crime, inadequate provision of educational and social services), political exclusion and powerlessness, extensive mistrust of the police, especially among youths subjected to 'stop and search' procedures and related forms of harassment and abuse cumulate in specific urban spaces (Benyon, 1987, 33–34).

With globalization, inequalities have skyrocketed in cities, creating more polarization between London and Paris centers, for instance, and their distant urban outskirts or working-class peripheries (the manufacturing cities in the North of England, the *banlieues* of Lyons or Paris). The transformation to a post-industrial economy and the impact of globalization have reinforced a pronounced economic Mismatch between job offered by firms and job residents can fill (in Europe, 14.4 per cent of the eighteen to twenty-four-year-olds drop out of school each year with no degrees. According to a 2011 European Union report on education, they are 12.3 per cent in France, that is, over 252,000 students).

In Burnley, the large public housing estate where two thirds of Asians live is among the ten poorest areas of the United Kingdom; 85 per cent of those under sixteen live in dependent families; 60 per cent of young Asians drop out of school with no degree (King and Waddington, 2004). In the 2011 events, two thirds of youths brought to the courts lived in the 10 % lowest income areas and received free school meals. Of the 66 riot areas, 30 were in the top 25% most deprived (Singh et al., 2012, 11).

French disorders erupted in areas benefiting from a form of territorial affirmative policy, the urban policy (*politique de la ville*), which is a redistributive policy justified by the areas' poverty, illiteracy, unemployment, of the number of youths under twenty-five, single-parent families, foreign households experiencing most of the urban violent incidents in France, has in the last thirty years the highest unemployment rate in the country. It also has the youngest population and the highest number of foreign families in comparison. The unemployed households totalled 13.9 per cent at the end of the summer of 2005, versus 9.8 per cent nationally. The number of households receiving public assistance went from 38,000 to 48,000 between 2002–05 (Kokoreff, 2006, 156). Clichy-sous-Bois is the poorest locality in this department. Its rate of unemployment rate reached 23.5 per cent in 2004 (and 16 per cent in 1993) and 31 per cent of youths under twenty-five. Dependent families make up 67.4 per cent of the population, and 46.6 per cent of households are under the poverty threshold. One third of the residents are non-national immigrants and among them, 60 per cent are jobless (Kokoreff, 2006:166).

The relative deprivation theory reconsidered

While there is something to be said for deprivation theory, it does not provide a sufficient explanation for the events which transpired in Britain and France. First, levels of poverty, unemployment and other distress factors show that other cities that were just as deprived as those that erupted did not experience disorder. Second, it is not when governmental subsidies decreased (in France in 2002) that disorders occurred in marginalized areas. The projected cuts had not yet been implemented in 2011. Third, the deprivation theory depends upon violence being caused by a vertical hierarchical relationship between the establishment (in the form of dominant elites or a controlling government) and minorities at the bottom. In fact, in the British examples, until 2011 the major conflicts were lateral, between ethnic/racial groups occupying the same city space (Nottingham and Notting Hill, Burnley, Oldham and Bradford). In France, while lots of disorder opposed youths and police, a majority of them were caused by youth feuds. These factors suggest that a complex skein of factors, including but not limited to deprivation, interact (Body-Gendrot and Savitch, 2012, forthcoming).

A correlation to deprivation theory is affected by a complexity of factors. Firstly, the data provides a static picture of neighbourhoods and does not reveal the high turnover of residents, which is more important in these zones than elsewhere. As better off families move out of public housing projects, the statistics of a place worsen. Secondly, in France, the maximum redistribution priority is given by authorities to sites according to risks of violence, and less to their level of deprivation. Many outbreaks of disorder involved youths occurred in free enterprise zones (Lagrange, 2009, 111) where expectations were high and, when unmet, open frustration. In Britain in 2011, poor neighbourhoods as those more affluent were subject to rampage, with as yet no convincing explanation as to why this was the case (cf. Reading the riots 2012).

5.4.2   The ideological/political level

This approach refers to attitudes in neighbourhoods perceived as tinder boxes. These attitudes have been shaped by various time lengths: the long time of colonization and decolonization and of migrations; the median time, the thirty years of urban confrontations; and the short time of disorders in specific contexts. Such various spans of time may influence the nature of the interaction between police and protesters (Blanchard, 2007; Jobard and Levy 2011, 190). In England, British citizens from the Commonwealth arrived as early as the end of the late 1940s. They were recruited by firms looking for increasing their additional labour force. A similar situation took place in France, at the end of the Algerian colonization in 1962, but immigration had started much earlier. There was a bureau for the surveillance and control of North Africans at the Police Prefecture as early as 1925.[13] An important difference is that a British 1948 law gave migrants the right to settle wherever they wanted without any restriction and with the same social and political rights as old-stock British. In France, however, immigrants from the colonies and former colonies did not benefit from the same social and political rights as the French (Joly, 2007). In both countries, these migrants' arrival did cause concerns in commotions in working-class neighbourhoods where they settled; they disrupted previous arrangements, compromises and norms of social control, and as a result xenophobia hardened. Migrants often went to neighbourhoods which were already experiencing social disorganization. They imported perceptions of the police linked to their home country where enforcement of codes of ethics hardly existed. Yet, until the first oil shocks of the 1970s, in both countries, full-employment economies allowed new and old residents to live side by side, without major conflicts.

The popularity of far-right ideas is probably more pronounced in France, but groups of White youths in Britain have also been motivated by a nationalist ideology. The intrusion of hooligans on soccer stadiums has been analysed at length as translating a malaise with nationalist and generational connotations (Cohen, 1972; Elias and Dunning, 1986; Tsoukala, 2009). Notting Hill and Burnley are also such cases where far-right ideologies fuelled racist views among working-class youths. More generally, vulnerable categories in the two countries feel threatened by immigrant newcomers and their offspring and express their resentment to visible neighbours whom they perceived as the cause of their downward social mobility (Body-Gendrot, 2010a, 194). The concept of multiculturalism is, as a result, questioned as in other European countries.

It is usual for political elites, when order is breached, to refer to urban unrest in problem neighbourhoods as external to mainstream culture and traditions. The rhetoric emphasizes an external provocation upsetting inclusive values (Benyon, 1987; Body-Gendrot, 1993). In 2011, Prime Minister David Cameron highlighted on the moral decay and 'sick' culture of the looters who were not part of mainstream society. Meeting with ad hoc groups in charge of domestic security crises, he correlated violence with a lack of social responsibility. The problem, he stated was not poverty, but a culture that glorified violence, showed disrespect to authority and said everything about rights but nothing about responsibilities, he said.

What occurred in France in the 1980s is related to the progressive autonomy of the issue of juvenile delinquency, formerly linked to immigration. It was also during those years that the beginning of a civil rights movement emerged. It collapsed however after three years due to internal divisions, localism and the cooptation of the issue by the Left, in power. At that time, many French became aware that immigrant families would not return to their home countries and that integrating (i.e., assimilating) them in the mainstream would take longer than with previous immigrant (frequently Catholic) waves. This is in part because of the association of violence with Islam in the imagination of an old Roman Catholic country which had prevailed for centuries.

Successive governments in Britain and in France have thus been confronted by the negative reactions of lower middle-class populations who resent the competition and disruptions brought by newcomers. In return, those newcomers were frustrated by their inability to compete on an equal basis due to racism and over discrimination.

But while the media's and politicians' interpretation was to emphasize a deficiency in immigrant families' social integration, mobilized protesters had another explanation. They wanted to confront police officers living happily in their own world and to fight them, one on one (Jazouli, 1992, 22). The same claims were heard again in 2005 and also in Britain in 2011.

5.4.3   The cultural level

The importance of subcultures cannot be ignored and point at misunderstandings between the police culture and the cultures of various youth groups' cultures.

Young British Whites' aggressive behaviour has been interpreted as overcompensation due to their social marginalization, their poverty and their contempt for established norms. Being unable to find ready access to the labour market, they take pride in an exacerbated masculine culture, leading them to lethal behaviour, to confrontation and to continuously challenging the police (Campbell, 1993). Consequently, any police force intervening at the residents' request becomes a flashpoint in a tinderbox.

Disenfranchised youths resort to physical violence when no other channel of political and ideological expression is available to them. Another dimension was put forward during the unrest of 2011. A subculture of 'greed', granting excessive importance to consumption led many individuals to loot stores and enjoy it, without any sense of displaying hardly any guilt in at doing so. But late-night shopping (looting) is not a subculture per se.

Young policemen share a professional culture after they enter the police, as shown by numerous research. Maintaining order in city streets which mainstream society ignores frequently appears as 'dirty work' to them. In France, police recruits almost never come from high-risk urban zones. Ninety per cent of those coming from provincial localities and assigned to those areas share a middle and lower middle-class culture influenced by negative images seen continuously on television. They are not familiar with multicultural high-risk zones and were not trained to be. It is difficult for them to distinguish among youths with hooded sweatshirts and hip-hop-style clothes, and to spot actual offenders from other youths (Bellot and Thibau, 2008). In 2007, an 86 per cent turnover of police chiefs (not to mention the high turnover rate in police rank-and-file) was observed in Seine-Saint Denis.

5.4.4   The contextual level

The circulation of rumours, the history of the location, the media coverage of issues in these localities – these all contribute to the understanding in the unfolding nature of specific disorders. In most cases, rumours have started a spiral of amplification. In Burnley, rumours mentioned that a large fascist march was about to take place and that Asian neighbourhoods would be attacked. The new Asian generation resents the political compromises of its community leaders. It denounces police passivity. Consequently, it organizes for confrontation. In a mirror effect, each group exacerbates its stereotypes, its intolerance, and its hostility (Waddington, 2001, 455). According to official reports, racism certainly played a role in the escalation of tensions, but only a partial. Alcohol and drug disputes increased the antagonisms felt by Whites and the desire for revenge among Asians.

In the 2005 French incidents, a series of mishaps helped explain the virulence. At the beginning of the mobilization, the local mayors' emergency calls were not received at the police headquarters in Paris. Thereafter, the media's extensive coverage generated a 'copycat element'. They could not resist counting the number of burnt cars, the number of impacted neighbourhoods. The result was a Top Ten of the '"hottest" cities, which stimulated youth of nearby cities to engage in still more violence and damage' (Cincelli et al., 2006, 35). The same observation applies to White British youths, who became icons from Toulouse to Tokyo in the 1990s, although they had never left their public housing projects (Campbell, 1993, 3).

Youths whose culture has been moulded by television are eager to be seen on the evening news. In 2005, reporters observed that these youths would mass around cell phones in the hope that journalists would speak about them. Why was such extensive coverage given to repetitive events dominating prime-time news for three weeks? The media and Sarkozy's political opponents were probably hoping that he would repeat the mistake the previous government had made in 1986 when, during a student demonstration, a young man, Malik Oussekine, died while being chased by a motorcycle police squad. The national upset caused by this event is said to have helped the victory of his opponent in the presidential election (Fillieule and Jobard 1998, 82).

What happened in 2011 in England is a different matter. Many youths did not hide their face with bandanas or hoods; they celebrated their loot in the public spaces and were caught by cameras then used by the police to prosecute them.

In 2011, howing how easy looting was, the media bear a responsibility for attracting opportunists to specific locations. They act as a magnifying glass, playing on the same images and using the same terms over and over, weaving a narrative to make sense out of isolated acts taken out of their context. With this rewriting function, the media create movements *à distance*.

5.4.5 The situational level

Divergent interpretations given to a specific territory, involving adversaries with different cultures may ignite confrontations. Besides, for instance, the racial dimensions of the conflict in Sheffield, a generational claim was formulated: Blacks felt that they were targeted in a place that they regarded as their sanctuary, distinguished by their regular presence, a space where, they felt safe from customers and storekeepers hostile to them. By contrast, for the police, a mall is a public space allowing very diverse group of people to come and go and shop without being bothered. It is their conception of order. Forms of gathering in a 'black space' are thus perceived by them as a nuisance hampering the flow of people. Controlling a mall is a potentially dangerous situation for the police, due to fluctuating crowds and uncertainty regarding the media's support. The will of the desire for containment may explain why the head of the police brigade wanted to display force as fast as possible.

Space was also a source of contention in Burnley between White youths and Asian households in public housing projects. The issue of space, of territory ownership, isomnipresent in all the French cases: youths defend their turf against the intrusion of the police, perceived as a hostile gang. Due to power associated with place, conflict is inevitable in most cases. Space is to be understood as a composite of multiple differences. It is a construct, resulting from social practices, ideologies and power relations. It questions shared uses, opposed to 'gated' ones, permissive tolerance contrasting with rigid codes of enforcement.

Why unrest spread rapidly from one neighbourhood to another in 2011 in London provides an interesting difference with Paris. Seen from London, affluent Paris looks like a medieval fortress, well protected by two ring roads. Outbreaks thus usually take place at the margins, where households' social handicaps multiply. The boundaries of London neighbourhoods and of other British cities are less sharply delineated. There are mixed areas near the center within walking distance from less well off areas. The unrest spread in a limited number of London neighbourhoods, from east to west, according to opportunity. As in Los Angeles in 1992, fluidity and mobility allowed youth bikers, their BBM in hand, to move on rapidly from one area to another, taking advantage of what was at hand, or with an objective in mind that must only be revealed later. Vandalism also hit socially mixed areas.

5.4.6   The interactional level

In the outbreaks analysed above, social ties, structures and processes interfere. 'Ideas about proper and improper uses of violent means, about differences among social categories, and about justice and injustice undoubtedly shape people's participation or non-participation in collective violence' (Tilly, 2003, 5–6). Some groups are more ready than others to inflict violence. 'Relations certainly matter as well ... Official defence forces ... play significant parts in collective violence' (Ibid.). The specific circumstances which triggered the events and the structural dimensions brought forward in the interpretation interplay to various degrees, according to context. In Clichy-sous-bois, a fraction of fifteen to twenty-year-old male youths from poor areas, frequently of immigrant/minority origin (because their families are the major component of the less well off) acted out of emotion and anger after a trauma. The incidents involved young cohorts of Arab, African, French and Muslim backgrounds clashing with the national police in impoverished localities. By any measure, it was not, however, most of the youths nor all the subsidized localities which mobilized (60 per cent of them did not). Youth – a deceptive word – is very diverse, some may be students, some have regular jobs and keep away from the justice system, some are high school students eager to have fun and others are idle and resentful – attitudes and trajectories vary along a wide spectrum. Resentful youths frequently (maybe 5 per cent of a cohort?) set fire to public property, including some primary schools (close to their housing projects, schools are the symbol of their frustrated hopes for mobility) but, according to Mohammed (2006), it seems that the choice of targets is discussed collectively and the risks assessed. In the 2011 events, youths reported a wide range of motivations.

Facing them, inexperienced or under-manned policemen interact with crowds of angry youths. They do not understand their codes of behaviour nor their frustration at having to share space with the police or show their IDs to them. In return, these youths resent police domination but they also feel numerically superior. Respect is an important value for both groups of contenders. When it is ignored in interactions, when all channels of communication are blocked or absent, disorder represents one form of interaction. After the 2011 unrest, some of the judges asserted that they wanted to restore 'respect, rectitude and responsibilities', that is, the mainstream moral codes supporting personal responsibility.

5.5   A comprehensive approach

The variables examined above influence the explanations of disorder. However, a comprehensive approach and a comparative analysis of national interpretations also seem justified and will be added to the overall frame. In a work comparing the unrest in Los Angeles in 1992 and in Greater Paris in 2005, Savitch and Sophie Body-Gendrot (2012) supported a comprehensive approach, emphasizing the operation of multiple forces which, in the course of events, came together to produce a particular outcome. Initially, these forces may be independent of each other, but interpenetrate as events unfold. Thus, the decline of employment opportunities for inner city residents may be independent of discord between police forces and city hall, yet in combination with other circumstances debilitating the community (among youths, increased school dropout rates, inter-ethnic tensions, drug trafficking and alcoholism). Those elements can combine to create a highly combustible compound.

The murky problem of why disturbances occur can also be illuminated by thinking about the obverse: why do not they occur more often in situations where we might expect them? The answer can best be obtained, initially, by acknowledging that civil strife is relatively rare and, next, by suggesting that when collective violence does occur, it is catalyzed through a labyrinth of relatively discrete, highly dispositional events which, at a defining moment, fold into one another. It is this combination of chance, context and causation, which may explain why disorders occur (Tilly, 2003; Body-Gendrot, 2010a). In Britain and in France, the demonstrators were not drawn from Bond Street or the Champs Elysées, but from depressed housing projects in the northern suburbs (*banlieues*) of Paris, at the periphery of other cities or within poor English inner cities. In both countries, segregation is an important factor in both countries. The idea of political regime is commonly applied to urban politics (Stone, 1989). Regime stability is defined as formal and informal arrangements through which conflict and social change can be managed. In the French and British cases, the conservative coalitions in power had an agenda and launched policies of austerity that weighted more on vulnerable categories than on bankers. From one country to another, conservatives respond to expressions of violence differently. The national dimensions have thus to be examined with such parameters in mind.

5.6   National divergences in response to disorders

In examining urban unrest comparatively, it is one cannot help how much the explanatory dimensions are similar (economic hardship, political disenfranchisement, police–youth tensions, identity relations and territorial contests, flashpoint thesis and so on.) and yet, when it comes to responses how much they differ on either side of the Channel, when it comes to responses. Why refer to national parameters? First, Britain and France are two old nations with comparable national political traditions, colonial involvement and post-war immigrations (Favell, 2001, 8). Historically speaking, their political experience has been central to the development of enlightenment, democratic ideas, rules of law and so on. Yet dealing with the fate of poor youths of immigrant origin, policies of assimilation/racial and ethnic differentialism distinguish French and British approaches, as already stated. 'To make sense, each needs to be translated into the terms and language of the other...The tenacity of the nationally particular and idiosyncratic terms and ideas by which immigration and integration questions have been answered...has over time clearly created a series of anomalies in policy practice, hence new political problems' (Ibid.). Favell refers to this phenomenon as 'path dependency', *repli sur soi*. It is the power of path dependency that blocks internal adaptation and responsiveness to...problems' (Ibid., 26; 241). Thus, even, in a globalized world where low-intensity conflicts explode now and then, national paths of dependency explain why the state remains of central importance in handling issues of urban violence in France, and it also explains why subcultures impact on British political analyses and lead to reforms. In these strongly centralized countries, the upper levels step in, and the localities are not given real legal powers and resources to be on the front line to produce solutions to recurring urban disorders.

5.6.1   Violence, youth and state in France

The incidents evoked in the French case contain 'hundreds of different local and indeed parochial events, with each location unveiling its specific set of causes and forms of collective violence' (Jobard, 2009, 233). What is revealing is the scattering of different local revolts blurred by the media translation of events. Unlike May 1968, intellectuals have not participated in the *banlieues'* incidents, nor were they the youths' spokesmen during those nights of turmoil.

What can be learnt from the French perspective?[14] What are the differences between what looks like similar causes and processes and the numerous variations observed in time, place and social context?

To restrict the analysis to 2005, H. Lagrange (2009) remarks that, in the Parisian region, the new scenes of disorders appeared in a number of localities with large families of African origin. The strict segregation of these families translated into poor schooling, stigmatization, delinquency and economic disinvestment; the lack of stakeholding in the existing political and social order (and due to their isolation); and the absence of spokespersons, are all dimensions that overlap in any explanations. Community organizations delivering services are not usually the advocates or protest spokespersons for the have-nots. Mayors with police powers usually opt to call the national state to their rescue and put an end to the disorder. In the Parisian region, after the end of the long weekend brought residents back into the localities, they mobilized their own municipal policemen and private safety agents and summoned anti-violence cells, created years ago to confront disorders. In other words, they sought an alternative to mere repression and resorted to tools of social prevention. Mediators, volunteers (some of them religious leaders), parents and associations conducted surveillance at the locations at risk and talked to youths incessantly. In some places it was also the case that, after three nights of unrest, silent marches involved parents. These symbolic demonstrations of unity and solidarity reveal that the residents are not utterly without resources. But there is a time for residents' mobilization, which does not correspond with the time when civil unrest first erupts. Marseille, with numerous and accumulated civil resources and a real *savoir faire* in its deprived areas, has so far avoided civil unrest but is plagued by many crime problems.

Special mention should be made of public housing managers in charge of numerous housing units. Their accumulated expertise led them in case of disorders to: a) systematically review security systems, alarms, locks, CCTVs, lights, power rooms, elevators, basements, terraces, parking lots, vacant apartments and green spaces; and b) clear car wrecks immediately c) negotiate with youths, for instance, asking them to burn garbage cans elsewhere than on the project precinct. They had daily debriefing sessions with their partners (including local police) during the three weeks of outbursts. Yet these remain relatively minor responses.

The state did intervene to put an end to the disorders. Schmitt presents *order* as an effect and a major accomplishment of sovereignty. In principle, an unlimited competence for the state, an order not emanating from law, results from situations of exception, allowing the state to place its sovereignty above the law (quoted in Brown, 2009, 78; Agamben, 1998). In the French case, a state of emergency was pronounced by decree on November 9, referring to a law passed in 1955 at the beginning of the Algerian war.[15] Prefects were required to deport undocumented foreigners involved in the outbursts.

In terms of judicial efficiency, the curve of massive arrests (2,808 were stopped and frisked during the crisis) followed the curve of disorders and reveals that summary processes translated into heavy sentencing. According to a judge in the Parisian region, in more than one third of cases, charges were dismissed because the police evidence was not convincing enough. Most of the youths were accused of throwing stones (*caillassage*) and other objects at the police; others were indicted for arson or vandalism. Those convicted were sentenced, on average, to four months of incarceration, including two and a half months of suspended sentencing.

No commission of investigation was convened by the government. This can be interpreted as an unwillingness to implement significant changes before the national elections in 2007. Moreover any review of police behaviour was headed by an internal police corps. The reluctance of the state has to be emphasized, and in particular of the interior minister to publicly debate this on this topic, to explain and maybe to apologize (for instance for police behaviour relative to the tear gas at the entry of the mosque of Clichy-sous-bois). But perhaps top officials were cynical enough to bet on the lack of empathy from the French for these marginalized areas. They may have been right. After all, the stock exchange kept rising during the three weeks of disorders.

It is likely that the demonstrators' apparent powerlessness led to their orchestration of violence. As noted by Arendt (1972, 157; Braud, 1993, 22–23), the   use of public force, in return, may be interpreted as a failure of the central state and of political power to efficiently confront social problems in deprived areas with alternative strategies, as noted by Arendt (1972, 157; Braud, 1993, 22–23). No one will deny that urban regeneration policies in France have been launched by the state from the top down in an effort to purchase social peace via various schemes. But what is missing is citizens' participation in the solutions to their problems, which is a learning process. Disorders emanate from segments of the French population which are also the least connected to the mainstream and the least organized.[16] Ethnicity is not an organizing resource for visible minorities in France and does not even explain significantly the distrust some youths have for the police. The respect for fair procedures by the police, usually the case, or their denial is at stake. Other public employees' action in helping families, women, young children and older people should be mentioned, here, yet what civil unrest in deprived areas reveals is a symptom of the disconnection of distant governing coalitions from those youths who are the most difficult to reach. They are the most unable to form coalitions with political allies, a phenomenon best explained in *Protest is not Enough*, in the case of competing racial minorities in American cities (Browning et al., 1984).

The heart of the matter is that state agencies are ill-adjusted to these *banlieues*. The state knows how to act on long term trends, whereas media pressures require immediate responses. Its answers are usually technocratic, whereas à la carte, tailor-made measures are needed in terms of jobs, inequality, housing, education and civil rights. Large organizations and intellectuals speak in the name of the sensitive areas' residents and, in so doing, disempower them. Participatory democracy is considered negatively in France, due to the weight of a representative democracy not deserving of its name. The failure of integration in the sense of belonging and 'feeling part' of a multicultural society results from routine and conservative mechanisms characterizing French society and its system of political representation.

The disorders occur in zones where only 4 million residents live, out of 55 million nationwide. These zones are scattered, and this may explain the state's preference for incremental action.

5.6.2   The multicultural approach in Britain

In many respects, what has been said about France concerning the disorders could apply to Britain. However, due to the path of dependency identified to above, the governmental choice to analyse the disorders and put an end to them frequently has been, until recently when the theme of youths' moral decay has been prominent, done in terms of racial and ethnic issues. Regarding the 2001 disturbances, official reports suggested that multiculturalism allowed, or even created, the development of communities segregated by ethnicity. For instance, the Cantle report, points at 'parallel lives' preventing any form of understanding between Whites and Asians. Asian Muslims choose to self-segregate in order to protect themselves.

In that respect, the analysis of Amin, the editor-in-chief of *Ethnicities* (Amin, 2003) is noteworthy. Regarding racism, he points out that the British context has significantly changed in the last ten years and that this change had an impact on the disorders. When the Labour Party returned to power in 1997 and following the Stephen Lawrence case (MacPherson 1999; Rowe, 2007) there was a strong denunciation of institutional racism within the police, of discriminations and of hate crimes which stirred the public debate following the Stephen Lawrence case (Rowe, 2007). That such an issue was publicly discussed, he says points to a form of minority integration in British culture. This implies that belonging and citizenship cannot be reduced to the markers of the White race and to Old England values. Amin stresses that in parallel, nevertheless, the Thatcherite legacy persists, emphasizing 'the strangeness of Otherness'. It is within that trend that the nationalist reactions to the Burnley and Oldham disorders belong; they question cultural practices and the national belonging of British Muslims, a question met by the support to the National Front.

In 2001, the passive image of Asians broke into pieces.[17] The distressed condition of disadvantaged urban zones has been emphasized. This condition generated distrust in communities, exacerbated social jealousy, aggressive mutual surveillance and disenfranchisement on the part of many youths. In 2010, governmental action focused on education and improved policing. But, soon, with the budget deficit growing, spending cuts impacted on public services, including education and the police.[18]

Such cuts may increase distrust and encourage self-involvement. This observation points at leads to an important national difference in public reactions to urban violence.

Extensive British television coverage was devoted to victims and to their emotions during the 2011 events. Local authorities and methods helping citizens to do so via images caught by CCTVs called for public denunciation, while self-help and innovative collective actions aimed at repairing damage were praised. This trend supports conservative politicians' values and their goals. It would be unthinkable in France to publicly incite citizens to denounce troublemakers and have their pictures published on the front pages of newspapers. The very word 'denunciation' translates as *délation*, invoking dark episodes during the Vichy regime. French journalists and commentators (with a class-sensitive lens) enjoy blaming the state repeatedly for not implementing policies remedying structural deficiencies and inequalities. Blaming the police for causing social tensions, due to their lack of accountability, their methods of harassment and their disrespect is routine. Then, in a country with a strong Catholic tradition, which the revolutionary heritage of secular republican civic engagement has not succeeded in effacing, youths whose lives are chaotic, whose parents are over-whelmed and whose education is dysfunctional, are rarely identified as 'shaming' the nation. A culture of 'excuse' prevails. Juvenile court judges write editorials to support such a culture. That these youths belong to communities disintegrating from inside and outside is readily admitted. Nevertheless, in France this 'compassion' does not, among the majority, generate more public mobilization of solidarity with the *banlieues* British residents' spontaneous attitude of self-sufficiency, their expression of solidarity with victims and organization of collective actions, remind us of New Yorkers rushing to Ground Zero to help after 9/11. Although there seems to be growing incivility in sections of British society, declining civility and increasing non-cooperation with the police, surprisingly high levels of interpersonal trust distinguish British culture from that of the French.

The comparison of disorders in Britain and in France reveals convergences: urban outbreaks take place in territories bearing multiple indices of deprivation and housing populations of diverse cultural origins but with different trajectories of mobility. In such areas, the police/population relations are frequently tense and distinguished by distrust. However, it appears that Britain has been more successful at implementing reforms – or promises of reforms – in such areas. Urban unrest in the early 1980s had a positive effect on policing and race relations and for instance, more antidiscrimination measures were implemented, for instance. The recommendations of important commission reports opened the path to police reforms. Cuts introduced after large budget deficits in 2011 were partly blamed when significant unrest spread to British cities. However new reforms, such as cuts in the number of police officers and the election of 41 Police and crime commissioners (PCCS), while being temporarily held up by the House of Lords, may be will be introduced.

In France, there is no noticeable involvement of the far right and nationalist youths in the forms of urban violence analysed in this chapter. Conflicts are usually less perceived through a racial lens than a class lens. The police appear to be a more important key player in the processes of disorder due to the centralization, lack of accountability, its political instrumentalization. One can even speak of an over-investment by policy makers in attempts to secure sensitive areas distinguished by large public housing projects. It can in turn lead to paramilitary modes of policing and the saturation of space with officers. Conversely, disenfranchised youths may resort to disorder to intimidate local politicians and get from them what they would not get otherwise (summer camps for their younger brothers and sisters, public jobs, and so on.). Allocation processes would then rely more on bargaining processes and on tests of strength, than on routine multiculturalist policies (Jobard, 2009, 239–40). In France, another difference comes from cycles of unrest linked to recent migration patterns. It suggests that each cohort had in effect to find its own repertoire. Repetitive disorders since the 1990s have led nowhere, and there has been no significant difference of approach between Left and Right governments. 'The very essence of riots in France lies in their ritualized nature. By their low-intensity and their crumbly nature, they do not threaten mainstream society nor the very cities from which they emanate. They do not affect the balance of power nor the economy' (Ibid.). In comparison with other countries, many youths from poor immigrant families in France fail in the labour market, in higher education and in political representation more than others (Schain, 2008). Policies meant to buy social peace remain incremental and insufficient in improving their social mobility.

Currently, in the long term, civil unrest is a symptom of how institutions remain mentally cut off from populations that are unable to articulate their demands except violently, now and then, under the claim 'we are the 99 per cent'.

6
Conclusion: Global Cities' Challenges

Comparing is 'both about discovering surprising differences and unexpected similarities' (Nelken, 2010, 33). National and local histories, institutions, cultures, morals and political choices all lead to different options and various modes of *savoir-faire*, including law enforcement. Firstly, this research began by emphasizing the difficulty there would be in comparing global cities from the North and the South, the challenges regarding security that they confront and the responses that they offer. One of challenges, present all along, relates to notions of democracy, as anchored in Western history and culture, and to those in the new democracies of the South, where human rights count for less and struggles are more uneven and more contradictory.

Nevertheless, the vitality of the South's societies and their capacity for innovation is illustrated by the case studies presented above. Urban societies in the South have young democratic experiences. The optimistic presentations of current efforts – the policies of small steps – the involvement of various partners on the safety issue, better coordination of efforts, a more appropriate funding and training for public jobs meant to fight quality-of-life crimes, a vision of inclusion for the median-term future with new paradigm shifts, the articulation of a 'right to life' in some judges's decision: all these dimensions reveal that resilient social groups are aware of what is needed to establish alternatives for cities. 'It is indeed a great mystery: despite their colossal problems, global cities in the South are imbued with strong elements of hope, due to their past victory over military coups, apartheid regime, or castes' diktats and to the power that democratic processes generate' (Gervais-Lambony, 1995, xiii). Transnational solutions are in the making and globally, in a context of *openendedness*, ideas flow, are absorbed, transformed, experimented with and circulated again (Pain and Smith, 2008).

Secondly, the case studies also illustrate that similar terminology hides very different types of insecurity and urban challenges. Some of the causes and triggers of these are fairly obvious, while others are obscure, and even mysterious. Why unrest escalates, then abruptly fades or lingers, is also puzzling. The interaction of the global and the local in cases of terrorism and criminal gangs is straightforward, but less so for urban disorders.

Thirdly, part of the problem and part of the solution are to be found in the methods used by the police, the organization of policing, the nature of police–public relations and in the courts' processes. The term 'police' can be elusive: the nature, size and type of organization differ, although police missions in terms of order maintenance and crime solving are similar. Yet, some policemen are not adequately trained for order maintenance, as seen in the 2011 London case, while other police units resorting to paramilitary tactics cause numerous casualties and foment outrage among the citizens when checking riots, as in the case of São Paulo. Less dramatic stop-and-search approaches reveal more about police behaviour from one city to another than do statistics on the race and ethnicity of those stopped and searched. Linked to the issue of police capabilities, Sherman (1995, 36–37) wonders why there is so much focus on crime-prone individuals and not on dangerous spaces. Examining crime reports in Minneapolis, he found that crime was highly concentrated in a few locations, which he referred to as *hot spots*: 'Why aren't we thinking more about wheredunit, rather than just whodunit?' he asked. Shaw and McKay (1942) reached similar conclusions in their seminal study of high-crime and low-crime neighbourhoods in Chicago, showing how stable they were over time. My research follows this trend, examining spaces that produce deviant patterns. But what is also apparent is that the offender, the target and the external/internal control need to be understood jointly, since they involve features of urban governance which are to be compared.

Likewise, courts have diverse governing principles, although their missions are similar. Penal cultures differ along with population size, historical arrangements and features of criminal justice systems. Yet the case of Johannesburg reveals that the language of rights makes a difference in the context of a weak state. The South African Truth and Reconciliation Commission has sent an amazing message of courage and fairness to the whole world. Some institutions, still caught by their recent history, contribute to hope. So does the European Union, opting to govern through *security* rather than through *fear*. This examination leads us to wonder what a just and inclusive city is.

Fourthly, disorders and urban dysfunction point at acute problems of urban governance, of relations between levels of government as well as at flaws and obstacles in the policy-making process. Yet they also take initiatives and with their know how, demonstrate international capacities at conflict resolution. These points will be developed below.

6.1 The globalization context

Are there linkages between globalization inequalities and urban violence (such as crime, terrorism, riots, violent protest)? In other words, does the current influence of finance on various forms of capitalism promote and accommodate unbearable inequalities which, in turn, generate social tensions and dissent, thereby hampering the economic, political and social well-being of cities? If so, are global cities in less developed countries more vulnerable? (Body-Gendrot, 2011a).

There is no need to recapitulate that global (or globally aspiring) cities are in a prominent position to exert functions of command, control and planning in the organization of the world economy. Their wealth grows at a very fast pace and so does the power they exert on public and private sectors. Sassen (2009, 230) points out at new, distinct assemblages of territorial insertions, authority and national rights in specialized and highly singular fields allowing multiple transactions for various uses. She says that the eminent role played by technologies, by interactive numerical entities with their specific social logics, she says, introduce new boundaries and shifts of frontiers in more numerous places and institutions than one imagines when using the term 'city'. Competing bodies of law produce 'ambivalence but also enable divergent and competing city-law spaces' (Segbers, 2007, 11) meaning that cities can build alliances with each other and take initiatives. Expecting accountability and a sense of responsibility from such global players is utopian.

In this perspective, globalization – the interconnection of mass communication, finance, knowledge institutions, administration and force in a power network – yields an agreed view of the world for many decision makers in the financial, economic and political spheres of these world-class cities. Global dynamics do, indeed, generate jobs, profits, assets and power leadership and, although inequalities loom large between the advanced economic sector and the backward-looking sector of cities, as long as there is profit for everyone, little dissent is heard. But problems cannot be overlooked. On the one hand, these developments maximize the profits of a privileged stratum evolving in a fragile and unstable context. On the other, those whose skills do not match the new requirements of the global distribution of labour, or who do not have access to the appropriate spheres, or who cannot adjust to change – the 'useless normal' unfit or redundant – are set aside, 'downgraded', or excluded. Moreover, more and more members of the middle classes experience economic insecurity and downward mobility, especially at times of financial crises, as is the case since 2008. An additional problem comes from the crush of numerous locally transmitted traditions, reciprocal transactions, redistribution and specifics supporting democratic aspirations. Instead, a general homogenization of thoughts, practices and values is observed. While globalization favours competitiveness and winner-take-all attitudes (via flows of images, information and communication), dissent and conflict express forms of resistance in global cities. They vary greatly in function of national histories, cultures, inherited traditions, institutions, legal framework and accumulated expertise in development.

6.2   Urban inequalities

When examining urban inequalities, we should not simply focus on their extent, because they certainly were just as pronounced in the past,[1] but how the current phenomenon of globalization transforms their perception. Due to widespread global interdependence and communication networks, these inequalities are fully exhibited in numerous countries and foster a sense of injustice. In the 1980s, it was mainly the populace at the bottom who were affected. Since the 1990s, however, the middle classes started to feel the effects as well, while the upper classes have benefited after globalization and in 2010, the top 1 percent of Americans captured 93 percent of the income gains. The CEO of Walmart earns 900 times the wages of the average employee. In many companies, the chief executive is paid more in each day than the average worker receives in a year (Wilkinson and Pickett, 2010, 250).[2] The classic tool for measuring inequalities is the GINI coefficient, which gauges inequality across a society as a whole, rather than simply comparing the extremes. The higher the GINI coefficient, the less equal the society in question. In New York, it was (.50 in 2007), and in London (.32 in 1995). As for cities of the global South, inequalities are higher in Johannesburg (.75 in 2005) and in São Paulo (.61 in 2005), than in Mumbai (.35 in 2004). By comparison with developed cities, the GDP per capita is sharply lower in the South: $9,000 in Johannesburg (2005), $12,000 in São Paulo (2006) and $1,871 in Mumbai (2006) compared with $55,000 in New York (2007) and $60,000 (in London 2007) (Burdett and Sudjik, 2011, 296–300).

In an Institut Français d'Opinion Publique (IFOP) poll carried out in April 2010 among 7,200 people in twelve countries (including China and Poland), respondents expressed similar concerns regarding inequalities. In nine out of twelve countries, a majority perceived their society as unjust. This held for over 70 per cent of those polled in China, Italy, Germany and, first of all, Brazil. Europeans (83 per cent of Germans and 80 per cent of French) think that inequalities have increased in the last ten years. Strangely, in a country with extreme inequalities such as the United States, only 42 per cent of Americans do they are just 17 percent to think that it is extremely important for the government to try to reduce them (Gallup November 2011), the lowest on the list. Only in four countries (China, Poland, the United States and Brazil) does a majority state that globalization contributes to reducing inequalities, and for China and Poland, only, that it is not possible to really reduce them.

The consequences of such inequalities are, however, felt socially. They produce more fragmented societies and more distrust among citizens. Americans used to be a 'society of joiners', according to Tocqueville. Is it still the case? The global world, largely devoid of in-betweens and interactions, reveals the coexistence of isolated elites (dwelling in their own spheres, restricted to their insiders' references, spokesmen and power-brokers) with disenchanted, insecure and angry majorities of populations (especially disadvantaged young people who feel neglected by the governing coalitions and unable to modify these situations). This assumption needs to be re-examined, however. In August 2011, an American billionaire urged Congress to raise taxes on the highest wealth brackets. He was echoed by fifty rich Germans, more than a dozen French millionaires as well as by Italians. Was it merely, caring for other people? They may have been aware, watching social unrest spread in numerous cities of the world, that we are more interconnected than ever. Policies of austerity hit vast majorities, slashing public services, undermining economic growth and future competitiveness for generations to come, and making cities more dangerous. The social fabric is stretched, human capital squandered and the social contract linking all members of societies is open to question. A de-modernization of democracy takes place, in the sense that societies lack a powerful cement, a 'commonwealth' based on shared principles, values and practices. The level of inequality, however, is not automatically correlated with urban violence. New York City, for instance, has become a success story in that respect, but remains a very unequal city in terms of wealth. The curvilinear relationship between inequality and violence is difficult to establish (Wilkinson, Pickett, op. cit.).

6.3   Urban violence as an expression of the disempowered

Disorders that hit cities are both opportunities as well as events. They often highlight issues that are being ignored in the public discourse, such as situations of injustice and people's emotions. They do not make the headlines, but they make a difference. They form a connection between the global and the local (Body-Gendrot, 2011, 362). Urban outbreaks of disorder, disorder and, more generally, urban violence, are not just a threat for global economic players, investors, political elites and more generally, citizens whose daily life is disrupted. These disturbances give globalization its confrontational dimension, without immediately resorting to political claims. The urban sites targeted by terrorists, dissenters and demonstrators symbolize what global cities are in terms of flux and wealth, but also of social failures. These disturbances are a mode of social expression; they reinterpret public spaces as strategic sites and organize a drama in the context of marked and contentious territories (Sassen, 2010; Body-Gendrot, ibid., 362). They can also be perceived as a 'voice', or a least 'a cry', a signal that disjunctive democracies are going too far in their excess.

It would be hard to draw generalizations regarding the modes of violent expression described in the various case studies in this book. Events happening in the global cities of the South have been dissociated from those of the North and within each region, deconstructed one by one. Yet, they all convey ambiguities in the perception of disorder. Cities are both the material support and the symbolic (and strategic) stake that incidents of disorder need. It is rarely the rich categories who take to the streets and shout their discontent. In the case of terrorism, the so-called suicide bombers may also be regarded as fighters at war, denouncing the Westernization of the world, the domination of affluent societies, their grabbing of wealth, resources and assets, and the erasure of cultural diversity, as in the typology by Moisi mentioned in Chapter 1. The rich Western world fears the resentment of Arab/Muslim countries translated into terrorist *passage à l'acte*. In India, elites worry about Pakistani militant sects orchestrating violence for multiple reasons – including ideological – and aiming by those elites. If the world is in part safer since 9/11, old forms of urban violence, such as ethnic hatred or caste tensions, are continuously revived under new conditions. 'The fear of small numbers is intimately linked to the tensions produced by the forces of globalization' (Appadurai, 2007, 124).

Regarding notorious criminal gangs operating in São Paulo, Holston has powerfully analysed the use they made of the language of democratic citizenship, rights and justice to represent their own organizations and intentions and find support among working classes. Crime and terror were justified, in reference to the rationalities of citizenship: 'So ENOUGH, we only want our rights, and we are not going to give them up,' a leader of a Comando exclaims. 'It's no use, we are not joking, those who joke are in politics, with the total abuse of power and with this generalized robbery ... If the laws were made to be followed, why this abuse ?' (2008, 300–01). The gangs' public discourses denounce prisons' inhuman conditions, the inmates' humiliations and beatings and their request for minimal conditions for survival. Ironically, liberty, justice and peace are invoked as rights. Even killings of policemen are justified by the gangs because the killings often 'correspond to the expectations of citizens who are frustrated with the inefficacy of the justice system and who do not believe in the likelihood of security in a society with immense inequality. In this context, many citizens view police killing as a realization of their right to security' (Ibid., 307).

Similar analyses are held in Johannesburg. For masses of people living in slums, identifying with criminals is not justified, but it is easier to do so than with elites who are in another world. As remarked by Alinsky (1945) 'farm chickens are rarely the friends of foxes'. Every day, disorders in South African townships convey demands for public services. Elites evoke more distrust than gangs, some of whom are also distributing services to populations living at the urban margins, in the slums, the *favelas* or the townships.

Finally, protesting young people in disadvantaged localities, after incidents with the police, are blamed because of the damage they cause to the residents' everyday lives (burning their cars or vandalizing public schools, for instance) and, more fundamentally, because the disruption of order and of common rules cannot be tolerated. Yet parents, educators, teachers and religious leaders also point out that, although they do not excuse violence, they can understand it. Other forms of protest draw massive acquiescence. In the summer of 2011 80 per cent of Spaniards supported the protestors' demonstrations of resentment in the public space (*The Economist*, July 16, 2011, 32). A booklet published in France by Hessel (2010) and titled *Time for Outrage* has become an instantaneous best-seller in numerous countries. Even though urban violence was vehemently denounced in Britain in 2011, after the phone-hacking scandal urban outbreaks offered an opportunity for political opposition and the media to denounce ruling class excess, greed and moral decay,. This may explain why both Ms Thatcher, after the Brixton incidents of 1981, and D. Cameron in 2011, did not want to hear any sociological explanation regarding the linkages between inequalities, marginalization and delinquent behaviours – but, instead, only the advocacy of repression, better formulated by Tony Blair's sound bite, 'tough on crime, tough on the causes of crime'.

Urban violence is a mode of social expression, and cities are both the material support and the symbolic stake that disorders and protest need. Violence reveals issues with no political legitimacy, not on the government's agenda, and belonging to non-decision making. It is not clear what these issues stand for. Many of them have no worldwide echo, yet they resonate in the imaginaries, not in the communication, of youth cultures (Bertho, 2009). In troubled times, people walk out on the system and take to streets. In Tunis, Cairo or Tripoli, in Tel Aviv, Athens, or Latin American and American cities, disempowered citizens collectively measure their strength via the convergences that cities allow in their public spaces. In some cities, fear changes into indignation. Public protest and assembly are part of the social compact: such process breaks individuals' solitude and isolation. Urban space allows all kinds of grievances to overlap and bridge into a cementing ethos. The 'sense of place empowers protests' (Kimmelman 2011). The political power of physical space is too frequently ignored. 'Politics troubles our conscience but places haunt our imaginations' (*ibid.*). The interest of such mobilization comes from the very process and the visibility given to issues such as inequalities. 'The process is the message', wrote one occupier in Zucotti Park, New York ('We are the 99 per cent!'). There may, consequently, be a correlation between macro-economic developments, rising inequalities, the elites' loss of legitimacy and the dialectics of order and disorder. Where income differentiation is high, so is social stratification and distrust. Inequality is a powerful social divider but also, in times of stress, a unifier (Body-Gendrot, 2011a). Moreover, civil unrest is also a denunciation of the way public power-brokers have willingly supported, tolerated or been taken hostage by entrenched interest groups (such as bankers), fighting for the defence of their privileges all over the world.

As an important reminder, one should mention that only democracies can such urban violence break through. The Arab spring came as a surprise in 2011. Demonstrations are unlikely to happen, other than sporadically, in authoritarian political regimes and are violently repressed.

Violence signals, thus, a danger, a dysfunction and a general shortsightedness on the part of elites. National policies, strong in rhetoric ('doing something' to assuage public discontent), and incremental in enforcement (patchwork repair and interim solutions) characterize current urban governance (Body-Gendrot, 2011b).

6.4   Global cities' compromises

Before evaluating how global cities alleviate fear and insecurity, one should mention once more that national, state and regional governments (as well as private investors) maintain control over global cities and, when granting them power, do so in a limited way, whether in New York, London or Paris, or in the metropolises of the South studied here. In order to be able to pursue their own national or global goals, national and state governments ensure that global cities are not 'independent'. Dramatic social problems, conflicts, tensions and forms of violence resulting from global processes could be alleviated if, from the start, cities were included in the decision-making process and in transactions among various actors. Macro-level frames should be held accountable 'for the types of stress that arise out of everyday violence and insecurity in dense spaces' (Sassen, 2010, 1) – the type of issue that global governance discourse and its norms do not quite capture.

Cities are subject to domination by national and central governments, but, being closer to citizens, they also take advantage of their own perceptions of problems. Required to restore public order, states usually opt between policies of redistribution and/or punishment. 'Locking people up or giving them money might be considered alternative ways of handling marginal, poor populations – repressive in one case, generous in the other' (Greenberg, 2001, 70), a kind of trade-off between welfare and incarceration. By contrast, cities prove that multitudes of people may connect in harmony. They can act as sanctuaries for undocumented families and they know how to offer assistance and care to very diverse newcomers. As seen in the case studies, civic leaders at their best support values of reconciliation and tolerance.

Following Lijphart (1999), one should distinguish consensual (or socio-democratic corporatist) democracies (taking as many views as possible into account) – such as Switzerland and the Scandinavian countries, but also Austria, Belgium, France, Germany, Italy and the Netherlands in Europe – from majoritarian, neoliberal democracies (the majorities dictate the choices, and are also more populist), which include Australia, Canada, Ireland, New Zealand, the United Kingdom and the United States, among Western countries. Consensual democracies are more welfare-friendly, more prone to 'trade-offs' and incline toward leniency, while conflict democracies expresses more severity

(Ibid.). Moderate penal policies have their roots in consensual cultures and 'societies of equals' concerned with general well-being, whereas corporatist political cultures are more prone to apply punishment to 'others' and to the alleged undeserving (Lappi-Seppala, 2011; Whitman, 2003). Policing and justice functions are specific institutions held by national and regional governments in all the cases examined in this research.

Regarding the issue of the state as a vehicle for securing the maintenance of public tranquillity and safety, two conceptions of the state usually prevail. On the one hand (in Europe for instance), the ideal duty of the state in its sovereign role is to produce forms of trust and abstract solidarity via its hold on public space and services. This conception of security is social in the sense that the security of any individual depends in some important ways upon the security of others (Loader and Walker, 2006). The very idea of a 'private security' is odd, while 'commonality' or 'common public-ness' produced by the state and solidarity are not. On the other hand, the state may be perceived as tied to class interests, unfairly directed toward coercing the poor and the weak, unable to defend a common vision against narrowly defined private ones (Ibid.). This vision is shared in parts of the United States and in cities of the South.

The state's higher interest in terms of geopolitics, global aspirations and policies for the largest number of people are invoked for such a role. But they do not all choose the same course. In Norway, for instance, after the attack that took place during a youth conference in the summer of 2011, the government, the victims and the general public were unanimous in declaring that the best response would be to enhance democratic values and the rule of law. Norwegians turned to their leaders for answers after the shock, and received them. This country's consensual idea was that states have to support democratic values and tolerance to confront terror and not manipulate fear or play political games. Despite an aggressive presidential campaign, similar opinions were expressed in France in March 2012, after the killings of innocent soldiers and Jewish children by an Islamic terrorist were uniformly condemned. In the best cases evoked in this study, state institutions, such as the judiciary, may defend their own choices, refusing to yield to populist demands, for instance, and expressing the determination to treat offenders' rights with fairness. This is what the trend supporting restorative justice is about.

However, the identification, control, and surveillance of at-risk populations and places also show legal and empirical convergence with the United States. The social and cultural evolutions of the last fifty years display more emancipated, more individualistic, but more security-prone societies (Garland, 2001). That deviance is part of daily life has been accepted along with late modernity, yet tolerance of risk and danger remains low. Consequently, demand for zero-risk remains high in the case of centralized countries and subnational units and in cities in that of decentralized ones, states then pressure law enforcers and private forces to bring tangible results showing that control is exerted on offenders, opportunities for crime reduced and costs distributed fairly among offenders, victims and taxpayers. As remarked by Zedner (2009, 13; 21), 'the apparent inevitability of continuing crime, terrorism and other security threats underwrites the security industry and serves as an incentive for further investment'. It explains the proliferation of security hardware, services and technologies in all the examined cities.

Can cities in such context, when attempting to alleviate fears and insecurity, bypass states with their own innovative solutions? Friedman's hypothesis[3] has been tested all along this research, and the answer is negative, except for a few limited exceptions that will be clarified.

That states, empowered with a monopoly in the use of force, resort to repression to check urban violence and prevent its occurrence has been amply demonstrated throughout. In matters of terrorism, public opinion expects states to protect their citizens. There is no need to mention once more the use made of emergency legislation, specific counterterrorist laws, coordination of intelligence and enforcement services, reinforced police and courts with coercive powers, and accelerated judicial processes, not to mention the resources offered by the private security sector in terms of cameras, walls, bollards, and so on. But while states are, at least symbolically, regulators, they represent only one type of actor among other supranational and nonstate actors. Cities then continue to play crucial roles regarding rule-sharing and social integration, protection and equity-oriented redistribution, public housing provision, education, health and public transportation meant to improve mobility and to better conditions of living for those who cannot afford private services. Support is offered to victims. These policies produce more fairness, thus security in civil societies. But while states are regulators, at least symbolically, they represent only one type of actor among other supranational and nonstate actors.

Cities are powerless to change inequalities and power structures, but they can provide equity. Fainstein (2010, 36–37) suggests substituting the term *equity* for that of *equality* as a goal for a just city. The goal of equality is (indeed) too complex, demanding and unrealistic to be an objective in the context of capitalist cities'. Urban policies do not have sufficient scope to bring about equality but they can be more redistributive. Then, equity evokes 'fairness which is more broadly accepted value than equality' (ibid.). It is a 'more politically strategic term' and aims at bettering the situation of those who cannot cope without public intervention (ibid., 37). French historian Rosanvallon (2011) points out, however, that the use of equity is an attempt to mask inequality or to allay inequality's impact on the social fabric by incorporating notions of merit, skills, virtue or whatever. This may be so, but attempting to enforce equity is better than merely denouncing the rise of inequalities. This remark holds also for cities of the South.

The dilemmas confronting mega-cities come from the need to become, or remain, world-class cities and reduce crime, social disorder and threats of terrorism, on one hand, and on the other, to avoid and reduce the socio-economic fragmentation of their populations and the context boosting such risks. Should they pursue the dream of attracting global actors via efficient structures of control, organizing stock exchanges, attracting tourists and investors and creating financial opportunities? Or should their priority be alleviating poverty with larger redistribution, more basic public services and shared spaces? This option conveys the risk of greater deficits or even the threat of bankruptcy, (for example, the financial crisis New York City experienced in 1975 trying to accommodate too many demands). Political compromises are elaborated as second-best choices and should be evaluated case by case, the first-choice preferences (matching ideals and norms) being unreachable. 'Compromises are vital for social life, even though some compromises are pathogenic ... We need to actively resist rotten compromises that are lethal for the moral life of a body politic', Margalit observes (2010, 7).

This dilemma regarding compromises is felt more acutely in South metropolises characterized by a duality of globally connected elites on the one hand and, on the other hand, the larger populations living on the margins and engaged in daily struggles for survival with in-between classes trying to avoid a downward slide (Segbers, 2007). While the dilemmas faced by most world-class cities are different in scale, no option appears as being satisfactory in the long term.

6.5   Attempting solutions

Innovative solutions have been tested in the South, but face formidable difficulties. Take Mumbai, for example. Visions for promoting Mumbai as a global city region do not exist, according to Segbers (2007, 348). The power to implement any political agenda related to public safety is split among rival institutions and hypertrophied political parties. The administration has its own autonomy, and its boundaries do not coincide with political gerrymandering. Such lack of coordination works against a coherent strategy. Mumbai is a 'patchwork city'.

Its governance structure is fragmented, vertically and horizontally. Mumbai's 'globalized service economy thrives next to a "bullock-cart economy" without interlinkage' (Ibid.). The city also lacks adequate public services and infrastructure. The global elite requires informal work but is not ready to pay for it at fair-market prices. In this violent and rough context, tensions abound and inequalities and ethnic fragmentation make Mumbai vulnerable. An improvement in public services, public housing and governance would alleviate conflicts (Lorrain, 2011, 38; 393). But the mayor of the Municipal Corporation of Greater Mumbai has limited powers, legitimacy and expertise. Among a plurality of actors, she is in a position to impose her choices. It is arduous in pluralistic games led by opaque actors to find compromises and, too often, zero-sum games prevail, encouraging the status quo. Efforts deployed at the governmental level, especially in matters of law and order, do not reach informally run territories (Lorrain, Ibid.) Yet good urban governance is not the alpha and omega. External factors and outer forces weigh on the future of neighbourhoods, as much as does their specific cultures. Optimism for Mumbai in terms of safety may come from strong social cohesion at the community level.

In Johannesburg, the strategy to make it a world-class city is ambitious, and its approach is more coordinated than in São Paulo or Mumbai. The region is run by one political party, the ANC, which rules at all levels. Balancing and negotiating take place within party structures. New instruments for citizen participation have been introduced, but the locus of power remains in a few hands, perpetuating the geography of exclusion due to what Murray (2011) calls 'the inertia of long-term deployments'. According to Beauregard and Tomlinson (2007), the issue of exclusion is politically ignored by the city administration, making Johannesburg vulnerable to crime and social tensions. There is no awareness of the need for solving problems of safety or of horizontal and vertical conflicts. As in the United States, new segmented forums at the community level and encouraging public debates challenge neither the overall governmental structure nor policies, thus maintaining the status quo in favour of the affluent groups.

The authorities' long-term perspective is, however, that by the year 2030 Johannesburg will be a 'city of possibilities and promise, excitement and hope for the future' (City of Johannesburg, 2002, 3). There are doubts that this assumption may come true, due to the rate of poverty, unemployment, lack of public services, crime, and rates collection shortfalls, among other issues (Beauregard and Tomlinson 2007, 251). The truth probably lies in between: Johannesburg is not a kind of urban *noir*, as seen by architect Rem Koolhas, but more likely, a city of all possibilities.

São Paulo for its part appears to be a globalized but uncoordinated metropolis.

In the past, São Paulo overcame Portuguese domination and subsequent dictatorship before finding its own autonomy and modernity. Nevertheless, the top problems of the city are related to a lack of cohesion and to fragmented spaces and sectors. The elites' specific local culture tolerates high levels of inequalities and violence as long as they themselves are not threatened by it. There is a lot of work still to be done to provide equal justice to all and to improve safety.

Unlike global cities in developed countries that complain that they are bankrupt after each major financial crisis, the cities in the South come across as young, energetic and resilient. Which of these cities will succeed the best? It depends what their priorities and goals are. When designing growth strategies for global cities, it is important to keep 'the city' in mind. Only if the essence of the city is maintained and citizenship rights guaranteed (Beauregard and Bounds, 2000) can a project be successful in a sustainable manner. The essence of a city is urbanity, which can be translated as shared public space, where different cultures and classes can meet safely. Under such conditions, encounters with other people can serve as sources of ideas and innovations. But creating a shared vision for the city remains incredibly arduous.

The accumulation of sources of wealth and power, and the concentration of populations, will always make global cities targets for potential human-induced risks. While reducing inequality is beyond the cities' capacities, it remains in their power to choose measures and policies that will alleviate risks and make a difference.

What they can do in terms of cohesiveness relates to their unique cultures (inherited from decades of experience), to the supply of public services, to the use they make of public space, to architectural solutions, and so on. The social question is also a law enforcement question that can be interpreted in various ways. The cities' reservoir of resources is illustrated with a few examples related to urban cultures and to the use of public space.

6.5.1   Making use of urban cultures

Regarding the terrorist threat, cities are vulnerable, but they are also resilient.[4] A city's specific cultural assets have to be taken into account. Most residents of the cities hit by terrorism decide that, after the attacks, life has to go on as usual. Collective strength shows that a city does not die after a massive attack, not even Dresden or Hiroshima. People can make sense of bombs and suicide bombers; they are aware of what violence can do and why certain targets are chosen. 'People can handle their fears', Y. Rubenstein, a researcher at Tel Aviv University observes. 'They do so by acquiring the necessary skills' (Rosenthal, 2005). They are selective in their fear of certain risks, which allows them to get some control over their lives. In Madrid after March 11, 2004, the public transportation ridership dropped for two months, psychologist A. Lopez-Rousseau discovered. But on the day after the bombing, train travel was four times higher than normal as Spaniards attended huge antiterrorism demonstrations (Rosenthal, 2005, 2).

Many people refuse to dramatize risks. In a 2010 poll from the Pew Research Center, 65 per cent of Americans said that they would not renounce certain rights and liberties for the sake of the antiterrorist struggle (in 2002, in a *Newsweek* poll, 55 per cent had said they would). They thus showed that they were not mere passive recipients of experts' know-how, but had selective perceptions. The extreme care paid to other citizens in situations of crisis, and the subtle skills deployed to summon collective energies, appear to be as typical of large cities' capacities to allow many diverse people to live together safely. After each tragedy, residents tend to find the most adaptable solutions to confront fate, using their own repertoire of strengths.[5] A 'capital of sympathy' shared by individuals who do not know each other is what makes them gather in the streets, in forums and in public places. 'Against terrorism, the strong values of democratic regimes act as the best urban defence: an alert citizenry, a vigilant, honest and consistent press, a vigorous legislature, and an independent judiciary power', Savitch optimistically remarks (2008, x).

Proximity, indeed, is obviously not synonymous with social solidarity and, in that respect, the notion of community has to be deconstructed. Neighborhood watch raise (as many) of surveillance set up as many problems as they solve, and there are other solutions besides cameras in public places. In risk management, the notion of trust is a major requirement. French revolutionary Sieyès used to say that authority comes from the top, and trust from the bottom. The awareness is widespread that safety is not just a private commodity, but also a fragile 'public good' (Loader and Walker, 2006).

New York Mayor Michael Bloomberg, a Republican supported by a majority of Democratic constituents, promoted innovative urban transformation regarding the reconstruction of the World Trade Center in Lower Manhattan, the development of a new business area on the West Side, called Hudson Yards, and of a residential and commercial zone in Brooklyn, known as Atlantic Yards. Such post-9/11 developments, supported by public and private partnerships, involved groups emanating from civil society as well. The decision makers, the governor, the Lower Manhattan Corporation, the mayor, the developer and so on, had at one point in the process to 'listen to the city' and hear critical viewpoints which forced them to modify what they had designed in the secrecy of closed rooms – listening in part because it would improve their plans.

In brief, it would be erroneous to think that, after terrorist attacks, global cities become safer for the mere purpose of attracting and keeping world investors. Having them in the city rather than in a nearby state is indeed a concern. Yet, after each catastrophe all kinds of reactions from people, firms and officials are formulated: leave the city, gate the city, express solidarity, offer protection to the most vulnerable, or do nothing. Each city tends to intensify its essence and be more itself than ever, they make the realistic choice of promoting dreams and utopias.

6.5.2 Public spaces as resources

The resources coming from public spaces must be appreciated and assessed in diverse ways. Public space symbolizes a collective feeling of belonging to a larger political entity. A common foundation of convictions, cultural evidence and mutual expectations are needed which, by sedimentation, forms the public space (Sennett, 1970). The sense of safety in cities depends also on the mixed uses of their public space. 'City-centers represent possibly the last significant concentrations of universally accessible, urban public space where people of different classes, races and cultures can meet' (Tiesdell and Oc, 1998). Ideally, in a metropolis, people in public space enjoy 'the pleasures of anonymity' and feel included, regardless of their differences (Sandercock, 2003).

Not all large cities, however, provide shared open spaces, but even in the global cities of the South, some do, and the celebration of sports victories, a national event or the need for protest demonstrations take place in spaces where people gather, with their differences, and together feel safe . They need, however, to overcome apprehension and can be educated to do so. Acting 'under conditions of ambivalence and uncertainty, born of difference and variety', Bauman observes, is a difficult art. Morally mature persons grow 'to need the unknown, to feel incomplete without a certain anarchy in their lives' and to learn 'to love the otherness among them' (1998, 46–47). A large city is 'so full of unexpected interactions and so continuously in movement that all kinds of small and large spatialities continue to provide resources for political invention as they generate new improvisations and force new forms of ingenuity' (Amin and Thrift, 2002, 157).

How can a sense of safety emanate from public space? What mechanisms maintain social inclusion, mutual trust and civic involvement? Many green visions of parks or 'high lines' allowing a diversity of people to walk and enjoy selective moments currently develop in global cities. Their goal is to coalesce a great variety of people together at the same time and in the same space. Their creators have opted for a social vision transcending class divisions and founded on universal needs for public tranquillity, entertainment and recreation. One example of such initiative is Chapultepec Park in Mexico City, partly financed by the million-plus residents, each giving one peso for the renovation of this large public space. Every weekend, 17,000 users mix and mingle in the park because signals of quietude abound. As in other large parks, micro-control systems are at work: acting invisibly, public employees make sure that the processes organizing smooth movement are respected. They interpret situations and make sense of them. In summary, they represent an alternative to CCTVs and high-end surveillance technologies. The same could be said of cultural events attracting diverse crowds in low-income neighbourhoods of the city. Such actions are based on public trust, on mayors and their teams, local organizers' *savoir-faire* and on the presence of street-level mediation agents.

Density remains a controversial issue, especially for population categories that have fled inner cities. For a long time, observers of cities shared a consensus: diversity and density of populations using public space for various purposes had to be perceived as an asset for cities because if public space generates contacts, frictions, investment, competition, it also create a visible vitality and vibrancy. This urban vision, as an opportunity for cities, has been developed by J. Jacobs (1961), who praised complexity, diversity and dissonance: the unexpected encounter, the chance discovery, the disorderly innovation in both public and private spaces. Sennett (2007, 295–96) goes further and champions incomplete urban designs – that is, sites for unregulated development which pave the way for innovation. He compares walls to cell membranes: they should be porous but resistant, block or yield passage when needed. He illustrates the current phenomenon of walls blocking contacts. In London, social housing estates have aged and become places where the poor are gated in, sealed off from daily contact with other Londoners (Sennett, 2011, 327). City Hall is surrounded by glass walls. No one on the outside can touch, feel or hear what is seen to be going on inside. There is only one entrance door, and dead spaces on both sides. By contrast, on both sides of porous walls in medieval cities, there were houses, merchants, and these were sites for passages. The walls of the *New York Times* building, designed by Renzo Piano, open a dialogue with the open space of Times Square; they are like a weather skin, reflecting the colours of the sky. The inner garden, the restaurants, the auditorium can be seen from the street as well as the offices where journalists and employees work (Masboungi, 2005, 38). Architectural innovation seeks to establish a balance between equilibrium (order) and disequilibrium (the disruption of a freezing order).

Similar paradoxes apply to security and insecurity. With time, what at first appears as tensions, arduous interconnections, blurring and overlapping eventually may produce inclusion, transitivity, proximity and flux, breeding a 'civility' which emanate from space. Such a view challenges the prevailing idea that mixed uses of space lead to social avoidance, self-segregation, gating in and out, and the suppression of the 'other otherness'. However, 'neighborliness' can be oppressive, especially for those at the social margins and, when people are dissimilar, proximity is not necessarily synonymous with social solidarities (Molotch and McClain, 2003, 688). Gans (1968, 28–29), analysing American places and people, goes further, stating that 'middle class people, especially those raising children, do not want working-class – or even bohemian – neighbourhoods. They do not want the visible vitality of the North End, but rather the quiet and the privacy, obtainable in low-density neighbourhoods and elevator apartment houses'. Putnam (2007, 150–51) adds that 'diversity, at least in the short run, seems to bring out the turtle in all of us' or a will to control its process.

It is all a question of dosage, of timing, place and subjectivity, it seems. Remarks applying to New York, Paris or London would be inappropriate for a majority of neighbourhoods in Mumbai, Johannesburg or São Paulo. Density and diversity are challenging notions. They 'may or may not be desirable, depending on their contribution to equity and culture' (Marcuse, 1987; Fainstein, 2010, 76).

Density is better accepted with green spaces and well-designed environments. It allows those who are 'different' to meet and to talk but, again, not everyone may wish to do so. It is important for planners and architects to take into account the models of a city that the residents have in mind.

These few examples demonstrate that global cities have leverage in their choices. World city mayors may value inclusive cities and act to support that goal with appropriate public policies and pressures exerted on local institutions, such as the police in some cases. Others may favour the status quo or defend privileged constituencies. Yet only a limited amount of de-pacification is tolerable in a city, as seen in São Paulo. Analysing how public services and architectural design and planning can make a difference (they do) would take another book (see Burdett and Sudjik, 2007; 2011).

6.6 Empowering citizens

When coping with assemblages of fear and insecurity, global cities face a multitude of difficulties, some arising from general causes and others from highly specific ones. Among these difficulties are the rise of populist movements based on disenchantment and anger with elites. Organized citizens may influence elections, pressure city officials for greater accountability, sometimes exert veto power over policy, and act as a countervailing power if they are given the opportunity to do so. If none of these options is available, groups may also resort to taking their own initiatives. When attempting to manipulate fear, authorities may face civic resistance. 'Everyday life always and already speaks back, resists' and challenges political attempts to manipulate fear. 'Grounded approaches to fear challenge the politics embedded in the scalar, top-down view of fear assemblage', Pain and Smith observe (2008, 249). Urban democracies need counter-powers and accountability. Mobilized constituencies act as a bulwark against institutional abuse and corruption, demanding accountability from institutions and law enforcement. They express shared values or formulate alternatives to elected officials' decisions. People can be vigilant; they can be judges or denunciators; they can exert sanctions and vetoes or they can recall elected officials, if there is an opportunity to do so. It is easier for dedicated officials to 'imagine, articulate, pursue and actualize the vision of a just city' if they work along with motivated groups (Fainstein, 2010, 181).

New forms of involvement – some of them quiet and personal, others large-scale and spectacular, as in the case of insurgent citizens in São Paulo – characterize such engagement (see below). Within global processes, local actors, some of them illiterate, may via technologies of communication such as the Internet, acquire a *presence* on a global and political scene when they connect to other local actors in the same country or elsewhere in the world. In return, they may receive proposals for action from world organizations in need of a local basis for their transactions. Non-governmental organizations (NGOs) and the third sector are a must for making a city work. In the best cases, they infuse trust, confidence and cooperation. Here, 'it might be the mere political and social feature of the scale as action that needs to be underlined' (Sassen, 2009, 219). With globalization, new social patterns emerge within traditional social conditions. Impoverished immigrants who have lived in cities for many years take on a new relevance, become aware of it and act consequently. Other poor citizens in cities may well act similarly (Ibid.).

In such a way, cities can provide a dense articulation of global and local dynamics, in response to which people think, and insert themselves into politics, becoming new kinds of citizens. Participation – a learning process – empowers citizens who are organized. Community-based associations may teach people how to get what they need, once they are organized. In that process, cities become both the site and the substance of not only the uncertainties of modern citizenship but also of its emergent forms. The politicization and capacity for resilience of 'people at the bottom' (*les gens de peu*) require those practices of everyday city life, unveiled by de Certeau (1984), which mingle the illegal and the legal, the just and the unjust, the public and the private, the political and the domestic.

An innovative and survival perspective, more appropriate for cities of the South, points at the self-sufficiency of the poorer populations, which can be interpreted as a quiet hold of daily life over collective property, that is: alternative decisions made at the margins in order to survive in a dangerous environment. What Bayat (2000, 533) calls 'a quiet encroachment of the ordinary', refers to marginalized groups' individual direct actions and alternative outlooks in the city. What do these men and women aim for? Their agency is necessary for the basic necessities of daily life, for instance, for opportunities in the illegitimate and direct acquisition of collective consumption (land, shelter, piped water, electricity, roads), public space (street pavement, intersections, street parking places), opportunities (favourable business conditions, locations, brands) and security, essential for survival. The poor aim at autonomy outside the boundaries of the state and institutions, basing their relationships on reciprocity, trust and negotiation, resorting to informal dispute resolution rather than going to the police or to the courts. However, such actions remain particularized despite the legacy of urban social movements. 'For modernity is a costly affair; not everyone can afford to be modern... The disenfranchised are unlikely to become a more effective player in the larger sense'(Bayat, 2000, 533–54).

In Brazil, how poor citizens became empowered remains an interesting study.[6] What Holston calls 'insurgent citizenship' refers to claims concerning residence, neighbourhood life, infrastructure, transportation, consumption and so forth. This insurgency has cracked open the principles of differentiation that, for centuries, legitimated a particularly inegalitarian formulation of citizenship. Such insurgent movements are not be romanticized however, and the destabilization created by democratization sustains part of current violence, injustice and incivilities in Brazilian cities. Holston's research illustrates how alternative changes happen in global cities via empowered citizens.

Long-term studies show that patient, modest, almost invisible processes of mediation among diverse old and new class-differentiated residents and urban decision makers can prove efficient (Amin and Thrift, 2002). Inviting people to think and express themselves about the spaces where they live and work or entertain themselves is a variation on this idea. Providing voices for the different groups that dwell together in the city without forming a community is an alternative to exclusion (Young, 1990, 227; Fraser, 1990). People invest in actions and places endowed with social and cultural meaning and thus empower themselves. But it is also well known that civic participation is not innate; only certain types of individuals participate in forums, community board meetings and other means of assembly, but not everyone does so. When participation is perceived as a redistribution of power – as was the case during the community-control mobilization in American cities in the 1960s – consensus on the principle of participation explodes, remarks Arnstein, the author of a seminal ladder of participation[7] (1969, 216). Separatism, inefficiency and opportunism are roadblocks hampering genuine participation. But without a redistribution of decisional power, she concludes, there can no redistribution of benefits, and inequalities keep growing, an idea formerly developed by the social organizer Saul Alinsky (1945). He criticized the anti-poverty programs of the Great Society launched by Lyndon Johnson as a top-down process, which did not allocate political power to the poor involved. Granting economic power was not enough. Poverty is about lacking political power, Alinsky said, and without a learning process for seizing power, there is no collective capacity to develop local leadership, and to teach people how to decide about their best interests after solving their conflicts. His lifetime goal was to show how to win power via a democratic organization and via various tactics and strategies, exerting and maintaining pressure on power-brokers. However, such a solution is short-lived. People cannot live in conflict continuously.

People get involved in mobilizations if they perceive a personal interest in doing so. The 'Olsen principle' (1990) – named for Olsen – is tested here. After the 2011 summer upheavals in London, numerous foreigners admired the moral sense and civic virtue which pushed many residents to clean up their neighbourhoods. They did it because it was something worthy of doing, but also because there was some advantage at recovering rapidly cleaned neighbourhoods.

The good governance is not however to advocate the philosophy of 'small is beautiful', as in the 1960s. Proximity has its limits, especially from the global players' viewpoints. Democratic decision making is not the answer to every urban problem. These do not fundamentally challenge existing relations of power and the weakness of democracy, exacerbated by the context of globalization. Insulated decision making may produce fair outcomes.

On the whole, global cities can do a lot they have possibilities and opportunities to become part of a larger approach of issues with international dimensions. As each of the aforementioned global cities demonstrates, ideas and experimentation are abundant – from the use of public spaces, to struggles against segregation, urban sprawl and social threats, and to trust and civic empowerment. The aura emanating from world cities extends beyond city leaders and residents. Pride is felt at mentioning such cities' names by many residents, visitors, businessmen, students, and so on. World cities' joint actions are required. Fragile optimism of will and pessimism of intelligence, according to the Gramci formula, should combine to bring hope as a response to fear, as an alternative against insecurity (Pain and Smith, op. cit., 250). It is not always the case, but it may be so. After evoking fears and feelings of insecurity, it would be a shortcoming not to mention hope as their corollary.

Political vision, will and involvement with the citizens' support are continuously needed to suffuse dynamism and fairness into the city. The role of urban condition is to favour and activate *vita activa* in both spaces and the flux of mobility. Away from an obsessive order-maintenance logic, the priority of urban government should be innovation and a vision linking urban past and future and, in its broad sense, citizenship.

Notes

Introduction

1. As conceptualized by Isin (2004), in a society governed by its aversion to risk, the subject seen as rational, responsible and autonomous is accompanied by a 'neurotic' subject whose conduct arises from and responds to fears, anxieties and insecurities. The neurotic subject wants absolute security. Governing through neurosis marks a new type of politics and power.
2. People ignore threats such as excessive consumption of salt in their daily diet. Reducing Americans' daily consumption of salt by 3g would 'reduce the annual number of deaths from any cause by 44,000 to 92,000' (Bibbins-Domingo et al., 2010).
3. As Prime Minister Margaret Thatcher told her constituents: 'Prisons work!', a political posture adopted by her successor, John Major. The Labour Party also opted for 'toughness'.

1   Old and New Fears in Cities

1. In 2007, less than 1 per cent of estimated remittances were sent by migrants to the poorest countries. In China, the impact of internal migration on poverty is estimated at less than 1 per cent, only reaching twelve millions of poor Chinese. In the United States and in Europe, the cost of immigration on the GDP is evaluated at more or less 1 per cent (0.65 per cent in United Kingdom).
2. This part borrows from Body-Gendrot, S., Garcia, M., Mingione, E. 'Comparative Social Transformations in Urban Regimes' in A. Sales (ed.) *Social Transformations at the Turn of the Century* (Sage, 2012c, chapter 16).
3. Seventy-five per cent of the French find their civil servants honest, 67 per cent competent and 63 per cent listen to them (Poll, April 13, 2011). Policemen benefit from such views on public services.
4. On the issue of trust, a recent Gallup poll among Muslims (a term to be clarified) indicated that 64 per cent of those living in London trusted justice, 51 per cent, the national government and the media (!) while for those living in Paris, the results were respectively 49 per cent, 40 per cent and 35 per cent, reflecting trends prevailing in their respective countries.

2   The Turning Point of 9/11

1. This expression entered policing discourse as early as the 1930s. FBI director, J. Edgar Hoover, sponsored a comic strip with that name. It appeared in forty-five newspapers through most of 1936 (Huq and Muller, 2008, 216).

2. In 1975–76, a Senate commission headed by Church offered the public an explanation for abuse (wiretapping without warrant, mail intercepted, files detained on a million and a half Americans, etc.): it showed that laws passed by Congress are deliberately ambiguous, instructions given to services evasive enough so as to allow possible violation or denial.
3. President George W. Bush used the term 'war on terrorism' on the evening of September 11, and adopted the truncated 'war on terror' in an address to Congress nine days later (Huq and Muller, 2008, 221).
4. Roosevelt's heroic posture recalls that of the fisherman evoked in Edgar Allan Poe's short story, a person who exalts other fishermen, curled up, muddled in adversity to react and not sink into the maelstrom. Norbert Elias (1993) offered his own interpretation of this short story, analysing the status of men in danger, unable to escape a high level of terror paralysing them, so strong is their representation of fear. Yet if man can control the violence of its effects, and evaluate realistically the disaster leading him to the maelstrom, then, Elias remarks, he might escape annihilation. This analysis fits into an American tradition valorizing solitary heroes confronted with danger.
5. The Patriot Act was amended considerably before it was enacted.
6. As an example, a recent immigrant of Mexican origin, M. Morales, a member of the St. James Boys gang, was consequently convicted under terrorist charges by a popular jury since his crime (killing a child during a party to which his gang was not invited) meant 'to intimidate or constrain by force a civil population'. Instead of homicide, his crime was labelled terrorism, the most-punished crime in the state of New York after 9/11, 2001.
7. Mohammed Ali Salih, a London correspondent for an American newspaper, remarked that in airports, suspicion targeted shoes, then water bottles, then baby food, then doctors from the Middle East and the Indian sub-continent (2007). What would happen if the police arrested someone with a dark suit and a briefcase carrying a bomb? Would all men carrying a briefcase be stopped and frisked?
8. Polls have to be taken cautiously. They are merely a snapshot of the public state of mind at one precise moment and the answers frequently mirror the questions that are asked. The distribution of answers and the 'don't knows' are most revealing. Their evolution is what counts most.
9. 'Viewing the relationship simply as a one-way street, media and politicians manipulating, and Americans sheepishly responding, is implausible' (Stearns, 2007, 210).
10. See Justice Brandeis's opinion in *Olmstead vs. United States* (1928): 'The greatest dangers to liberty lurk in insidious encroachment by men of zeal, well-meaning but without understanding.'
11. By comparison, Europe would have spent €93 million to fight terrorism since 2001, €9.5 billion for the war in Iraq and €16 billion for the war in Afghanistan. France has not revealed the amount of its war budgets, but Germany spent €6.7 billion in Afghanistan (Stroobants, 2011).
12. CCTVs were first introduced in 1985 in a resort town, Bournemouth, after a bomb had been thrown during a Conservative Party conference in Brighton, almost killing PM Thatcher. In the United States, casinos installed them to prevent fraud in the 1960s; then cameras moved to malls and theme parks. Fighting hooliganism, the United Kingdom became pioneer for urban spatial

control in Europe. The number of CCTVs is currently estimated at 4.2 million, one for every fourteen people. Every day, an individual in Britain may be identified three hundred times (Wyckes, 2009, 7; Coaffee et al., op. cit., 80).

13. When errors are made or when someone has been cleared by police or justice, it is very hard for anyone to extract one's name from the database. Moreover, the driving force behind such public policy of control is traceability. A symbol is sent that state authorities are watching citizens' behaviour.

14. This development follows Coaffee et al., op. cit., chaps 6 and 8.

15. For instance, in most Western countries, the training of imams emanating from Western countries rather than their import from home countries has appeared as a necessity, and its implementation is under study. Radical organizations perceived as risky for Western countries have been banned and troublesome places of worship closed. But prisons may be a breeding ground for young Muslim delinquents who convert to Islamic radicalism.

16. Since 1975, a forum for member state collaboration in policing and criminal matters has been functioning, called Trevi (Terrorism, Radicalism, Extremism, Political Violence). It covered threats to public order and forms of organized crime and was absorbed in 1993 by the third pillar.

17. When a commission of experts deem offenders dangerous to society after their prison time is complete, they remain detained. This concerns particularly sex offenders but the very principle of this measure marks a rupture with the functioning principles of justice. This measure was first introduced in Germany in 1933. It was almost extinct, but in 2004 it was reactivated by a court in Karlsruhe then transmitted to the European Court on Human Rights (Delmas-Marty, 2010, 24–25). In general, the German courts offer strong protection of offenders' rights.

18. Only the United Kingdom has an Internet register allowing the broadcast of information on sex offenders about to be released or just released.

3   Terrorism

1. Interview at John Jay College, November 2010.

2. The data regarding stop–and-frisk numbers are on the NYPD website. The Rand Corporation was required by the NYPD to analyse them. Cities like Chicago refuse to release their stop numbers, and Boston and New Orleans state that they do not keep such records.

3. Assistant professor at NYU Law School. Interview on November 11, 2010.

4. I wish to thank D. Richman, at Columbia University, for his useful comments.

5. The following development borrows from Dickey's analysis of the methods used by the New York Police Department counter-terror force. His account may appear laudatory, but it also brings information to which only an investigative journalist with wide credentials or an insider have access.

6. The most sophisticated weapon, sarin nerve gas, was used only once by the Aum Shinrikyo organization in Japan, with assets estimated at over one billion dollars. The gas released on five lines of the Tokyo subway in 1995 killed twelve people and severely injured a few dozen more. It has not been used since (Dickey, op. cit., 131).

7. Ian Blair, in a discussion we had during the Urban Age Berlin summit on November 10, 2006.
8. Two federal policies resulted from their recommendations – guaranteeing loans allowing modest households, especially veterans, to move to the suburbs and become homeowners in Levittowns or similar residential housing, on one hand, and, on the other, constructing highways connecting cities to the suburbs – (the bill of 1956 on interstate highways was submitted to Congress and introduced as a defence program to the public).
9. In a study carried out in California on whether local police would contact federal authorities if an individual in police custody was unable to produce a valid ID, 70 per cent of police officials answered that this was unlikely (which is in line with the position of the International Association of Chiefs of Police). Moreover, if this individual did not speak English, they answered that they would make efforts to provide an officer fluent in the required language.
10. The proof for deportation is made once the fingerprints of county or jail inmates are sent to the Homeland Security Administration, which then compares them with the prints in their files. Only twenty-seven of the sixty-two counties in New York State have cooperated so far (*New York Times*, June 2, 2011).
11. This part borrows from Body-Gendrot (2011d, chapter 6)
12. In a poll *Les Enjeux-les Echos* of August 2010, three out of five French require more regulations and refuse 'the diktats of neo-liberalism'; 66 per cent of the French would not mind their children being civil servants and 73% of the 15–30 children would opt for a job in the public sector (Landré, 2011; Peillon 2011; IPSOS-Logica Business, February 2012).
13. According to a 2010 report from the National Commission on Human Rights, forty eight per cent of the French think that Muslims are a group apart (an increase of four points compared with 2009); yet seventy four percent state that Muslims are French like other French. Twenty per cent admit that they are rather racist but fifty per cent that they are not. Strong feelings of distance and hostility are expressed towards Romas, as is the case elsewhere in Europe.
14. It is hardly surprising that in a Gallup poll conducted in fifty countries, the French are champions in economic pessimism, with 61 per cent of negative answers (versus 28 per cent on average and 22 per cent in Germany). Optimism is retained by Vietnam. Wealth per capita is $35,000 in France and $3,000 in Vietnam (Delhommais, 2011).
15. In a consultation about urban renewal, at Les Halles, in 2004, 12,000 ballots expressed views on architectural and environmental proposals. Safety and terrorism were just not issues mentioned on the ballots.
16. This information was provided by the mayor's cabinet. Other information comes from victimization surveys that take place every two years in the region.
17. This information comes from an exchange of letters I had with the Ministry of the Interior, spring of 2008.
18. Neighbourhood policing or 'proximity policing' models have never been popular among French police forces. Police officers usually do not have ties to the place where they work. In 2002, N. Sarkozy dismantled the proximity

policing approach launched by the Left in 1997 and enforced in 1999. It is difficult to evaluate a reform after only three years. Police unions claim that they never had enough resources to organize meetings with the public and to reduce crimes (the rates of crime clearance were under 9 per cent for all crimes and 5 per cent for street crimes in Paris in 1995). They complained that proximity policing missions were unclear and that they were not on the field to meet 'social goals' (*faire du social*). A majority of policemen shared the idea that community policing was not real police work, that they had nothing to learn from residents whose expectations were too diverse and incoherent. Moreover, since policemen in the field could report more crimes, delinquency curves were rising. It was politically costly. In brief, police chiefs claimed that they preferred to receive clear-cut orders from their hierarchy. There was also a deeper fear, that of balkanization, of becoming accountable to politically diversified mayors, some of them under pressure from politicized groups, whereas the police's shared motto was that citizens should never be partners of policemen, even less their advisors (Mouhanna, 2008, 78).

19. Interview with the author and participation.
20. 'A "community" can be considered to be under official suspicion if, and only if, a substantial majority of those who share its identity are under official suspicion, and/or if this identity is, in and of itself, sufficient to arouse systematic official suspicion' (Greer 2010, 1178).
21. This part draws partly on S. Body-Gendrot (2011) 360–67.
22. Conversation with the author in New York, January 2011.
23. According to a surviving Kurd couple in one attacked hotel, the young terrorist, Amir Kazal, told them that he came from an extremely poor background where the caste system is pervasive. He was sold by his parents to the Laskar-e-Taibi for about €1,000 to commit the attack. He had never seen a tap before and did not know how to run water (Kamdar, 2009). The extreme deficit of justice from which such youths suffer may explain their subsequent violence. They are a lost generation rather than a vanguard of warriors.

4 Criminals and Gangs in Global Cities of the South

1. As a poet once remarked: 'Man sticks to what he is and dreads to lose even this. Fear and hope move along, together. To lose hope is to lose all fear. Then, there is nothing left to dread' (Mandelstam, 1970, 42).
2. In Europe, judges condemn overreactions to acts of robbery, for instance. In such cases, the victim is indicted.
3. The United States has the most important share of the security services industry (43 per cent) in the world, followed by South Africa (37 per cent), Europe (only 6 per cent) and Latin America (3 per cent) (Phillips, 2002, 10). In 1999, there were over four private security guards for every uniformed member of the SAPS. More than half of the required services concern guarding, the rest addresses electronic monitoring, fencing and so on. 'Armed response' is a common sign in most of affluent areas of South Africa.
4. Private security companies are listed on the Johannesburg Stock Exchange: a few large businesses monopolize the South African private security market.

5. In a private conversation, a White participant at the 2006 Urban Age Conference remarked: 'Why should we be in charge of public parks, when we have them behind our walls?'

6. Justice Albie Sachs gave an early clarification of the positive duty of the state arising under section 12 (1)(c). He argued that constitutional rights oblige 'the state directly to protect the right of everyone to be free from private domestic violence'.

7. *State v Baloyi (minister of Justice intervening)* 2000; *Carmichele v Minister of Safety and Security and Another* 2001 (4) BCLR 938 (CC) para. 44, the decision states that 'in some circumstances, there would also be a positive component (to constitutional rights) which obliges the state and its organs to provide appropriate protection to everyone through laws and structures designed to afford such protection'.

8. *Rail Commuters Action Group and Others v Transnet Ltd t/a Metrorail and Others* 2005 (4) BCLR 301(CC) para. 48.

9. *Osman v UK* (1998) 29 EHRR 245, para. 115.

10. This development on Brazilian citizenship follows Holston (2008).

11. I am grateful to Carolina Grillo and Roberto Kant da Lima (1999) for pointing at that expression which means that the constitutional rules establishing juridical equality among people coexist with legal norms that spell out juridical inequality. See also Cardoso de Oliveira (1999).

12. The average per capita income was $12,000 (€8,807) in 2008. Some of the wealthy households only use helicopters to circulate, with landing spaces on top of high-rise buildings. São Paulo has more private helicopters registered to its citizens than any other city in the world (Sudjik, 2011).

13. I would like to thank Martin, Catherine and E. H. Tonkens for sharing their comments on Holston's work.

14. Such data, when collected and processed by the police or judicial authorities, yield very different results. They should be taken cautiously.

15. I am grateful to M. Anderson for this information.

16. It was agreed that cell phones would no longer be used in prisons, but that inmates would be able to watch the World Soccer Cup on flat screen TVs (Perétié, 2006).

17. I am thankful to C. Grillo for her useful information on the PCC. See also Cardoso de Oliveira (1999).

18. In February 2001, a very large rebellion in twenty-nine prisons had successfully taken place, the inmates making use of their cell phones.

19. Drauzio Varella, the prison doctor who had worked there for ten years, wrote his own account of the infamous episode and it rapidly became a best-seller, then a film by Hactor Babenco. This prison, built in 1956, was bulldozed in 2002. Governor Geraldo Alkmin from the Socio-democrat Party (PSDB) declared then that a new era would mark the prison system (Duarte, 2011).

5   Disorders in British and French Cities

1. Refusing such categories was justified by the HCI in 2006 as such: 'The model of integration "French style" is often derided. Like any "ideal type", it is confronted with a reality which is moving away from it. We remain

however convinced that one should not throw away the baby with the bathwater, because the only alternative suggested would consist in artificially imposing a foreign model – in substance an Anglo-Saxon model officially putting forward a system based on an organization of communitarian style. Not only would this approach contradict our tradition, our values, in one word, our very conception of life in society but also such a revolution would necessitate long delays of implementation incompatible with the urgency of the situation. Finally, it would be paradoxical to rely on a formula whose pertinence is strongly doubted by its chief promoters, as the situation in the U.K. or in the Netherlands, for example, demonstrates' (HCI, 2006, 18).

2. Many British do not understand why their country is characterized as communitarian when everyone is subject to the same law and has the same rights – though with some exceptions.
3. History offers an explanation. The Revolution abolished intermediary bodies between citizens and the state and the state constructed itself by eliminating intermediary bodies, parishes or communities seen as interfering with the state's aim of unifying society.
4. We are no longer, however, in the past when it did not make a difference 'whether protagonists fought with sharp words or with sharp knives' (Schwerhoff, 2002, 119). Historian of violence, Spierenburg (2007, 13) doubts that even pre-industrial people failed to draw a line between insult and physical attack. For him, 'aggressive speech', a form of hurt or violence is not homicide; words are words and bullets are bullets.
5. This account borrows from Body-Gendrot (2008).
6. In France, the law requires everyone to carry identity papers at all times in public space.
7. This policeman and the one receiving the call who did not alert other policemen were subsequently indicted and eventually found not guilty. At the time of this writing, the deceased boys' family lawyers were to appeal this decision.
8. Three days earlier, visiting one of the Paris suburbs, he had declared that he would rid the residents of the riff-raff (*racaille*), a term interpreted as an insult by the youths. The mention of a possible theft, reported as such by the media and discrediting the victims, shocked numerous youths who expected words of compassion or at least some respect towards the grieving parents and friends.
9. 741 urban areas, labelled 'sensitive' or high-risk by the French administration, are located in the three most industrialized regions, where 60 per cent of immigrant families live.
10. Sometimes stop-and-search approaches reveal more about police behaviour than about the ethnicity of those stopped and searched. Being young, exhibiting furtive or confrontational behaviour and a rowdy appearance may be more important in the police subculture than ethnicity.
11. The Scarman report confirms this assumption: 'The incident which sparked off the disorder...was nothing unusual on the streets of Brixton...Why, on this occasion, did the incident escalate into major disorder culminating in arson and a full-scale battle with the police?...The tinder for a major conflagration was there...Deeper causes undoubtedly existed, and must be

probed; but the immediate cause of Saturday's events was a spontaneous combustion set off by the spark of a single incident' (1985, 37).

12. 'Some territories cumulate too many handicaps, too many difficulties. Territories confronted to violence and to traffics. Territories where unemployment is massive and urbanism inhuman. Territories where children are school dropouts, where too many youths have trouble finding work, even with diplomas' (Scarman, 1985, 38).

13. I am grateful to M. Anderson for this information.

14. This part borrows from Body-Gendrot (2008).

15. The state of emergency was supposed to last three months but was terminated by President Chirac after January 4, 2006. It allowed curfews and home searches night and day all over the territory (only 5 per cent of localities resorted to them), banned group gatherings and closed cafés and entertainment places early in the sensitive zones of twenty-five *départements*.

16. In the movie *La Haine* by M. Kassowitz, the marginality of street educators or of mediators and their inability to relate to marginalized youths is striking.

17. A journalist, Kundnani (2001), refers to an 'amphibious generation, often straddling two worlds and cultures, frequently troubled and troublesome. Second generation angst is a problem. It can cause serious trouble as long as it lasts'. He denounces the neglect expressed by authorities regarding young Asians' calls: 'While in 1981 and in 1985, uprisings against the police in Brixton, Handsworth, Tottenham and Toxteth reflected the violence of a black and white united community, angered by the brutal treatment of the police, here, the fires were lit by youth from a community disintegrating from the inside and the outside, youth whose violence has a desperate character. It is the violence of a community fragmented by skin color, by class belonging and by policy choices. It is the violence of the hopeless. It is the violence of those whose rights have been violated'.

18. In 2011, it was announced that environmental budgets might be cut by 33 per cent before 2015, local government budgets by 27 per cent, the Home Office and Justice respectively by 23 per cent.

6   Conclusion: Global Cities' Challenges

1. Rousseau, praising equality in *Le Contrat Social*, expected that no citizen would be affluent enough to be able to buy another one and no one poor enough to be forced to sell oneself . He noticed the wicked effect (*gueuserie*) of inequalities on both the rich and the poor living in the same city (see for comparison, Rosanvallon, 2011, 353).

2. According to estimates from the American Congressional Budget Office, between 1979 and 2005 the median of the income distribution rose 21 per cent, a relatively slow growth. The income of the very rich (the top .01 of 1 per cent of the income distribution) rose by 480 per cent, translating from $4.2 million to $24.3 million. Yet the tax burden of the latter being less than that of many middle-class Americans, they seem exempted from the 'social contract' applied to everyone else, allowing a decent and functioning society, Paul Krugman remarks in his editorial (*International Herald Tribune*, September 24, 2011). According to the Tax Policy Center, two thirds

of entitlements and tax breaks benefit lower-income Americans. But the third fraction ($ 1 trillion) goes to those earning $1 million before taxes. They receive $447,259 vs. $427 for those earning $10, 000 or less (Porter 2012).

3. A specialist of world cities, Friedman (1995, 317), predicted that they would operate like 'city states in a networked global economy, increasingly inter-dependent of regional and national mediation'. The dream of sixteenth-century Italian city states would come true once more.

4. Coaffee et al. identified how resilience is now used as a label, and a frame-work, for a host of policies broadly connected to security, and particularly to the 'war on terror' (2009, 261).

5. The characters in *Smoke* (1995) and *Blue in the Face* (1995), films directed by Paul Auster and Wayne Wang, illustrate how they modestly unite their capacities and start to heal their wounds together, despite their differences and their exasperations.

6. The testimony of an insurgent citizen reminds one of the father of five in the United States expressing his indignation in the 1960s (see ch. 2, x): 'I am an honest person...I don't steal from anyone. I am a worker. I fulfil my obligations at home, with my family. I pay my taxes. But today I think the following: I have rights because the Constituinte (Constitution) gives me these rights. But I have to run after my rights...If you don't run after your rights, how are you going to make them happen?' (Holston, 2008, 253). After the 1988 Constitution enumerated more rights for the people, huge electoral mobilizations tackled major issues, for instance, police violence.

7. Arnstein's ladder measuring the intensity of participation runs from manip-ulation and therapy, that is, non-participation, to informing and consulta-tion offered by power-brokers to citizen recipients. Placation is a higher level of tokenism: the have-not citizens are consulted. Only with partnership and citizen control do they play their role fully. Arnstein acknowledges the limitations of this typology, it juxtaposes the powerless with the powerful, whereas such categories are not monolithic blocks.

References

Agamben, G. *Homo Sacer* (Paris: Le Seuil, 1998).

Agan, Y., and Cahuc, P. *La société de défiance* (Paris: Editions rue d'Ulm, 2007).

Alinsky, S. *Reveille for Radicals* (Chicago: Chicago University Press, 1945).

Amin, A., and Thrift, N. *Cities: Reimagining the Urban* (Cambridge: Polity Press, 2002).

Amin, A. 'Unruly Strangers? The 2001 Urban Riots in Britain', *International Journal of Regional and Urban Research* 27 (2) (2003), 460–63.

Anderson, M. *In Thrall to Political Change: Police and Gendarmerie in France* (Oxford: Oxford University Press, 2011).

Ang, I. 'After 9/11: Defending the Global City', *Ethnicities* 2 (2) (2010), 160–62.

Appadurai, A. *Fear of Small Numbers* (Durham, NC: Duke University Press, 2007).

Arendt, H. *Sur la violence* (Paris: Calmann-Levy, trans. 1972).

Arnstein, S. 'A Ladder of Citizen Participation', *Journal of the American Planning Association* 35 (4) (1969), 216–24.

Baker, A. 'Governing through Crime: The case of the European Union', *European Journal of Criminology* 7 (3) (2010), 187–213.

Bartkowiak-Théron, I., and Corbo Crehan, A. 'The Changing Nature of Communities', *Research and Public Policy Series* 111 (8) (Canberra: Australian Institute of Criminology, 2010).

Bauman, Z. *Globalization* (Cambridge: Polity Press, 1998).

Bayat, A. 'From Dangerous Classes to Quiet Rebels', *International Sociology* 15 (3) (2000), 533–57.

Beau, J., Owen, C., and Parnell, S. *Uniting a divided city governance and social exclusion in Johannesburg*, (London: Earthcan Publications, 2002).

Beauregard, R., and Tomlinson, R. 'The Discourse of Governance in Post-Apartheid Johannesburg', in K. Segbers (ed.) *The Making of Global City Regions* (Baltimore: Johns Hopkins University Press, 2007), 237–57.

Beauregard, R., and Haila, A. 'The Unavoidable Continuities in the City', in P. Marcuse and R. van Kempen (eds) *Globalizing Cities* (Oxford: Blackwell, 2000), 22–36.

Beauregard, R., and Bounds, A. 'Urban Citizenship', in E.F. Isin (ed.) *Democracy, Citizenship and the Global City* (London: Routledge, 2000), 243–56.

Beck, U. *Risk Society* (London: Sage, 1992).

Beetham, D. *The Legitimation of Power* (Atlantic Highlands, NJ: Humanities, 1991).

Bellot, M., and Thibau, A. 'Police and discrimination, an investigation', in France Culture Radio Program, June 25 (2008).

Benit, C., and Gervais-Lambony, P. 'La mondialisation comme instrument politique local dans les métropoles sud-africaines', *Annales de géographie* 633 (2004).

Benyon, J. 'Interpretations of Civil Disorder' in J. Benyon and J. Solomos (eds) *The Roots of Urban Unrest* (Oxford: Pergamon Press, 1987).

Bertho, A. *Le temps des émeutes* (Paris: Bayard, 2009).

Bibbins-Domingo, K., Chertow, M., Coxson, P., Moran, A., Lightwood, J., Pletcher, J., and Goldman, L. 'Projected Effect of Dietary Salt Reductions on Future Cardiovascular Disease', *New England Journal of Medicine* 362 (2010), 590–99.

Blanchard E. 'L'encadrement des Algériens de Paris (1944–54) entre contraintes juridiques et arbitraire policier', *Crime, Histoire & Sociétés/Crime History & Societies*, 11 (1) (2007), 5–25.

Bleich, E. *Race Politics in Britain and France* (New York: Cambridge University Press, 2003).

Bleich, E. 'The Legacies of History? Colonization and Immigrant Integration in Britain and in France', *Theory and Society* 34 (2) (2005), 171–95.

Boda, Z., and Szabo, G. 'The Media and Attitudes towards Crime and the Justice System: A Qualitative Approach', *European Journal of Criminology*, 8 (4) (2011), 329–42.

Body-Gendrot, S. *Ville et violence* (Paris: Presses Universitaires de France, 1993).

Body-Gendrot, S. *The Social Control of Cities?* (Oxford: Blackwell, 2000).

Body-Gendrot, S., Duprez, D. 'Security and Prevention Policies in France in the 1990s: French cities and Security', in P. Hebberech and D. Duprez (eds) *The Prevention and Security Policies in Europe* (Brussels: VUB University Press, 2002), 95–132.

Body-Gendrot, S. 'Confronting Fear' in R. Burdett and D. Sudjik (eds) *The Endless City* (London: Phaedon, 2007a), 352–63.

Body-Gendrot, S. 'Urban "Riots" in France: Anything New?', in L. Cachet, S. de Kimpe, P. Ponsaert and A. Ringeling (eds) *Local Security Policy in the Netherlands and Belgium* (Den Haag, Netherlands: Boom Juridische Uitgevers 2008), 263–80.

Body-Gendrot, S. 'From Old Threats to Enigmatic Enemies', in S. Body-Gendrot and P. Spirenburg, (eds) *Violence in Europe* (New York: Springer, 2009), 115–37.

Body-Gendrot, S. 'Police, Marginality and Discrimination in the *Banlieues* of France', *Ethnic and Racial Studies* 33 (4) (2010a), 656–74.

Body-Gendrot, S. 'European Policies of Social Control Post-9/11', *Social Research* 77 (1) (2010b), 181–204.

Body-Gendrot, S. 'Uneven Landscapes', in R. Burdett and D. Sudjik (eds) *Living in the Endless City* (London: Phaedon, 2011), 360–67.

Body-Gendrot, S. 'Power and powerlessness in global cities' <www.opendemocracy.org>, February 7 (2011a).

Body-Gendrot, S. 'Disorders in World cities' <www.opendemocracy.org>, August 15 (2011b).

Body-Gendrot, S. 'The Police and the Cities: the French experience', in A. Mehra and R. Levy (eds) *The Police, State and Society* (Dehli: Longman, 2011d), 133–146.

Body-Gendrot, S. 'Globalization and Urban Insecurity: Comparative Perspectives', in K. Fujita (ed.) *Cities and Crises: New Critical Urban Theory* (Sage, 2012a, forthcoming).

Body-Gendrot, S., and Savitch, H.V. 'Urban Violence in the United States and France: Comparing Los Angeles (1992) and Paris (2005)', in K. Mossberger, S. Clarke, and P. Jones (eds) *Oxford Handbook of Urban Politics* (Oxford: Oxford University Press, 2012b).

Body-Gendrot, S., Garcia, M., and Mingione, E. 'Comparative Social Transformations in Urban Regimes', in A. Sales (ed.) *Sociology Today: Social Transformations in a Globalizing World* (Thousand Oaks, CA: Sage, 2012c), 703–42.

Boisteau, C. 'Sécurité, Dynamiques urbaines et privatisation de l'espace à Johannesburg', *Cahier du LaSur* (7) (2003).

Borradori, G. Le 'Concept' du 11 Septembre: Dialogues à New York avec Jacques Derrida et Jurgen Habermas (Paris: Galilée, 2003).

Bourdieu, P. *Outline of a Theory of Practice* (New York: Cambridge University Press, 1987).

Bourke, J. *Fear* (London: Virago Press, 2006).

Bratton, W., and Kobler, P. *Turnaround* (New York: Random House, 1998).

Braud, P. (ed.) 'La violence politique dans les démocraties occidentales' (Paris: L'Harmattan, 1993).

Bremner, L. 'Recovering from Apartheid', in R. Burdett and D. Sudjik (eds) *The Endless City* (London: Phaedon, 2007), 203–13.

Brown, G. Speech at the Royal United Services Institute (London, February 13, 2006).

Brown, W. *Murs* (Paris: Les prairies ordinaires, 2009).

Browning, R., Marshall, D., and Tabb, W. *Protest Is Not Enough* (Berkeley: University of California Press, 1984).

Bui-Trong, L. 'L'insécurité dans les quartiers sensibles', *Cahiers de la sécurité intérieure* 14 (1993), 235–40.

Burdett, R., and Sudjik D. (eds) *The Endless City* (London: Phaedon 2007).

Burdett, R., and Sudjik, D. (eds) *Living in the Endless City* (London: Phaedon, 2011).

Burdett, R., and Rode, P. 'Living in the Urban Age', in R. Burdett and D. Sudjik (eds) *Living in the Endless City* (London: Phaedon, 2011), 8–40.

Cahn, O. 'The Fight Against Terrorism and Human Rights: the French Perspective', in M. Wade and A. Maljevic (eds) *A War on Terror?* (New York: Springer), 467–504.

Caldeira, T. 'Worlds Set Apart', in R. Burdett and D. Sudjik (eds) *Living in the Endless City* (London: Phaedon 2011), 168–75.

Campbell, B. *Goliath* (London: Methuen, 1993).

Campbell, D. *Writing 'Security'* (Minneapolis: University of Minnesota Press, 1998).

Canada, G. *Fist Stick Knife Gun* (New York: Beacon Press, 1996).

Cantle Report. *Community Cohesion* (London: Home Office, HMSO, 2001).

Cardoso, R. 'Republican Rights and Nationalism: Collective Identities and Citizenship in Brazil and Quebec', *Antropologia* 259 (1999), 1–23.

Castells, M. 'The Information Age: Economy', *The Rise of the Network Society* (Oxford: Blackwell, 1996).

Ceyhan, A. 'Sécurité et patriotisme: les identités sous surveillance', *Cultures et conflits* 44 (2001), 117–34.

Chevalier, L. 'Classes laborieuses et classes dangereuses' (Paris: Hachette, 1984).

Cincelli, V., Galland, O., de Maillard, J., and Misset, S., 'Enquête sur les violences urbaines. Comprendre les émeutes de novembre 2005. L'exemple d'Alnay sous bois' (Paris: Centre d'analyse stratégique, 2006).

City of Johannesburg Metropolitan Municipality. 'Reflecting on a solid foundation. Building developmental local government' (2000–05), City Council Report (2006).

Clarke, Lord. *The Burnley Task Force Report* (Burnley: Burnley Borough Council, 2001).

Coaffee, J., Murakami, W.D., and Rogers, P. *The Everyday Resilience of the City* (New York: Palgrave Macmillan, 2009).

Cohen, S. *Folk Devils and Moral Panics: The Creation of the Mods and the Rockers* (London: MacGibbon & Kee, 1972).

Cohen, R. '10 Reasons Terror Meets Silence from Muslims', *International Herald Tribune*, October 26 (2005).

Crawford, A. 'From the Shopping Mall to the Street Corners: Dynamics of Exclusion in the Governance of Public Space', in Crawford, A. (ed.) *International and Comparative Criminal Justice and Urban Governance* (Cambridge: Cambridge University Press, 2011), 483–518.

Crawford, A. 'Regulating Civility, Governing Security and Policing (Dis)order under Conditions of Uncertainty', in J. Blad, M. Hildebrandt, K. Rozemond, M. Schuilenburg and P. van Calster (eds) *Governing Security under the Rule of Law* (The Hague: Eleven International Publishing, 2010), 9–35.

Crime Information Analysis Center 'The Reported Serious Crime Situation in South Africa', *Crime Intelligence* (Pretoria: SAPS, Head Office, 2001).

Dawson, A. 'Geography of Fear: Crime and the Transformation of Public Space in Post-Apartheid South Africa', in S. Low and N. Smith (eds) *The Politics of Public Space* (Oxford: Routledge, 2006), 123–43.

De Certeau, M. *The Practice of Everyday Life* (Berkeley: University of California Press, 1984).

De Haan, W. 'Violence as an Essentially Contested Concept', in S. Body-Gendrot and P. Spierenburg (eds) *Violence in Europe* (New York: Springer, 2008), 27–40.

Defoe, D. *An Effectual Scheme for the Immediate Prevention of Street Robberies* (1730).

Delbès, C., Gaymu, J. and Springer, S. 'Les femmes vieillissent seules, les hommes vieillissent à deux. Un bilan européen', Paris: INED, *Population et sociétés*, 419 (2006) editorial.

Delhommais, P.A. 'Les Chinois, eux, ont le champagne gai', *Le Monde*, January 10, (2011).

Della Porta, D., and Reiter H. (eds) *Policing Protest* (Minneapolis: University of Minnesota Press, 1998).

Delmas-Marty, M. *Libertés et sûreté dans un monde dangereux* (Paris: Le Seuil, 2010).

Delumeau, J. *Peur en Occident, XIVe-XVIIIe siècles* (Paris: Fayard, 1978).

Denham, J. *Building Cohesive* (London: Home Office, 2001).

Dickey, C. *Securing the City* (New York: Simon and Schuster, 2009).

Dladla, J. *Homelessness in Inner City Johannesburg* (Johannesburg: CSVR, 2002).

D'Monte, D. 'A Matter of People', in R. Burdett and D. Sudjik (eds) *Living in the Endless City* (London: Phaedon, 2011), 94–101.

Dolnick, S. 'Even Mayor Cannot Escape Complexity of Immigration Issue', *New York Times*, January 21 (2011).

Douglas, M., and Wildavski, A. *Risk and Culture* (Berkeley: University of California Press, 1984).

Duarte, C. 'Carandiru' in a paper presented at a conference on Violence latente vs. violence explosive dans les villes des Amériques, LISST research center, Toulouse, France, February 25 (2011).

Dupuy, J.P. *Le catastrophisme éclairé* (Paris: Le Seuil, 2002).

Durose, M., Smith, E., and Lagan P. 'Contacts between the Police and the Public 2005' (NCJ 215243) (2007).

Elias, N. 'Les pêcheurs dans le maelstrom' *Engagement et distanciation* (Paris: Fayard, 1993).

Elias, N., and Dunning, E. *Quest for Excitement* (Oxford: Blackwell, 1986).

Esping-Andersen, G., Gallie, D., Hemerijk, A., and Myers, J. *Why We Need a New Welfare State* (Oxford: Oxford University Press, 2002).

European Commission Communication from the Commission on the Precautionary Principle, February 2 (Brussels: European Commission, 2000).

Ewald, F. 'The Return of Descartes' Malicious Demon: An Outline of a Philosophy of Precaution', in T. Baker and J. Simon (eds) *Embracing Risk* (Chicago: University of Chicago Press, 2002), 273–301.

Ewald, F. 'Usages et portée', *Constructif, 27* (2010), 10–12, <www.constructif.fr>.

Fagan, J. and T. Meares 'Punishment, Deterrence and Social Control: the Paradox of Punishment in Minority Communities', *Ohio State Journal of Criminal Law*, 6 (1) (2008), 173–229.

Fagan, J., and Wilkinson, D. 'Situational Contexts of Adolescent Violence in New York City', *Revue européenne des migrations internationales* 14 (1) (1998), 63–76.

Fagan, J. Expert report in *Floyd v City of New York* (2011).

Fagan, J. 'Indignities of Order Maintenance Policing', memo (New York University Straus House workshop, 2011a).

Fagan, J., West, V., and Holland, J. 'Reciprocal Effects of Crime and Incarceration in New York City Neighborhoods', *Fordham Urban Law Journal*, July, 30 (5) (2010), 1551–99.

Fainstein, S. *The Just City* (Ithaca: Cornell University Press, 2010).

Faleiro, S. 'Dreams of Mumbai', *International Herald Tribune*, July 21 (2011).

Favell, A. *Philosophies of Integration* (New York: Palgrave Macmillan, 2001).

Feierabend, I. 'Aggressive Behaviors within Polities 1948–1962: A Cross-National Study', *Journal of Conflict Resolution*, 10 (1966), 249–71.

Ferrero, K. *Fear of crime* (Albany: University of New York Press, 1995).

Fillieule, O., and Jobard, F. 'The Maintenance of Order in France: Toward a Model of Protest Policing', in D. Della Porta and H. Reiter (eds) *The Policing of Mass Demonstrations in Contemporary Democracies* (Minneapolis: University of Minnesota Press, 1998).

Flamm, M. *Law and Order* (New York: Columbia University Press, 2005).

Foucault, M. *A vida dos homens invame* (Rio de Janeiro: Forense Universitaria, 2003).

Fraser, N. 'From Distribution to Recognition ? Dilemmas of Justice in a "post-socialist" Age', *New Left Review* 212 (1995), 68–93.

Fraser, N. 'Rethinking the Public Sphere: A Contribution to the Critique of Actually Existing Democracy', *Social Text*, 25–26 (1990), 56–80.

French Ministry of the Interior, *Annual Survey*, 2009. http://www.interieur.gouv.fr

Friedman, J. 'The World City Hypothesis', in P. Knox and P. Taylor (eds) *World Cities in a World System* (Cambridge: Cambridge University Press, 1995).

Frug, G. 'Democracy and Governance', in R. Burdett and D. Sudjik (eds) *Living in the Endless City* (London: Phaedon, 2011), 350–55.

Fuchs, L. *The American Kaleidoscope* (Middletown: Wesleyan University Press, 1990).

Fukuyama, F. *Trust* (New York: Simon & Schuster, 1995).

Furedi, F. *Culture of Fear* (London: Continuum, 2002).

Furstenberg, F. 'Public Reaction to Crime in the Streets', *American Scholar* 40 (1971), 601–10.

Gans, H. *People and Places* (New York: Basic Books, 1968).

Garbaye, R. *Emeutes vs Intégration* (Paris: Presses de SciencesPo, 2011).

Garland, D. *The Culture of Control* (Chicago: University of Chicago Press, 2001).

Gasnier, A. 'Le baril de poudre des prisons de São Paulo', *Le Monde*, October 28 (2006), 20–21.

Gerstle, G., and Mollenkopf, J. (eds) *E Pluribus Unum?* (New York: Russell Sage, 2001).

Gervais-Lambony, P. 'Avant-propos', in J.M. Rennes (ed.) *La recherche sur la ville en Afrique du sud* (Paris: Anthropos, 1995), i–xiii.

Gitlin, T. *The Twilight of Common Dreams* (New York: Metropolitan Books, 1995).

Glassner, B. *Narrative* 'Techniques of Fear Mongering', *Social Research* 71 (4) (2004), 819–26.

Glassner, B. *The Culture of Fear* (New York: Basic Books, 1999).

Goffman, E. *Asylums* (Garden City: Doubleday, 1961).

GOM. 'Transforming Mumbai into a World-Class City', *First Report of the Chief Minister's Task Force*, Mumbai, Government of Maharashtra (2004).

Goodstein, L. 'Poll contradicts many stereotypes on Muslims in U.S.', *New York Times*, August 3 (2011).

Grabe, M.E., and Drew, D.G. 'Crime Cultivation: A Comparison across Media Genres and Channels', *Journal of Broadcasting and Electronic Media* 51 (1) (2007), 147–71.

Graham, H.D., and Gurr, T.R. (eds) *Violence in America* (Beverley Hills: Sage, 1979).

Greenberg, D. 'Novos ordo saeclorum ? A Commentary on Downes, and Becket and Western', in Garland, D. (ed.) *Mass Imprisonment: Social Causes and Consequences* (London: Sage, 2001), 70–81.

Greer, C. 'Crime and media: understanding the connections', in C. Hale et al. (eds) *Criminology* (Oxford: Oxford University Press, 2005), 157–80.

Greer, S. 'Anti-Terrorist Laws and the United Kingdom's "suspect community": A Reply to Pantazis and Pumberton', *British Journal of Criminology* 50 (6) (2010), 1171–1190.

Gurr, T.R. 'Historical Trends in Violent Crime', *Crime and Justice* 3 (1981), 295–353.

Hall, S., Critcher, C., Jefferson, T. Clarke, J., and Roberts, B. *Policing Crisis* (Houndmills, Basingstoke : Palgrave Macmillan, 1978).

Hamilton, A., Madison, J., Jay, J., and Clinton, R. *Federalist Papers* (New York: Signet Classic, 1961).

Harcourt, B. 'Unconstitutional Police Searches and Collective Responsibilities', *Criminology and Public Policy* 363 (2004), 1201–16.

Haut Conseil à l'Intégration 'Le bilan de la politique d'intégration 2002–2005', *Rapport au Premier Ministre* (Paris: La documentation française, 2006).

Her Majesty's Inspectorate Constabulary (HMIC) 'Keeping the Peace: Policing Disorder' (London: HMIC, 1999).

Hervieu, S. '50 meurtres sont commis chaque jour en Afrique du sud', *Le Monde*, September 24, (2009).

Hessel, S. *Indignez vous! transl. Time for Outrage* (London: Charles Glass, 2011).

194   *References*

Hobbes, T. (1651) *Leviathan*, R. Tuck (ed.) (New York: Cambridge University Press).
Hobsbawn, E. *Primitive Rebels* (Manchester: Manchester University Press, 1959).
Hoffmann, S. 'Thoughts on Fear in Global Society', *Social Research* 71 (4) (2004), 1023–38.
Home Office Report. *Secure Borders Safe Heaven* (London: HMSO, 2002).
Hunt, A. 'Immigrants, Votes and a Party Divided', *International Herald Tribune* January 17 (2011).
Huq, A. and Muller, C. 'The War on Crime as Precursor to the War on Terror', *International Journal of Law, Crime and Justice* 36 (2008), 215–29.
Ignatieff, M. *The Warrior's Honor* (New York: Henry Holt, 1997).
Isin, E. 'The Neurotic Citizen', *Citizenship Studies* 8 (3) (2004), 217–35.
Jackson, J. 'Introducing Fear of Crime to Risk Research', *Risk Analysis*, 26 (2006), 253–64.
Jacobi, P. 'Two Cities in One: Diverse Images of Sao Paulo', in K. Segbers (ed.) *The Making of Global City Regions* (Baltimore: Johns Hopkins University Press, 2007), 279–94.
Jacobs, J. *The Life and Death of American Cities* (Hardmondsworth: Penguin, 1961).
Jacobs, J. *The Economy of Cities* (New York: Random House, 1970).
Jazouli, A. *Les années banlieue* (Paris: Le Seuil, 1992).
Jobard, F. 'An Overview of the French Riots', in D. Waddington, F. Jobard, and M. King (eds) *Rioting in the UK and France* (Cullompron: Willan, 2009), 27–40.
Jobard, F., and Levy, R. 'Police, justice et discriminations raciales en France: état des savoirs', in *La lutte contre le racisme et la xénophobie* (Paris: Commission nationale consultative des droits de l'Homme, 2011), 167–98.
Joly, D. *L'émeute* (Paris: Denoël, 2007).
Jones, G. 'Social Engagement in Latin American Cities', in D. Sudjik and R. Burdett (eds) *Living in the Endless City* (London: Phaedon, 2011).
Jones-Brown, D., and Gill, J. 'Stop, Question and Frisk Policing Practices in New York City: A Primer' in John Jay College, Center on Race, Crime and Justice. *Report: Stop, Question & Frisk Policing Practices in New York City: a Primer* (2010).
Joppke, C. 'The Retreat of Multiculturalism in the Liberal State: Theory and Policy', *British Journal of Sociology*, 55 (2) (2004), 237–57.
Joshua, H., Wallace T., and Booth, H. *To Ride the Storm* (London: Heinemann, 1983).
Kandar, M. 'Yaad. La mémoire', *Courrier International*, 26 November (2009) http://www.courrierinternational.com/article/2009/11/26/yaad-la-memoire
Karstedt, S. 'Handle with Care: Emotions, Crime and Justice', in S. Karstedt, I. Loader and H. Strang (eds) *Emotions, Crime and Justice* (Oxford: Hart 2011), 2–19.
Katane, D. 'Insécurités. Pour une sociologie générale des questions de société' (Paris EHESS: Ph.D. dissertation. Unpublished, 2005).
Keith, M. Race, *Riots and Policing: Lore and Disorder in a Multi-Racist Society* (London: UCL press, 1993).
Keith, M. 'Making the Street Visible: Placing Racial Violence in Context', *New Community* 21 (4) (1995), 551–65.
Kerner Report (National Advisory Commission on Civil Disorders) (New York: Pantheon Books, 1988).

King, M. and Waddington, D. 'Coping with Disorder? The Changing Relationship between Police Public Order Strategy and Practice – A Critical Analysis of the Burnley Riot', *Policing and Society* 14 (2) (2004), 118–37.

King, D. 'Making Americans', in G. Gerstle, and J. Mollenkopf (eds) *E Pluribus Unum?* (New York: Russell Sage, 2001), 143–74.

Kitano, C. 'African Urbanism', in R. Burdett and D. Sudjik (eds) *The Endless City* (London: Phaedon, 2007), 214–17.

Kokoreff, M. 'Le sens des émeutes de l'automne 2005', *Regards sur l'actualité* 319 (2006), 15–26.

Kundnani, A. 'From Oldham to Bradford: The Violence of the Violated', *Race and Class* 43 (2) (2001), 105–31.

Lafree, G. Keynote presentation at the *European Society of Criminology Annual Meeting* (Liège, September, 2009).

LaFree, G. and Dugan, L. 'Research on Terrorism and Countering Terrorism', *Crime and Justice* 38 (1) (2009), 413–77.

LaFree, G., Morris, N., and Dugan, L. 'Cross-National Patterns of Terrorism', *British Journal of Criminology* 50 (2010), 622–49.

Lagrange, H. 'La structure et l'accident', in H. Lagrange and M. Oberti (eds) *Emeutes urbaines et protestation* (Paris: Presses de SciencesPo, 2006).

Lagrange H. 'The French Riots and Urban Segregation', in D. Waddington, F. Jobard, and M. King *Rioting in the UK and France* (Cullompron: Willan, 2009), 107–23.

Landré, M. '66 pourcent des Français verraient bien leur enfant devenir fonctionnaire', *Le Figaro*, June 16 (2011).

Lane, R. *Murder in America* (Columbus: Ohio State University Press, 1997).

Lappi-Seppälä T. 'Explaining imprisonment in Europe', *European Journal of Criminology* 8 (4) (2011), 303–28.

Lazarus, L., and Goold, B. (eds) *Security and Human Rights* (Oxford: Hart, 2007).

Lazarus, L. 'Mapping the Right to Security', in B. Goold and L. Lazarus (eds) *Security and Human Rights* (Oxford: Hart, 2006).

Lefebvre, H. *La révolution urbaine* (Paris: Gallimard, 1970).

Leggett, T. 'Just Another Miracle', *Social Research*, Fall 72 (3) (2005), 581–606.

Levi, M., and Maguire, M. 'Violent Crime', in M. Maguire, R. Morgan, R. Reiner (eds) *Oxford Handbook of Criminology* (Oxford: Oxford University Press, 2002), 795–843.

Levy, R., and Jobard, F. 'Les contrôles d'identité à Paris', *Questions pénales* (23) (2010).

Lewis, P. and Ramakrishnan, S. 'Police Practices in Immigrant-Destination Cities: Political Control or Bureaucratic Professionalism?', *Urban Affairs Review* 42 (2007), 874–99.

Lijphart, A. *Patterns of Democracy: Government Forms and Performance in Thirty-Six Countries* (London: Yale University Press, 1999).

Loader, I., and Walker, N. 'Necessary Virtues: The Legitimate Place of the State in the Production of Security', in B. Dupont and J. Woods (eds) *Democracy, Society and the Governance of Security* (Cambridge: Cambridge University Press, 2006).

Logan, J., and Molotch, H. *Urban Fortunes* (Berkeley: University of California Press, 2007).

Lorrain, D. (ed.) *Métropoles XXL en pays émergents* (Paris: Presses de Sciences Po, 2011).

Loveday, B. Paper presented at the International Conference 'Public safety. Legal and Organization Functioning of Municipal Policy in Europe', Krakow, Poland October 10–11, 2011.

Lyon, D. *Surveillance after September 11* (Cambridge: Polity Press, 2003).

Mabin, A. 'Johannesburg : (South) Africa's Aspirant Global City', in K. Segbers (ed.) *The Making of Global City Regions* (Baltimore: Johns Hopkins University Press, 2007), 32–63.

Mabin, A., and Harrison, P. 'Security and Space: Managing Contradictions of Access Restrictions in Johannesburg', *Environment and Planning B: Planning and Design* 33 (1) (2006), 3–20.

Machiavelli, N. *The Prince* [1515] trans., C.K. Marriott (New York: J.M. Dent, 1908).

MacPherson, W. 'The Stephen Lawrence Inquiry' (London, SMSO, 1999).

Mandelstam, N. *Hope against Hope* (New York, 1970/1999).

Marcuse, P. 'Neighborhood Policy and the Distribution of Power: New York City's Community Boards', *Policy Studies Journal* 16 (1987), 277–89.

Marcuse, P. 'Urban Form and Globalization after September 11th: The View from New York', *International Journal of Urban and Regional Research* 26 (3) (2002), 596–606.

Margalit, A. *On Compromise and Rotten Compromises* (Princeton: Princeton University Press, 2010).

Marx, G. 'Civil Disorder and the Agents of Social Control', *Journal of Social Issues* 26 (1) (1970), 19–57.

Masboungi, A. (ed.) *Penser la ville heureuse: Renzo Piano* (Paris: Editions de la Villette, Projet urbain, 2005).

Mayer, J. *The Dark Hour* (New York: Doubleday, 2008).

McKendrick, B., and Hoffman W. *People and Violence in South Africa* (Cape Town: Oxford University Press, 1990), 446–82.

Méda, D. *Le travail* (Paris: Aubier, 1995).

Mehra, A. 'Mumbai Again', *Geopolitics* (2011) editorial.

Mehta, S. 'Looking for the Bird of Gold', in R. Burdett and D. Sudjik (eds) *Living in the Endless City* (London: Phaedon, 2011), 102–07.

Mehta, S. *Maximum City* (New York: Knopf, 2004).

Metropolitan Police Service *4 Days in August. Strategic Review into the Disorder of August 2011* (London: Metropolitan Police March 2012).

Mirza, M., Senthilkumaran, A. and Ja'far, Z. *Living Apart Together:British Muslims and the Paradox of Multiculturalism*, Policy Exchange Report (2007).

Mingione, E. 'Urban Social Change: A Socio-Historical Framework of Analysis', in Y. Kazepov (ed.) *Cities of Europe* (Oxford: Blackwell, 2005), 67–89.

Mingione, E. *Urban Poverty and the Underclass* (Oxford: Blackwell, 1996).

Misse, M. 'O Rio como um bazar: a conversao da ilegalidade em mercadoria politicas', in *Crime e violencia no Brasil contemporaneo* (Rio de Janeiro: Lumen Juris, 2006), 179–210.

Mohammed, M. 'Youth gangs and "troubles" in the projects', *Penal Issues*, <www.cesdip.org/spip.php?article332> (2006).

Moisi, D. 'The Clash of Emotions', *Foreign Affairs* (2007), 1–2.

Molotch, H., and McClain, N. 'Dealing with Urban Terror' *International Journal of Urban and Regional Research* 27 (3) (2003), 679–98.

Mongin O. *La conditions urbaine: La ville à l'heure de la mondialisation* (Paris: Le Seuil, 2005).

Monjardet, D. *Ce que fait la police* (Paris: La découverte, 1966).

Monkkonen, E. *Murder in New York City* (Berkeley: University of California Press, 2001).

Montaigne, M. [1575] *Les Essais*, trans. (Stanford: Stanford University Press, 1955).

Mucchielli, L. 'Insécurité ou sentiment d'insécurité', <http://insecurite.blog. lemonde.fr/2011/05/01/securite-et-sentiment-dinsecurite/> (2011).

Mumford, L. *The Culture of Cities* (New York: Harcourt Brace, 1938).

Muncie, J. *The Trouble with Kids Today* (London: Hutchinson, 1984).

Municipality of São Paulo. 'Document Postulating São Paulo for 2012 Olympic Games, theme 1, item 1.8', *Economic Resources and Dynamics of the City*, mimeo (2002).

Murakami Wood, D. (ed.), Ball, K., Lyon, D., Norris, C. and Raab, C. *A Report on the Surveillance Society* (Wilmslow, UK: Office of the Information Commissioner (ICO), 2006).

Murray, M., *City of Extremes: The Spatial Politics of Johannesburg* (London: Duke University Press, 2011).

Mythen, G., and Walklate, S. 'Terrorism, Risk and International Security: The Perils of Asking What If?', *Security Dialogue*, 39 (2–3) (2008), 221–42.

National Association of Latino Elected Officials Education Fund. 'A Profile of Latino Elected Officials in the United States, and Their Progress Since 1996' (Washington, D.C.: *NALEO*, 2007).

Naudé, B., Prinsloo, J., and Snyman, R. 'The Third International Crime Victim Survey in Johannesburg, South Africa' (Kampala: UNAFRI, 2001).

Nelken, D. *Comparative Criminal Justice* (London: Sage, 2010).

Nevanen, S., Didier, E., Robert, Ph., Zauberman, R. 'Enquête locale sur la victimation et l'insécurité: uvervilliers, Guyancourt: Centre d'études sociologiques sur le droit et les institutions pénales' (2005) www.cesdip.fr

Newburn, T. ' "Tough on crime": Penal Policy in England and Wales', in M.Tonry (ed.) *Crime, Punishment, and Politics in Comparative Perspective* (Chicago: Chicago University Press, 2007), 425–70.

Newman, O. *Defensible Spaces* (London: Architectural Press, 1973).

Oc, T., and Tiesdell, S. 'The Fortress, the Panoptic, the Regulator and the Animated', in J.R. Gold and G. Revill (eds) *Landscape of Defence* (London: Prentice Hall, 2000), 188–208.

Olson, M. *The Logic of Collective Action* (Cambridge, MA: Harvard University Press, 1966).

Otten, M., Boin, R., and van der Torre, E. *Dynamics of Disorder* (The Hague: Crisis Research Center, Leiden University, 2001).

Pain, R. and Smith, S. (eds) *Fear: Critical Geopolitics and Everyday Life* (Aldershot: Ashgate, 2008).

Palmary, I., Rauch, J., and Simpson, G. 'Violent Crime in Johannesburg', in R. Tomlinson, L. Bremner, R. Beauregard and X. Mangcu (eds) *Emergent Johannesburg Perspectives on the Post-Apartheid City* (London: Routledge, 2003), 101–22.

Pantazis, C. and Pemberton, C. 'From the "Old" to the "New" Suspect Community: Examining the Impact of Recent UK Counter-Terrorist Legislation, *British Journal of Criminology* 49 (5) (2010) 646–66.

Paquot, T. *L'espace public* (Paris: La Découverte, 2009).

Parnell, S. 'Polics of Transformation: Defining the City Strategy in Johannesburg', in K. Segbers (ed.) *The Making of Global City Regions* (Baltimore: Johns Hopkins University Press, 2007), 139–67.

Patillo, M. 'Searching for Loic Wacquant', *International Journal of Urban and Regional Research* 33 (3) (2009), 858–64.

Peach, C. 'Muslims in the 2001 census of England and Wales: Gender and Economic Disadvantage, *Ethnic and Racial Studies* 29 (4) (2006), 629–55.

Peillon, L. 'Les fonctionnaires bien aimés des Français', *Libération*, May 5 (2011).

Penalosa, E. 'Politics, Power, Cities', in R. Burdett and D. Sudjik (eds) *The Endless City* (London: Phaedon, 2007), 307–19.

Pew Research Center; Pew Hispanic Center. 'America's Immigration Quandary' (Washington, D.C.: Pew Global Attitude Project, 2006).

Phillips, R. 'Cash Security in a Violent South Africa', *Security Focus* 20 (9) (2002).

Porter, E. 'Wealthy in the U.S. get handouts, too', *International Herald Tribune*, March 3 (2012).

Power A., and Turnstall, R. *Dangerous Disorder* (York: York Joseph Rowtree Foundation, 1997).

Proband, S. 'European Prison Populations Stable', *Criminology in Europe*, May (2008), 11–14.

Putnam, R. 'E Pluribus Unum: Diversity and Community in the Twenty-First Century', *Scandinavian Political Studies* 30 (2) (2007), 137–74.

Putnam R. *Making Democracy Work* (Princeton: Princeton University Press, 1993)

Ranci, C. 'Social Vulnerability in Europe', *The New Configuration of Social Risks* (Palgrave Macmillan, 2010).

Reading the Riots. Investigating England's summer of disorder: report (London: The Guardian and the London School of Economics, 2011).

Richman, D. 'The Past, Present, and Future of Violent Crime Federalism', in M. Tonry (ed.) *Crime and Justice: A Review of Research* 34 (2006), 377–439.

Rifkin, J. *The End of Work* (New York: Putnam, 1995).

Robbins, L. 'By Sept. 11, Unit at Trade Center will be Policing', *New York Times*, January 19 (2011).

Robert, A. Beauregard, 'Radical Uniqueness and the Flight from Urban Theory', in Dennis R. Judd and Dick Simpson (eds) *The City Revisited, Urban Theory from Chicago, Los Angeles New York*, (Minneapolis: University of Minnesota press, 2011), 186–204.

Robert, P. *Le citoyen, le crime et l'Etat* (Genève: Droz, 1999).

Robin, C. *Fear : The History of an Idea* (Oxford: Oxford University Press, 2004).

Roché, S., and de Maillard, J. 'Crisis in Policing: The French Rioting of 2005', *Policing* 3 (1) (2009), 34–40.

Roosevelt, F.D. *The Public Papers and Addresses of Franklin D. Roosevelt,* 13 vols, 1938–1950 (New York: Random House).

Rosanvallon, P. *La société des égaux* (Paris: Le Seuil, 2011).

Rosenthal, E. 'New Insight on Coping with the Risk of Terror', *International Herald Tribune*, July 30–31: 2 (2005).

Roux, G., Roché, S., and Astor, S. 'Ethnic Minorities and Trust in Criminal Justice: Report on the French pilot', in M. Hough and M. Sato (eds) *Trust in Justice* (Helsinki: EUNI, 2011), 43–47.

Rowe, M. (ed.) *Policing beyond MacPherson* (Cullompton: Willan, 2007).

Salih, M. 'Of course, I carry a bomb in my briefcase', *International Herald Tribune*, June 25 (2007).

Sandercock, L. *Cosmopolis II* (London: Continuum, 2003).

Sassen, S. *The Global City.* 2nd edn. (Princeton: Princeton University Press, 2001).

Sassen, S. *Territory-Authority-Rights* (Princeton: Princeton University Press, 2006).

Sassen, S. *La globalisation* (Paris: Gallimard, trans., 2009).

Sassen, S. 'The City: Its Return as a Lens for Social Theory', *Theory, Culture and Society* (1: 2010), 3–10.

Sassen, S. 'The Economy of Cities', in R. Burdett and D. Sudjik (eds) *Living in the Endless City* (London: Phaedon, 2011), 56–67.

Savitch, H.V. *Cities in a Time of Terror* (Armonk, NY: M.E. Sharpe, 2008)

Scarman, Lord. 'The Brixton Disorders 10th–12th April, 1981' (London: HMSO, 1985).

Schain, M. *The Politics of Immigration in France, Britain and the United States* (New York: Palgrave Macmillan, 2008).

Schain, M. 'Immigrant Integration: A Transatlantic Perspective', paper prepared for the *Seventeenth International Conference of Europeanists* (Montreal: April 15–18, 2010).

Scheingold, S. *The Politics of Law and Order* (New York: Longman, 1984).

Schlesinger, A. *The Vital Center* (New York: DaCapo Press, 1988 [1949]).

Schwartz, F., and Huq, A. *Unchecked and Unbalanced* (New York: Free Press, 2007).

Schwerhoff, G. 'Criminalized Violence and the Process of Civilization: A Reappraisal', *Crime, History and Societies* 6 (2) (2002), 103–26.

Segbers, K. (ed.) *The Making of Global City Regions* (Baltimore: Johns Hopkins University Press, 2007).

Sekhonyane, M., and Louw, A. 'Violent Justice, Vigilantism and the State's Response', *ISS Monograph Series* (72) (Pretoria: April 2002).

Sennett, R. *Uses of Disorder Life* (New York: Knopf, 1970)

Sennett, R. 'Boundaries and Borders', in R. Burdett, and D. Sudjik (eds) *Living in the Endless City* (London: Phaedon, 2011), 324–31.

Sennett, R. 'The Open City', in R. Burdett, and D. Sudjik (eds) *The Endless City* (London: Phaedon, 2007), 290–97.

Sessar, K. and Kury, H., 'Risk and insecurity as broader concepts behind fear of crime and punitiveness', Crimprev conference 'Deviance, Crime and Prevention in a punitive age', (Milton Keynes: Open University, 2009).

Shapiro, J. and Suzan, B. 'The French Experience of Counter-terrrorism', *Survival* 45 (1) (2003), 67–98.

Shaw, C. *The Jack Roller* (Chicago: University of Chicago Press [1930], 1966)

Shaw, C., and McKay, H. *Juvenile Delinquency in Urban Areas* (Chicago: Chicago University Press, 1942).

Shearing, C., and Stenning, P. *Private Policing* (London: Sage, 1987).

Sheehan, M. *Crush the Cell* (New York: Crown, 2008).

Sherman, L. 'Hot Spots of Crime and Criminal Careers of Places', in J. Eck and D. Weisburg (eds) *Crime and Place* (Monsey, NY: Criminal Justice Press, 1995).

Sigelman, L., and Sampson, M. 'A cross-national test of the linkage between Economic Inequality and Political Violence', *Journal of Conflict Resolution* 21 (1977), 105–28.

Simon, J. *Governing through Crime* (Oxford: Oxford University Press, 2007).

Simon, J. *Poor Discipline* (Chicago: University of Chicago Press, 1993).

Simpson, G. 'Shock troops and Bandits: Youth, Crime and Politics', in J. Steinberg (ed.) *Crime Wave* (Johannesburg: Witwatersrand University Press, 2001), 115–28.

Singh, D., Marcus, S., Rabbatts, H. and Sherlock, M. *5 Days in August. An Interim Report on the 2011 English Riots* (London: Riots, Communities and Victims Pannel November, 2011).

Sivaramakrishnan, K. 'Democracy and Self-Interest', in R. Burdett, and D. Sudjik (eds) *Living in the Endless City* (London: Phaedon, 2011), 90–93.

Sklar, J. *Political Thought and Political Thinkers* (Chicago: University of Chicago Press, 1998).

Skolnick, J. *The Politics of Protest* (New York: New York University Press, 2010).

Smelser, N. *Theory of Collective Behaviour* (New York: Free Press, 1962).

Smith, A. 'Le NYPD, police municipale et armée antiterroriste', *Le Figaro*, September 9 (2011).

Spierenburg, P. 'Violence: Reflections about a Word', in S. Body-Gendrot and P. Spirenburg (eds) *Violence in Europe* (New York: Springer, 2008), 11–26.

Stearns, P. *American Fears* (Oxford: Routledge, 2006).

Stearns, P. 'Fear and Contemporary History: A Review Essay', *Journal of Social History* (Winter, 2006), 477–84.

Stone, C. *Regime Politics* (Lawrence, KS: University of Kansas Press, 1989).

Stroobants, J.P. 'Les dépenses militaires se sont envolées aux Etats-Unis et au Royaume-Uni après les attaques d'Al-Qaida', *Le Monde*, September 11 (2011).

Sudjik, D. 'The View from Outside' in R. Burdett and D. Sudjik (eds) *The Endless City* (London: Phaedon, 2007) 200–202.

Sudjik, D. 'Fine Tuning South American Cities', in R. Burdett and D. Sudjik (eds) *Living in the Endless City* (London: Phaedon, 2011).

Sunstein, C. 'Fear and Liberty', *Social Research* 71 (4) (2004), 967–96.

Svendsen, L. *A Philosophy of Fear* (London: CPI, Reaktion Books, 2008).

Taylor, D. *The New Police* (Manchester: Manchester University Press, 1997).

Telles, V. 'Paper presented at a conference on Violence latence vs. violence explosive dans les villes des Amériques' (Toulouse: LISST research center, February 25, 2011).

Telles, V. 'Ville et pratiques urbaines: aux frontières incertaines entre l'illégal, l'informel et l'illicite', in *Estudos Avançados* (French trans.) (São Paulo: IEA/USP, 21, (61) (2007)), 173–91.

Thomas W. *The Child in America* (New York: Knopf, 1928).

Thoreau, H.D. [1837–61] *Journal*, vol. 7, B. Torrey (ed.) (New York: Houghton Mifflin, 2008).

Thrasher, F. *The Gang* (Chicago: University of Chicago Press, 1927).

Tiesdell, S. and Oc, T. 'Beyond "fortress" and "panoptic" cities – towards a safer urban public realm', *Environment and Planning B: Planning and Design* 25(5) (1998), 639–55.

Tilly, C. *The Politics of Collective Violence* (Cambridge: Cambridge University Press, 2003).

Tocqueville, A. de [1830] *De la démocratie en Amérique* (Paris: Gallimard, 1961).

Todorov, T. *La peur des barbares* (Paris: Robert Laffont, 2008).

Touraine, A. 'Face à l'exclusion', in J. Donzelot (ed.) *Citoyenneté et urbanité* (Paris: Ed. Esprit, 1991), 165–73.

Tsoukala, A. *Football Hooliganism in Europe* (Basingstoke: Palgrave Macmillan, 2009).

Tsoukala, A. (ed.) *Terror, Insecurity and Liberty* (London: T and F Books, 2009).

Tulchin, J. 'Crime and Violence: The Threat of Division and Exclusion in Latin American Cities', in C. Wanjiku, Kihato, M. Massoumi, B. Ruble, P. Subiros and A. Garland (eds) *Urban Diversity* (Baltimore: Johns Hopkins University Press, 2010), 301–22.

Tyler, T. *Why People Obey the Law* (New Haven: Yale University Press, 1990).

United Nations. 'World Population', Department of Economic and Social Affairs, Population Division, December (2009).

Valéry, P. [1931] *Reflections on the World Today* (New York: Pantheon, 1948).

Vico, G. [1744] *The New Science* (Ithaca: Cornell University Press, 1984).

Waddington, D. *Contemporary Issues in Public Disorder* (London: Routledge, 1992).

Waddington, D. *Policing Public Disorder* (Cullompron: Willan, 2007).

Waddington, D. 'Trouble at Mill Towns', *The Psychologist*, September 14, 9, (2001), 254–55.

Waddington, D. and Critcher, C. *Flashpoints* (London: Routledge, 1989).

Waddington, D., Jobard, F., and King, M. *Rioting in the UK and France* (Cullompron: Willan, 2009).

Waddington, D., and King, M. 'Coping with Disorder?' *Policing and Society* 14 (2) (2004), 118–37.

Waddington, P.J. *The Strong Arm of the Law* (Oxford: Clarendon, 1991).

Waddington, P.J., Badger, D., and Bull, R. 'Appraising the Inclusive Definition of Workplace "Violence"', *British Journal of Criminology* 45 (2004), 141–64.

Weber, M. [1922] *Economy and Society*, G. Roth and C. Wittich (eds) (Berkeley: University of California Press, 1991).

Webster, C. *Understanding Race and Crime* (London: McGraw Hill, 2007).

Weinstein, L. 'Mumbai's Development Mafias: Globalization, Organized Crime and Land Development', *International Journal of Urban and Regional Research* 32 (1) (2008), 22–39.

Whitman, J. *Harsh Justice* (Oxford: Oxford University Press, 2003).

Wilheim, G. 'São Paulo', in K. Segbers (ed.) *The Making of Global City Regions* (Baltimore: Johns Hopkins University Press, 2007), 329–34.

Wilkinson, P., and Pickett, K. *The Spirit Level* (London: Penguin, 2010).

Wirth, L. 'Urbanism as a Way of Life', *American Journal of Sociology* 44 (1938), 1–24.

Wyckes, M. 'The English Experience', a paper presented at CRIMPREV, University of Porto, Law School, January 16–17 (2009).

Young, I. *Justice and the Politics of Difference* (Princeton: Princeton University Press, 1990).

Zauberman R., Robert Ph., Névanen S., Bon D. 'Victimation et insécurité dans les espaces franciliens: une diversité de combinaisons', *Revue française de sociologie* (sp 2012, forthcoming).

Zedner, L. *Security* (Oxford: Routledge, 2009).

Zehra, M.-H. 'Mumbai ou les enjeux de construction d'un acteur collectif', in D. Lorrain (ed.) *Métropoles XXL en pays émergents* (Paris: Presses de Sciences Po, 2011) 139–214.

Zimring, F. *The City That Became Safe: New York and the Future of Crime Control*, mimeos (New York: New York University Straus House workshops, 2010 and 2011).

Zolberg, A., and Wong, W.L. 'Why Islam Is Like Spanish: Cultural Incorporation in Europe and in the U.S.', *Politics and Society* 27 (1) (1999), 5–38.

Zolberg, A. *A Nation by Design* (Cambridge, MA: Harvard University Press, 2006).

Index